music
in the
united states

 The Brown Music Horizons Series

Books now available

MUSIC IN THE UNITED STATES—*Arthur C. Edwards and W. Thomas Marrocco,* U.C.L.A.

MUSIC THROUGH THE RENAISSANCE—*James C. Thomson, University of Kansas*

The tremendous growth and interest in basic music appreciation and literature courses and the increasing emphasis on music for the general college student demands fresh approaches to teaching and learning at the introductory level.

The Music Horizons Series represents a significant attempt to meet these needs by providing students with stimulating material of high quality by an authority in the field as well as providing instructors with the advantage of complete flexibility in organizing and teaching their course. Although the individual titles are self-contained, collectively they cover the full scope of music appreciation, literature and history.

music
in the
united states

Arthur C. Edwards
University of California, Los Angeles

W. Thomas Marrocco
University of California, Los Angeles

WM. C. BROWN COMPANY PUBLISHERS, *Dubuque, Iowa*

THE

VVHOLE

BOOKE OF PSALMES

Faithfully
TRANSLATED *into* ENGLISH
Metre.

Whereunto is prefixed a difcourfe declaring not only the lawfullnes, but alfo
the neceffity of the heavenly Ordinance
of finging Scripture Pfalmes in
the Churches of
God.

Coll. III.

*Let the word of God dwell plenteoufly in
you, in all wifdome, teaching and exhort-
ing one another in Pfalmes, Himnes, and
fpirituall Songs, finging to the Lord with
grace in your hearts.*

Iames V.

*If any be afflicted, let him pray, and if
any be merry let hims fing pfalmes.*

Imprinted
1640

introduction

Fortunately, the beginnings of music in the United States are not shrouded in darkness, nor are they obfuscated by myths and misinformation. Unfortunately, American music before 1900 has never been taken seriously, for there are thousands upon thousands of compositions which unjustly lie dormant in our libraries, archives and other repositories. Even among our more dedicated performers, there are very few indeed who are aware of the treasures which have accumulated in our libraries. Our early music has also been sadly neglected by European musicologists, and what is unforgivable, is the scant attention given to it by our own musicologists, music historians and music educators. Karl Nef stated, "Only the music composed after 1860 in America merits consideration."[1] Paul Rosenfeld declared, "American music, the body of music rooted in American soil, begins with Edward McDowell."[2] David Ewen, in *Music Comes To America*, titled his first chapter, "When Music Was Very Young" and completely ignored all musical activity in the United States before 1850.[3] In 1952 Sidney Finkelstein stated, "There is nothing in the past of the United States music comparable to the place in our culture of the poetry of Whitman, or the novels of Cooper, Hawthorne, Melville, and Mark Twain."[4] Earle Johnson stated in his article, "The Need for Research in the History of American Music," that the role of music in America is not overplayed in the most widely used texts available to our young people.[5] He mentions *The Rise of American Civilization* by Charles and Mary Beard who sum up in four pages our musical activity during the eighteenth and nineteenth centuries.[6] H. V. Faulkner devoted six lines to music from 1840 to 1948.[7]

Was there really a musical hiatus in our culture? Was there a lack of music appreciation among our forebears? Were they exposed only to the music of second and third-rate composers? Was our native music so innocuous that the less said the better? Were our compositions buried so deeply in archives and libraries that the energy required to retrieve them far exceeded the meager catch? Did eighteenth- and nineteenth-century Americans participate in musical activity? The authors hope they have found the answers to these questions in the following pages.

This is an historical survey of music in the United States; however, no amount of scholarly disputation, factual listing of chronological events, or mere presentation of musical landmarks will give an accurate summation of music in America. In the authors' opinion, no matter how much one discusses the merits or demerits of a composition, no matter how cleverly it is dissected and analysed, the composition will not sound any better. The ultimate goal of music is performance. With this thought in mind the authors have given sources of musical examples in an extensive bibliography. Examples from Marrocco-Gleason, *Music in America — An Anthology* (footnoted, Ma-GlA) are indicated by number. The reader will derive greater benefit and satisfaction by examining and performing or hearing a performance of the composition.

Some of the greatest twentieth-century composers born in Europe have produced important works in the United States and indeed have had a pervasive influence on American music. Béla Bartok, Paul Hindemith, Arnold Schoenberg and Igor Stravinsky come immediately to mind. Detailed discussion of their music lies outside the scope of this book; however, various aspects of their styles and wide influence will be included.

Because of the size of this book, whom and what to exclude were particularly vexing problems. Many readers will question the absence of a favorite composer or composition. But to enumerate every American composer, past and present, would have necessitated a volume of monumental proportions. As a result, many able composers have been excluded; for these omissions the authors offer their regrets and apologies.

Arthur C. Edwards
W. Thomas Marrocco

FOOTNOTES

[1] NefO, p. 334.
[2] RosH, p. 31.
[3] EweM, p. 31.
[4] FinH, p. 105.
[5] JohR, p. 44.
[6] BeaR, I, pp. 142, 798-803.
[7] FauA, pp. 295, 637, 730.

contents

1. First Arrivals 1
2. The Psalters 5
3. The Rise of American Music 11
4. The Influx of Professional Musicians 16
5. The Minority Sects and Their Music 20
6. Fasola, Doremi and Revivalism 29
7. Patriotic and National Songs and Our Lighter Side 38
8. Nineteenth-Century Musical Sophistication 41
9. New England Academicians 47
10. Music Education 53
11. Native Musical Activity 57
12. Nationalistic Elements I 66
13. Nationalistic Elements II 78
14. Nationalistic Composers I 91
15. Nationalistic Composers II 100
16. Contemporary Development of Traditional Styles 109
17. On New Paths 122
18. Twelve-Tone Techniques 132
19. Electronc Music 136
Discography 143
Bibliography 159
Index 173

first arrivals

The Pilgrims. We may well be thankful to James I, King of England (1603-1625), who began his reign by demanding complete fealty of his subjects. Singling out the noncomformist Puritans, he stated, "he would make his subjects conform in religion or be harried out of the land."[1] Electing the latter, the Puritans began their exodus in 1608 and chose Holland, the land of religious tolerance; however, not desirous of losing their identity through absorption by the Dutch, they sought permission to settle in the New World. It was granted in 1620 and forthwith a hardy band of one hundred and one pioneers left Delfthaven for Southampton on the first leg of their journey to the land of freedom. Upon arrival in Southampton, a serious leak in their ship, the Speedwell, forced the pilgrims to transfer to the Mayflower. On this vessel the pilgrims set sail from Plymouth on September 16, 1620. After a journey fraught with danger, they dropped anchor on November 11 off the shore of what is now Cape Cod, thus founding the first permanent colony in the New World.

The Spaniards. There were, of course, earlier arrivals. Had Columbus' crew broke out in song and worship upon landing on San Salvador, it would have marked the first time European music was heard on this continent. In 1565 the Spaniards founded St. Augustine, Florida. Moving westward they founded what is now called New Mexico. In San Felipe (New Mexico), Father Cristobal de Quinones had a small organ installed in the town's first church and taught the Roman liturgy between 1598 and 1604. Father Junipero Serra established the first mission in San Diego in 1769. Twenty-one other missions were to follow, all in Cali-

fornia. Indians were taught to sing and play an instrument and were
employed to perform during the Mass, the music often composed by
Father Duran.[2]

The French.   It is known that Jacques Cartier celebrated his arrival
on the coast of Labrador with a sung Mass on June 14, 1534. Unlike the
English, the French in Canada and the Spaniards in the Southwest and
Mexico were deeply interested in converting the Indians. Sister Marie
de l'Incarnation wrote on September 27, 1650 that it was the desire of
the King to "Frenchify" the Indians, and to do so, one began with the
children. The schools had already taken in a number of them, where they
were all dressed *a la française* and taught to read and write as in
France.[3] In 1676 Father Jean Enjalran reported that "the nuns in France
do not sing more agreeably than some Indian women here."[4] So successful were their missionary efforts that the Iroquois Indians received Papal
permission in 1668 to have their services, including the Mass, celebrated
in their native tongue, not Latin. It is said that this privilege is still
observed at the mission in St. Regis, Quebec.[5] The ill-fated Huguenots
who settled along the coast of South Carolina and Florida between 1562
and 1565 sang from their Geneva psalter.[6]

The English and Dutch.   In 1607 Jamestown was founded by the
English; its inhabitants sang from the Sternhold and Hopkins psalter,
often adapting its verses to Thomas Est's harmonic settings.[7] The Dutch
claimed land in North America as a result of Henry Hudson's expedition
in 1609 and also founded Albany in 1614. According to Ellinwood, the
Dutch Reformed congregations sang the tunes to the metrical psalms in
Dutch verse by Peter Datheen until 1767, when, after the introduction
of English preaching, Francis Hopkinson was commissioned to adapt
English words to their traditional tunes.[8]

All these nations contributed to the development and culture of our
country, but it was principally the English culture (into which all other
cultures were assimilated) which gradually enveloped the country.

THE PURITAN: MUSICAL OR ANTI-MUSICAL?

Music for Worship.   Much has been written relative to the place of
music in the Puritanical society. It has been maligned and praised. In
spite of the many references to music making and instruments in seven-
teenth- and eighteenth-century New England, the Puritans (spiritual
brethren of the Calvinists) did not encourage musical activity except
for use in worship. Phillip Stubbes's *Anatomie of Abuses* (London, 1583)

clearly describes the Puritan attitude toward music, which, because of its association with dancing and bawdy texts, was considered the agent for the "dissemination of scurrility." He stated:

> But if musick openly were used . . . to the praise and glory of God, as our Fathers used it, . . . would comfort man wunderfully, and moove his hart to serve God better; but being used as it is, it corrupteth good minds, maketh them womanish, and inclined to all kinde of whordome and mischeef.[9]

Macknerness is of the opinion that we shall not understand the Puritan standpoint properly if we fail to bear in mind the length to which hatred of Rome — the subject of dozens of ballads — was carried during this period.[10]

Undoubtedly, the overly zealous fanatics among the Puritans were responsible for carrying out the desecration or silencing of organs. There was a precedent in Geneva in which the Council ordered the organ in the Rive Cathedral to be dismantled and its pipes melted down. Calvin opposed instruments and part singing. With reference to the metrical psalms sung in unison and unaccompanied, Calvin stated in his *Institutes of the Christian Religion*:

> . . . if songs be tempered to that gravity which becommeth the presence of God and Angels, it both procureth dignity and grace to the holy action . . . . But wee must diligently beware that our eares be not more heedfully bent to the note, than our mindes to the spirituall sense of the words.[11]

In Boston, Cotton Mather opposed the installation of an organ in the Brattle Street Church. And in so far as singing was concerned, he said, "the human voice is significant and edifying by signification, the voice of instruments is not."[12]

Music for Entertainment. John Milton, father of the poet, is often mentioned as having Puritanical leanings. But Brennecke writes that there is ample evidence the Miltons eagerly embraced rather varied opportunities to cultivate the enjoyment of the worldly arts — painting, for instance, as well as poetry and music.[13] It is well known that Milton was on friendly terms with Ben Johnson, William Shakespeare, Alfonso Ferrabosco and Thomas Lupo. When Thomas Morley envisaged his musical bouquet for Queen Elizabeth, *The Triumphs of Oriana* (1601) he invited England's foremost composers to contribute to his collection. It would indeed be difficult to explain the name of John Milton on the roster of contributors had he been a hard-core Puritan.

Certainly Puritanical ethics and philosophy were far removed from
the sophisticated and pleasure-seeking aristocracy of the Elizabethan
and Jacobean courts.

> Tudor church music was remarkable, but it is the secular forms of
> English music — the madrigal, lute ayre, virginal music, and fancies for
> viols — that embody most richly the spirit and power of the English
> Renaissance.[14]

It has been said that no gentleman would have considered himself as
such unless he could sing at sight or play on an instrument. In fact,
gitterns and lutes were placed at the disposal of gentlemen in tonsorial
parlors while waiting their turn to have their hair groomed or to be
fitted for a wig. Fortunately, there were many Anglicans and sophisticated Puritans in the Colonies to somewhat offset the austerity of the
Calvinistic Puritans. Covey writes:

> In America during the Colonial period, the concerts, opera, oratorio,
> and balls . . . were all patronized, composed for, and performed by
> Anglicans, with a sprinkling of Roman Catholics and Lutherans, but no
> Puritans.[15]

FOOTNOTES

[1]ColF, p. 127.
[2]DaSM, pp. 5-8.
[3]KalMC, p. 10.
[4]KalMC, p. 12.
[5]HiggH, p. 13.
[6]First published in Geneva, 1551.
[7]*The Whole Booke of Psalmes,* London, 1592.
[8]EllinR, pp. 296-297.
[9]FurP, pp. 170-171.
[10]MacS, p. 79.
[11]Translated by Thomas Norton, London, 1634, p. 435.
[12]CovP, p. 384.
[13]BrenM, p. 95. See also Ma-GlA, No. 6.
[14]ReeR, p. 815.
[15]CovP, p. 382.

the psalters

The Music of the Pilgrims. *The Booke of Psalmes, Englished both in prose and metre,* known as the *Ainsworth Psalter,* was printed in Amsterdam in 1612 for the Separatists. Henry Ainsworth, a biblical scholar, forced to leave England in 1593 as a result of active participation among the Separatists, found a haven in Amsterdam where he remained until his death in 1622. It was here that he came into contact with Dutch and French tunes, which no doubt influenced him in his selection of the tunes included in his psalter.[1] A blend of English, Dutch and French music, this psalter is characterized by the presence of a variety of meters (there are 15) and a predominance of the longer ones. Containing thirty-nine monophonic tunes printed with diamond-shaped notes without bar lines and servicing one hundred fifty psalms, it remained the official psalter of the Plymouth colony when it merged with the Massachusetts Bay colony in 1692.

The Music of the Puritans. The *Whole Booke of Psalmes,* by Sternhold and Hopkins, first published in London in 1562, enjoyed great diffusion among English Protestants, reaching seventy-eight editions. The forty-two monophonic tunes mostly borrowed from French and English sources also contained a few original tunes.[2] As in the case of the Ainsworth psalter, the French tunes show more variety in meter, but the English tunes show a predilection for the shorter lines and for common or ballad meter. In all, seventeen different meters were supplied for the one hundred fifty psalms. The non-Separatist Puritans came directly from England and settled along the Massachusetts Bay in 1630.

5

The Bay Psalm Book.   The full title of this, the first book printed
in North America, is *The Whole Booke of Psalmes Faithfully Translated
into English Metre.* Dissatisfaction with the translation in the Ainsworth
and the Sternhold and Hopkins psalters soon became apparent. It was
claimed that the translations did not always reflect the meaning of the
original Hebrew. Moreover, seventeen different meters in the Sternhold
and Hopkins and fifteen in the Ainsworth were far too many meters to
cope with. Thus in 1640, the New England Divines, headed by Robert
Mather, Thomas Weld and John Elliot, revised the translations and
reduced the meters to six, retaining, however, one hundred twelve in
common meter. This edition contained no music; its users were advised

Bay   Psalm   Book,   Boston,
1698.

John Tufts, *Introduction to the
Singing of Psalm-Tunes*, 5th ed.,
Boston, 1726.

to turn to either Thomas Ravenscroft's *Whole Booke of Psalmes* (London, 1621) for the many harmonized tunes to which metrical versions
of the Psalms in common meter could be sung,[3] or to the Sternhold
and Hopkins which contained unharmonized tunes.[4] At the end of
the book an admonition to the reader lists the tunes selected from the

Ravenscroft, and possibly the Sternhold and Hopkins psalters, that could be sung to the six meters of the psalms as follows:

> The verses of these psalmes may be reduced to six kindes [meters], the first whereof may be sung in very neere fourty common tunes; as they are collected, out of our chief musicians, by Tho. Ravenscroft. The second kinde may be sung in three tunes as Ps. 25. 50, & 67. in our english psalm books. [Sternhold and Hopkins]

> The third. may be sung indifferently, as ps. the 51. 100. & 10 commandments, in our english psalme books. which three tunes (meters aforesaid, comprehend almost all this whole book of psalmes, as being tunes [meters] most familiar to us.

> The fourth. as ps. 148. of which there are but about five.

> The fift. as ps. 112. or the Pater Noster, of which there are but two. viz. 85. & 138.

> The sisxt. as ps. 113, of which but one, viz. 115.

In 1651 Reverend Henry Dunster, first president of Harvard College, with the assistance of Richard Lyon, carried through the first major revision of the *Bay Psalm Book*. It was the third edition in 1698, however, that is of major interest to the music student, for this edition, the ninth, contained thirteen tunes for treble and bass.[5] The music is notated with diamond-shaped notes without bar lines, and, as an aid to new singers, the letters of the solmization system, f[a], s[ol], l[a], m[i], are placed below the notes in lieu of the text. Irving Lowens informs us that the music in the 1698 edition was borrowed from the 1674 and 1679 editions of John Playford's *A Brief Introduction to the Skill of Musick* (London).[6]

MANNER OF SINGING PSALMS

Common Way. Not until the ninth edition of the *Bay Psalm Book* in 1698 does one suspect that all was not well with the singing in churches. Apparently, later generations, forced to endure the hardships and privation encountered in the land of freedom and promise, found little or no time to devote to the cultural pursuit of music and a serious decline in the cultivation of sacred music took place. The ability to read music was neglected and with this shortcoming there arose the practice of "lining-out," in which the congregations sang by rote rather than by note. This method was accomplished by a deacon or precentor who read or sang one line of the Psalm and then led the singing of what had

been read, repeating the process after each new line. It can readily be
seen how a melody could have been changed unintentionally. The battle
lines were clearly drawn between those in the rural areas who favored
an oral tradition of singing by rote "common way" and those zealous
reformers who insisted on singing by note "regular way."

Regular Way. The most vocal opposition to the "common way"
came, as would be expected, from the clergy, namely, Reverends Thomas
Symmes, John Tufts, Thomas Walter, Cotton Mather and Nathaniel
Chauncey. Symmes pointed out in his *The Reasonableness of Regular
Singing, or Sing by Note* (1720):

> singing by note is giving every note its proper pitch, and turning the note
> in its proper place, and giving to every note its true length and sound.
> Whereas, the usual way [common way] varies much from this.
> In it, some notes are sung too high, others too low, and most too long,
> and many turnings or flourishings with the voice (as they call them)
> are made where they should not be, and some are wanting where they
> should have been.[7]

Cotton Mather in his *The Accomplished Singer* (1721) claimed that his
publication was "intended for all that sing psalms with grace in their
hearts: but more particularly to accompany the laudable endeavors of
those who are learning to sing by Rule, and seeking to preserve a *Regular
Singing* in the Assemblies of the Faithful."[8] Nathaniel Chauncey's publication was self-explanatory in the title which read:

> Regular Singing defended and proved to be the only true way of
> singing the songs of the Lord.[9]

FIRST INSTRUCTION BOOKS

Introduction to the Singing of Psalm-Tunes. In search of a more
efficient system of notation which would enable the reader to sing a
tune at sight and to combat the haphazard psalm singing resulting from
the lining-out practice, the Reverend John Tufts spearheaded the sing-
ing-school movement through the publication of his *Introduction to
the Singing of Psalm-Tunes.*[10] Tufts employed letters used in solmization:
F[a], S[ol], L[a] and M[i], and placed them (in lieu of the conventional notation) on the appropriate lines and spaces. The Appendix to
his book made it clear that the length of the note was governed by the
presence or absence of a dot or dots. Tufts was not the originator of the
system, for we were introduced to this novel approach for the first
time in the Colonies in the 1698 edition of the *Bay Psalm Book.* The new
feature in Tuft's method was the substitution of the solmization letters

for the conventional notation placed on the staff. This ingenious American has earned the distinction of being the originator of the first American music textbook, for this brief work contains an appendix dealing with the rudiments of music, tuning the voice, notation, intervals, scales, clefs and time signatures. This publication became the prototype of thousands of hymn-tune books published in the service of church music. It must be admitted that the use of solmization syllables was not accepted without some initial opposition from those who maintained that the new way made disturbances in churches, grieved good men, exasperated them and caused them to behave disorderly, was popish and required too much time to learn and so forth. Tuft's "100 Psalm Tune New" may possibly be the first sacred tune composed by a native American.

The Grounds and Rules of Musick. The Reverend Thomas Walter stated in this publication:

> Once the tunes were sung according to the rules of music but are now miserably tortured and twisted. . . .
>
> There are no two churches that sing alike . . . .
>
> Somebody or other did compose our tunes, and did they, think ye? compose them by rule or by rote? If the latter how came they prick'd down in our Psalm books? . . .
>
> For want of exactitude, I have observed in many places one man is upon a note, while another a note behind, which produces something hideous and is beyond expression bad . . . . Our tunes are, for Want of a Standard to appeal to in all our Singing, left to the Mercy of every unskilful Throat to chop and alter, twist and change, according to their infinitely divers and no less Humours and Fancies. . . .[11]

Perhaps anticipating the opposition to the use of letters, Walter's publication was notated in the conventional manner. There are twenty-four tunes in three parts neatly engraved with regular bar lines by James Franklin, older brother of Benjamin.[12] Walter's "Southwel New" could well vie with Tuft's "100 Psalm Tune New" for being the first sacred composition by a native American.

Other Collections. An entry in Judge Sewall's Diary of March 16, 1721,[13] informs us that he and another "sung four times out of Tate and Brady." The book referred to is *A New Version of the Psalms of David Fitted to the Tunes Used in Churches* by Nicholas Tate and Nicholas Brady. Although it did not supersede the Sternhold and Hopkins (which became known as the Old Version), it provided an alternate version, the two existing side by side until the end of the eighteenth century. In 1700 there appeared *A Supplement to the New Version* containing a selection of tunes from earlier psalters. It is, however, the 1708 edition of the *Supplement* which is of special importance to us, for this one contained seventy-five tunes set in two parts.[14] In 1713 the King's Chapel in Boston, an Episcopalian Church, adopted the New Version. Another *Supplement to the New Version* was published by Thomas Johnston in 1755, Boston. This publication contained perhaps for the first time a three-part setting of the tune "Mear."[15]

A publication which greatly influenced our first American composers was William Tans'ur's *The Royal Melody Compleat,* or *The New Harmony of Sion* in three volumes with music in two, three and four parts. In his preface the compiler admonishes the singer(s):

> such Tunes that are in Four Parts may be sung in Three parts; omitting anyone of the Upper Parts. But if the Altus or Contra-Part be omitted, then must the Treble be used as a Cantus; Or both the Upper Parts may be omitted, and sung but in Two Parts; When Voices can't be had. But it is better to omit the Treble in Tunes of Four Parts, than the Cantus; unless there are voices to sing the Treble in the Eighth above.[16]

Aware of the favor with which this publication was received in the colonies, Daniel Bayley published *The American Harmony,* or *Royal Melody Complete*, joining it with that of another Englishman, Aaron Williams' *The Universal Psalmody*.[17] With disarming frankness, Bayley stated in his preface: "my design was to have a large Collection of Musick, at a low price."[18]

FOOTNOTES

[1]Ma-GlA, Nos. 1 through 5.
[2]Ma-GlA, Nos. 7 through 11.
[3]Ma-GlA, No. 6.
[4]Ma-GlA, Nos. 7 through 11.
[5]Ma-GlA, Nos. 12 through 17.
[6]LowB, p. 27.
[7]Boston.
[8]Boston News Letter (February 6-13, 1721), advertisement.
[9]New London, 1728.
[10]Boston, 1721. The first-known edition, the fifth, was published in 1726. It contained thirty-seven tunes in three-part harmony.
[11]Boston, 1721.
[12]Ma-GlA, Nos. 24, 25, and 26.
[13]SewD, III, p. 285. Sewall does not specify whether he used the supplement, or if he fitted the Tate and Brady text to the tune in either the *Bay Psalm Book* of 1698 or the Sternhold and Hopkins.
[14]Ma-GIA, Nos. 18 and 19.
[15]Ma-GlA, Nos. 20 and 20a.
[16]London, 1734.
[17]Newbury-Port, 1767.
[18]Ma-GlA, Nos. 27, 28 and 29.

the rise of american music

Determining Factors. Allied to England in spirit, blood and outlook, even after the umbilical cord was severed from the mother country by the Revolution, our composers remained strongly influenced by the collections of church music by William Tans'ur and Aaron Williams. With William Billings, however, a characteristically American idiom began to appear, finding its greatest expression in unconventional if not primitive harmonies. The catalytic agent was not the work of one man, but of two forces: the great religious awakening and a unique American phenomenon, the singing school movement. Although the primary function of the singing school was a pedagogical one, its popularity was no doubt enhanced by the fact that a social hour usually followed the termination of a lesson.

The Great Awakening. Undoubtedly, the most radical change in hymnody was brought about by the nonconformist divine, Dr. Isaac Watts (1674-1748) whose publication, *Hymns and Psalms*[1] was widely circulated in England and in the American colonies. Watts was a Congregationalist, but his paraphrased hymns were readily accepted by other denominations from Massachusetts to Virginia. (For examples of Watt's hymn texts, see footnote 2.) The popularity of his paraphrased hymns coincided with the revival movement and the great awakening which aroused congregational participation. The two figures directly responsible for this awakening were the Reverends Jonathan Edwards (1703-1758), a fiery and persuasive American Congregational clergyman and theologian and George Whitefield (1714-1770), an eloquent English evangelist and organizer of the Calvinistic Methodists, who spent several

years in the Colonies.[3] Among other hymn writers may be mentioned
John Newton (1725-1807), William Cowper (1731-1800), John Cennick
(1718-1755), James Relly (c. 1722-1788), John Wesley (1703-1791) and
Charles Wesley (1707-1788). The Wesleys, founders of Methodism, wrote
the texts to many hymns which found their way into many southern
hymodies. In 1737 John Wesley published his *A Collection of Psalms
and Hymns* in Charleston, South Carolina.

The Singing School Movement. The typical New England singing
school teacher of the period 1770-1830 was a hardy and enthusiastic
individual steeped in the heritage of psalm singing, a man of modest
circumstances and humble occupation. He was a composer, a compiler
of tune books and a singing master by avocation, who traveled through
the countryside holding classes in taverns, schools and churches. Most
of these men had a limited education, a few were college graduates, some
were prominent in politics and became prominent citizens.[4] Among the
more successful composers and tune book compilers were William Billings, (1746-1800), Abraham Wood (1752-1804), Jacob French (1754-?),
Justin Morgan (1747-1798), Supply Belcher (1751-1836), Daniel Belknap (1771-1815), Samuel Holyoke (1762-1820), Jeremiah Ingalls (1764-
1828), Jacob Kimball (1761-1826), Daniel Read (1757-1836), Lewis
Edson (1748-1820), Timothy Swan (1758-1842), Oliver Holden (1765-
1844), Eliakim Doolittle (1722-1850) and Stephen Jenks (1772-1856).
Their compositions are contained in books that measure approximately
six by ten inches and open lengthwise. In these one finds a variety of
compositions — psalm tunes, hymn tunes, fuging tunes, odes, anthems, set
pieces, sentences — set for four voices (sometimes three): treble, counter,
tenor (which carried the tune) and bass — all intended for church and
home use.

Musical Forms: Psalms and Hymns. Apart from their origins, psalms
and hymns are similar in musical treatment and form. Both are short —
fifteen to twenty-two measures in length; the texts are set syllabically;
the music is homophonic with no musical repetition.[5] *Fuging tune*: In
two parts, the first section is homophonic ending either on the tonic
or dominant. At the second section each voice enters successively, the
imitation not longer than one or two measures. This is followed by a
concluding homophonic phrase. The second section is then repeated
making an ABB form.[6] *Set Piece*: This form may be a lengthy, sectional
composition with changing moods and time signatures, chordal and imitative treatment, solo passages interspersed among the choral, or the form
may be a brief one in AAB form and in homophonic (or familiar) style.
The meeting ground of these two techniques is found in the choice of

subject matter taken not from the Scriptures, but prepared especially for a particular occasion or an important ceremony and set to a tune that was used only once with its one original text.[7] *Anthem*: This is an extended, through-composed composition consisting of several sections of changing moods and time signatures and each thematically unrelated. It is generally arranged for mixed voices in two-, three- and four-part writing, with occasional solo parts, chordal and imitative texture and sacred or secular text.[8] *Sentence*: A short scriptural text set to music, which seldom extends beyond one or two periods. Musically, it is in a slow tempo, in one meter, usually in a major key and presents a homophonic texture. *Miscellaneous compositions*: Several compositions in the form of a canon have come down to us by William Billings. His most successful is his "When Jesus Wept," a canon of four in one.[9] *Patriotic Tunes*: "Chester," words and music by William Billings, became the battle cry of the Revolution.[10] In 1775 Nathaniel Niles wrote a broadside which was printed in Norwich, Connecticut titled "Bunker Hill." The poem proved so popular that Andrew Law set it to music.[11]

The Stylistic Traits. In this strong and highly original American music, one finds folklike tunes, irregular phrase lengths, natural minor (Aeolian) and gapped scales and virile rhythms. Unconventional harmonic progressions, parallel fifths and octaves, triadic and dyadic harmonies, occasional rhythmical independence of voices (fuging), sudden dissonances derived from contrapuntal part writing and the lack of suspensions are among some of the other important characteristics of this music.

MUSIC FOR ENTERTAINMENT

Williamsburg. Since New England prior to the Revolution appears to have neglected music for entertainment, we must look to Virginia, the Carolinas and Pennsylvania. That there were instrumentalists in Williamsburg and Jamestown is not disputed. Whatever music making took place in those cities was arranged by local or traveling musicians, or, in some instances, by British officers who found time to play the role of impresarios and to stage ballad operas. Peter Pelham appears to be the only musician mentioned in the annals of Williamsburg, a city whose musical taste had Italianate leanings. In his dual capacity as jail-keeper and keyboard performer, Pelham often and conveniently brought a prisoner to pump the church organ, and is remembered for having given the first performance of the *Beggar's Opera*. In a letter to John Page, Thomas Jefferson lamented of a hang-over after a dance:

Last night, as merry an agreeable company and dancing with Belinda in the *Apollo* could make me, I never could have thought the succeeding Sun would have seen me so wretched.[12]

No native composer, whether by vocation or avocation, seems to have been encountered in these cities before the Revolutionary War.

Charleston. A prosperous city of over seven thousand, Charleston had caught the attention of Edmund Burke, the English statesman, who wrote in his *Early Settlements in America* (1757), that "Charleston approached more nearly to the social refinement of a great European capitol than any other American city.[13] In 1762, a musical organization, the Saint Cecilia Society was founded. By 1794, the city boasted of an orchestra of thirty-two musicians, and had become a center for the performance of ballad operas.

Philadelphia. Philadelphia, the largest and wealthiest city in the Colonies, was dominated by the Quakers, who, like their concordant brethren, the Puritans, did not encourage fine arts and music. Yet, among the more sophisticated citizens of Philadelphia, many musical soirées were held, often at the mansion of the Governor, John Penn.[14] Francis Hopkinson (1737-1791), a signer of the Declaration of Independence, composer, harpsichordist, inventor, painter, and our first Secretary of the Navy, was perhaps our first composer. It appears that his song, "My Days Have Been So Wondrous Free,"[15] composed in 1759, is the first secular composition composed by a native American. His collection, *Seven Songs for the Harpsichord or Forte-piano,* dedicated to George Washington (1788) is a landmark in our music history, for it is the first-known collection of art songs to be published in the American colonies. His style was that of the English composer, Thomas Arne. The only other Philadelphian who may be considered a composer was Benjamin Franklin, who not only perfected the glass harmonica and printed music collections, but is also named as the composer of a string quartet found in Paris after the close of World War II. It is written in *scordatura* in which all four performers (three violins and one cello) play open strings only.[16] Two copies of this suite are preserved in the Musikarchiv in Göttweig, Austria and in the Christian-Weise Bibliothek in Zittau, East Germany.

FOOTNOTES

[1]London, 1707.
[2]MaGlA, Nos. 48, 49, 50, 52, 53, 56, 57, 58, 60, 66, 91, 93, 94 and 99.
[3]Ma-GlA, No. 40.
[4]Ma-GlA, p. 98. The reader is urged to consult MetA for a detailed account of our early composers.

[5]Ma-GlA, Nos. 45, 51, and 69.
[6]Ma-GlA, Nos. 48, 49, 52, 55, 58, 60, 61, 62 and 68.
[7]MarrS, pp. 348-352.
[8]Ma-GlA, Nos. 45, 51 and 69.
[9]Ma-GlA, No. 42.
[10]Ma-GlA, No. 43.
[11]Ma-GlA, No. 47.
[12]ForJ, I p. 353.
[13]ChaA, p. 107.
[14]The first public concert in Philadelphia took place on January 20, 1757 under the direction of John Palma.
[15]Ma-GlA, No. 38.
[16]A facsimile edition of this quartet and transcription was published by Odete Lieutier, Paris, 1946. It was arranged for string orchestra, using normal tuning by John Vincent and published by Mills Music, Inc., New York, 1963.

chapter **4**

the influx
of professional
musicians

Pre-Revolution. Only a few professional musicians in pre-Revolutionary times are known to us. They are Theodore Pachelbel (son of the famous organist and composer, Johann Pachelbel) who gave New York City its first concert in 1736; Phillip Ludwell Lee of Stratford, Virginia; William Selby,[1] organist, harpsichordist, teacher and composer, who settled in Boston in 1771; John Palma, composer, harpsichordist and teacher in Philadelphia about 1750;[2] Giovanni Gualdo, composer, teacher, impresario and performer who settled in Philadelphia in 1767; W. S. Morgan, violinist, conductor, teacher, impresario and performer who set up a studio in Portsmouth, N. H. and gave some concerts in Boston; the many unknown instrumentalists who played in orchestras for theatrical entertainments such as ballad operas and dances. Arriving in this country, such musicians could not live entirely on their musical talents — most of them turned to more substantial and steady employment such as selling wine, tobacco, groceries, and so forth. Posterity has been unkind to the mere performer, for he has been completely forgotten. With the end of the Revolutionary War, the influx of English, French and German immigrants, many of them musicians, (not to mention the captured Hessians and English troops who chose to remain in the land they came to conquer) a resurgence of secular musical activity took place.

Post-Revolution. Among the better musicians to arrive may be mentioned Alexander Reinagle (1756-1809), a dominant personality who settled in Philadelphia in 1786 and who guided the musical destiny of that city almost singlehandedly, and Raynor Taylor (1747-1825),

Reinagle's teacher, who settled in Philadelphia and played a dual role as organist in St. Peter's church and an impressario-entertainer of comic skits known as olios. His works are mostly secular and include a ballad opera, cantatas, songs and chamber music. Jean Gehot (1756-c. 1820) played violin in London under Joseph Haydn and under Reinagle in Philadelphia after 1791, wrote on violin pedagogy, composed string quartets and some orchestra compositions. The musician who not only took part in the musical life of his city as a performer, teacher, impresario-composer and conductor, but was also shrewd enough to publish his own compositions and "new tunes recently arrived from England," was not compelled to seek outside employment. Among those remembered in this connection are Peter von Hagen (1750-1803), John Moller (d. 1803),[3] James Hewitt (1770-1827) and Benjamin Carr (1768-1831). The cities most often chosen to carry on the music profession were Boston, Philadelphia, New York and Baltimore. Somewhat akin to the game of musical chairs, some musicians began in Philadelphia and settled in New York, others began in Boston and found Philadelphia more to their taste. Some settled in New York and left only to return.

Thanks to our newly arrived musicians, our musical fare was European. We need not look for American compositions, for despite the fact that hundreds of compositions were composed in American cities, the style was transplanted English, French or German. Our early programs consisted of ballad operas or concerts of instrumental and vocal solos, orchestral, keyboard and chamber music. Alexander Reinagle's piano sonatas are in the style of C.P.E. Bach and Joseph Haydn,[4] as are Raynor Taylor's sonatas for piano and violin.[5] Benjamin Carr was perhaps the most energetic and successful of the professional emigrants. A versatile musician, his greatest contribution lies in the publication of the *Musical Journal* and his *Musical Miscellany,* both containing his own music as well as those of other composers. One of his most successful songs, "Why Huntress, Why?" composed for his ballad opera, *The Archers,*[6] in 1796, appeared later in his *Musical Journal.* The first ballad opera to be composed in the United States was *Tammany* in 1794 by James Hewitt. The sole surviving excerpt from this work is a short air titled, "The Death Song of the Cherokee Indians."[7] The tune, completely devoid of any Indian characteristics, enjoyed wide favor in Scotland, England and in the Colonies and eventually found its way into Southern folk hymnody under the title "Morality."[8]

Hewitt and Carr have left us two examples of "battle music," a descriptive and naïve genre of musical compositions quite popular in Europe in the eighteenth and early nineteenth centuries. Many European composers (including Beethoven) were attracted to this type of bloodless warfare in which battle cries, trumpet calls, drum beats, clash of steel and cannon shots were translated into musical sounds — with each stratagem briefly described in advance. Hewitt composed *The Battle of Trenton,* which depicted the battle and defeat of the Hessians. Carr published *The Siege of Tripoli, an Historical Naval Sonata for the Pianoforte,* which vividly described the prodigious deeds of American tars aboard the *Constitution* in clearing the Mediterranean of Pirates in 1804. Both compositions contain "Yankee Doodle," perhaps the most popular tune during and after the Revolution. Other eminent musicians were Gottlieb Graupner (Germany, 1767?-Boston, 1836) whose paucity of compositions is laid to his various other activities such as that of publisher, conductor (of the Handel and Haydn Choral Society) and instructor of a newly founded Music Conservatory. As a result only four compositions have come down to us.

Hans Gram (born in Denmark) arrived in Boston about 1789 and was the organist at the Brattle Street Church. He collaborated with Oliver Holden and Samuel Holyoke on the *Massachusetts Compiler* (1795). Several of his compositions appeared in the *Massachusetts Magazine.* His *Death Song of an Indian Chief*[9] is the first orchestral score to be published in the United States; Phillip Phile, (Germany, c. 1734-Philadelphia, 1793), a violinist, composed his *Hail, Columbia* about 1798;[10] Victor Pelissier (dates unknown) was a horn player from France and settled in New York where he composed several ballad operas and incidental music for plays;[11] George K. Jackson (Oxford, England, 1745-Boston, 1823) settled in Boston and became the organist of the Handel and Haydn Choral Society. He published hymn books, a treatise on music theory and many compositions;[12] William Tuckey (Somersetshire, England, 1708 - Philadelphia, 1781) was active as a performer and teacher. He organized a choir at Trinity Church in New York and is credited for presenting parts of Handel's *Messiah* for the first time in the United States;[13] Chevalier Marie Robert de Leaumont (dates unknown) came to America about 1790, conducted an orchestra in Boston in 1796 and then settled in Charleston; Jacob Eckhard (Germany, 1757-Charleston, 1833), a composer and organist, arrived in America in 1776 and settled in Charleston where he was an organist and choirmaster at the German Lutheran Church.[14] Louis Picchieri[15] mentions Horatio Garnet, Winthrop Bennet, J. H. Smith and John L. Berkenhead.

FOOTNOTES

[1]Ma-GlA, Nos. 72 and 73.
[2]HowP, p. 22.
[3]Ma-GlA, No. 79.

[4]Ma-GlA, No. 74. See also his song in MilP, p. 19.
[5]Ma-GlA, No. 75. See also MilP, p. 22, and HowP, p. 20.
[6]Ma-GlA, No. 76. See also MilP, p. 28 and his *Rondo* in HowP, p. 28.
[7]Ma-GIA, No. 77.
[8]Ma-GlA, No. 92. See also his song in HowP, p. 26.
[9]Ma-GlA, No. 80.
[10]Ma-GIA, No. 111.
[11]Ma-GlA, No. 78. See also MilP, p. 5 and 2 keyboard pieces in HowP, p. 24.
[12]Ma-GlA, No. 82.
[13]Ma-GlA, No. 70.
[14]Ma-GlA, No. 71.
[15]PicM, pp. 112-36.

the minority sects
and their music

Land of Religious Freedom. In March 1681, William Penn, a Quaker and prominent reformer, obtained a large region west of the Delaware River in exchange for a debt of about 16,000 pounds owed to his father by Charles II. At first called "Sylvania," later "Pennsylvania" in honor of his father, William Penn offered land at attractive terms and complete religious freedom to all settlers. The Quakers first came to America in 1653 to preach the doctrines of religious and political independence, but were cruelly persecuted by the Puritan authorities in Massachusetts. By 1776 over one hundred thousand Lutherans, Moravians, Mennonites, Pietists, Quakers, Catholics and Anglicans made Pennsylvania their home, and many thousands more settled on the frontiers of Maryland, Virginia, North Carolina and Georgia. Thus Pennsylvania not only attracted emigrants from the Rhineland and northern Ireland, but also from New England.

Moravians. The Moravian brethren, who founded Bethlehem in 1741, left us a sizable body of sacred and secular music, both their own compositions and many brought from Europe. The research division of the Moravian Music Foundation discovered and authenticated several compositions by Johann Christoph Bach and Johann Ernst Bach in the church archives, and these compositions are the only ones known to exist in the world. John Antes (1740-1811), born in Frederick, Pennsylvania, the most famous of the Moravians, is known to have composed at least twenty-five sacred, concerted vocal compositions, thirteen chorales and three trios for two violins and cello. The last mentioned represents the first examples of chamber music composed in America and are very favorably compared with similar works by Joseph Haydn.[1]

Two of his most expressive compositions in the sacred genre are *Go, Congregation, Go* for soprano solo and keyboard accompaniment and *Surely He Has Borne Our Griefs,* anthem for mixed voices.[2]

Among Moravian-Americans may be mentioned Johann Friedrich Peter (Holland, 1746-Bethlehem, 1813) who composed some one hundred sixteen anthems[3] and six string quintets,[4] and David Moritz Michael (Germany, 1751-1827) who spent several years in Nazareth and Bethlehem. It was during his sojourn in Bethlehem that he composed his "water music," intended for alfresco performances on barge excursions on the Lehigh River. These delightful compositions are titled *Parthien* (Suites) and are scored for two clarinets, two horns, one or two bassoons and an additional flute or trumpet.[5] Unfortunately, very little of Moravian-American music entered the main stream of musical activity in America. Their greatest period was between 1750 and 1850, during which time they founded the first collegium musicum, organized the first trombone choir, constructed organs, many of which are still in use, and gave first performances of major European oratorios and symphonies.

Seventh-day Baptists. Pennsylvania became a haven for another band of refugees, Seventh-day Baptists, who established a semimonastic community in 1732 called Ephrata in Lancaster county. The chief figure was Conrad Beissel, an indefatigable composer of over a thousand hymns and musical settings based on the Old Testament. In addition to directing the destiny of his community, Beissel organized and trained a chorus to sing his music, which had as many as eight parts (the lowest of which was played on an instrument), with antiphonal singing an important feature. A primitive in musical composition, Beissel developed his own music theory and musical style. The music was sung rather freely with the rhythm following the natural accents of the text. Among his many harmonic liberties are parallel fifths and octaves, chords in root position interchanged with those in the second inversion and almost no modulations or suspensions.[6]

The Mennonites. Founded in Zurich in 1525, the Mennonites extended their religious beliefs throughout Switzerland, Germany, Austria, Holland, Russia, and eventually, the United States, where the first settlement was made in 1683. William Penn's offer of religious freedom induced the Mennonites to settle in Germantown and Philadelphia, and later, in Minnesota, Kansas and the Dakotas. They sang from *Das Ausbund: Das ist Etliche Schöne Christliche Lieder,* a hymn book printed in Schaffhausen, Germany in 1583. In 1742 an edition was published for them in Germantown and it is still being used by the Amish in Pennsylvania. The 1940 *Mennonite Hymnary* contains six hundred eighteen chorales, metrical psalms, gospel songs, responses, doxologies and Amens in four-part harmony. Catholic in its taste, the *Hymnary* has drawn its repertory from Lutheran, Catholic and Jewish sources, specifically from the *Genevan Psalter* (1551), *Damon's Psalter* (1592), *Est's Psalter* (1592), *Scottish Psalter* (1615), *Ravenscroft's Psalter* (1621) Italian opera composers, English madrigalists and German chorale books. In fact, nineteen of the hymns are in German. The preface to the *Hymnary* does indeed inform us that such a book should contain a great variety of hymns and songs which will lend themselves to the use of all services carried on in the church.

The Pietists. Led by Johannes Kelpius, the German Pietists established a community in Pennsylvania in 1694 on the banks of the Wissahickon River not far from Philadelphia. The Gloria Dei Church, a Swedish-Lutheran Church in which the members were choristers, was the scene of elaborately sung services which were often accompanied with viols, hautboys, trumpets and kettledrums.

The Shakers. Shakerism originated in the English Quaker Church about 1747. Nine members of the sect led by Mother Anne came to the United States in 1774 and settled in Watervliet, New York. When Mother Anne died in 1784 there were four colonies established in Massachusetts: Hancock, Tyringham, Harvard and Shirley; Alfred and New Gloucester were established in Maine, Enfield and Canterbury in New Hampshire and Watervliet and New Lebanon in New York. After 1800 the movement was extended to communities in Kentucky, Ohio, Indiana and Sodus, New York. At its zenith there were six thousand members. Its decline began after the Civil War, and today there are fewer than one hundred. This sect believed in divine revelation, the millennium, confession, separation and equality of the sexes, celibacy and the second coming of Christ.

The first Shaker songs were wordless tunes, not meant for instruments, for instrumental music was forbidden in the early years. An organ made its first appearance in the services in 1870, other instruments were added later. The first Shaker hymnal, *Millennial Praises*,[7] contained one hundred forty compositions, some borrowed, some original. During the Great Revival (1837-47), "vision songs" (which came as "gifts" to individuals who heard "beautiful music in the air") were added to the repertory. Many of these vision songs were set to nonsensical syllables, or in an "unknown tongue." Dancing was an integral part of their wor-

Shaker Music: A Collection of Songs of Various Kinds, 1839.

ship. During the early years, the "Shaking Quakers" as they were called —
because of their bodily contortions in the act of worship — employed a
kind of interpretive dance in which each participant danced as he saw
fit. Valentine Rathbun wrote in 1781:

> Everyone acts for himself, and almost everyone different from the
> other; one will stand with his arms extended, acting over odd postures,
> which they call signs; another will be dancing, and sometimes hopping
> on one leg about the floor; another will fall to turning around, so swift,
> that if it be a woman, her clothes will so fill with wind, as though they
> were kept out by a hoop; another will be prostrate on the floor; another
> will be talking with somebody; and some sitting by, smoking [sic]
> their pipes; some groaning dismally, some trembling extremely; others
> acting as though all their nerves were convulsed; others swinging their
> arms, with all vigor, as though they were turning a wheel, etc. Then
> all break off, and have a spell of smoking, and some times great fits
> of laughter. . . . They have several such exercises in a day, especially
> on a Sabbath.[8]

Toward the end of the century organized dances were introduced.
Among them may be mentioned the Square Order Shuffle (the first
distinct dance movement), then a later variant called the Square Step
and still later the Hollow Square. Marchlike dances were introduced
early in 1817; circle dances were not developed until after 1822 and
many variants of these ensued. Henry Tudor witnessed such dances in
1834.[9]

The Shaker melodies are simple and unharmonized and vary in
length from six to forty-five measures. The longer anthem-like melodies
are quite varied rhythmically with frequent time changes, a result of the
music yielding to the demands of the text. Most of the melodies are
gapped, that is, they are based on incomplete scales such as the pentatonic and hexatonic. The diatonic melodies are major and minor, rarely
modal. A pentatonic melody in major is usually without its fourth and
seventh degrees, or occasionally minus the seventh. Melodies in the
minor key or in a mode are usually not gapped. Most melodies are in the
natural minor, a few in the Dorian mode. According to Andrews the
Shakers embellished their tunes by using the following devices: (1) the
upward slide to the begining note of the tune; (2) bridging of intervals,
that is, raising or lowering the vocal pitch in the direction of the following note; (3) the pitch sag between two successive notes which have the
same pitch; (4) the Scotch Snap; (5) the use of trills.[10] One tune caught
the attention of Aaron Copland, "The Gift to be Simple," and was used
in his "Appalachian Spring." The Shakers experimented with various
notations, for they too were eager to use a notation that was easiest to

learn and that gave the singer the fullest amount of information as simply as possible. As a result, some manuscripts have come down to us using letters of the alphabet with and without a staff, and others in conventional notation. Toward the end of the century, the Shakers succumbed to the magnetism of harmony and published *Hymns and Anthems* in four parts (ed. by H.C.B., East Canterbury, N.H., 1892) and *Original Shaker Music* (2 vols., New York: Wm. Pond & Co., 1893) for the North family.

The Catholics. Through a grant obtained in 1632 from Charles I, George Calvert (Lord Baltimore) established an asylum in what is now Maryland for the persecuted Catholics of England. Nothing is known of its early church music. It was not until 1787 that John Aitken published the Compilation of the *Litanies, Vespers, Hymns, and Anthems As They Are Sung in the Catholic Church.*[11] Originally for unharmonized melodies, later editions contained music in three parts — the harmonic idiom similar to that used in Protestant churches. According to Ellinwood:

> an improvement began with the formation of the *Caecilian Society* in 1873 by John Baptist Singenberger. . . . Through annual conventions, lectures, and the pages of its magazine, *Caecilia*, the Society strove to purge Roman Catholic services of cheap, sentimental music, and to cultivate the use of plainsong and polyphony.[12]

In 1905, A. Edmonds Tozer in his *Catholic Church Hymnal*[13] brought together the best of those hymns which he claimed "have endeared themselves to so many thousands of people" and "to provide others of a more virile type expressed in the restrained language of the church's own song." The melodies are drawn from Gregorian chant set in four-part harmony and from other sources including newly composed melodies. Tozer himself contributed forty-eight compositions. Nicola Montani's *The St. Gregory Hymnal*[14] achieved wide diffusion for it was particularly adapted to the requirements of choirs, schools, academies, seminaries, convents and Sunday schools. This hymnal contains hymns arranged in unison, two, three or four part harmony. Many florid chants were borrowed from the Liber Usualis. These have been carefully pruned of their floridity for easier singing. The *Pius X Hymnal*[15] (1953) was published to commemorate the Golden Jubilee of the Motu Proprio of 1903. By all standards the best collection of hymns, this publication contains compositions for unison, two-equal or four-mixed voices by Pierluigi da Palestrina, Heinrich Isaac, Tomas Luis de Victoria, Roland de Lassus, anonymous ones taken from French and German psalters and others in addition to Gregorian chants. Of equal quality is the *Parish*

Mass Book[16] *prepared by the Committee of the Liturgical Conference* in 1959. The choice of melodies was not restricted to Catholic composers, for there are compositions borrowed from John Day's *Psalter* (1562), Tate and Brady (1698) and from other Protestant denominations, as well as Gregorian chant with organ accompaniment. Except in those large churches which encourage trained choirs, there is little or no singing in the average parish church. It may be that the recent changes in the Catholic rite will bring about greater congregational participation.

The Jews. The Jews who came to America before the Revolution followed the Sephardic ritual, which was predominantly Spanish and Oriental. In the nineteenth century, the bulk of the Jews came from the Germanic countries, which followed the Ashkenazic ritual. Today, there are orthodox, conservative and reform temples throughout the United States. The orthodox Jews have never felt the need for singing books in their temples, for whatever hymns were used were sung by cantors whose repertoire was based on an oral tradition. The conservatives allow the same traditional hymns, but depend almost completely on cantors and professional choirs with little congregational participation. Charleston, South Carolina was the birthplace of the reform movement led by Isaac Wise in 1824. Believing in the necessity of cultivating the manners and practices of the Protestant churches as a step towards assimilation into the American culture, reform congregations abbreviated Hebrew texts, introduced prayers and hymns in English, installed organs and engaged professional choirs.

In 1878 Simon Hecht published in Indiana his *Jewish Hymns for Sabbath Schools and Families.*[17] This collection contained forty-three hymns in English and nine in German. Hecht, himself, composed twelve. Another collection containing music by Mozart, Beethoven, Mendelssohn and others in four-part harmony was compiled by A. J. Davis, titled, *Music to Hymns and Anthems for Jewish Worship.*[18] The *Union Hymnal*[19] is used in most reformed temples and adopted many Protestant melodies which were intermixed with Jewish folk tunes. The 1940 edition contains two hundred sixty-six hymns in four-part harmony, many published for the first time. Among some Protestant hymns that found their way into the reformed Jewish hymnal are "O God, Our Help" by Isaac Watts, set to music by William Croft; "The Nation," Samuel A. Ward's setting of Katherine Lee Bates's text titled "America the Beautiful"; and Schiller's "Hymn to Joy" set to the theme of Beethoven's Ninth Symphony. Perhaps the melodies most loved are *Yigdal* ("Praise the Living God") and *Adon Olam* ("Lord of the Universe"). An examination of the two hundred sixty-six melodies in the *Union Hymnal* revealed that two hundred and one were cast in major tonalities, sixty-one in minor, and only four in modal; moreover, forty-two are gapped melodies, the majority of which lack the leading tone. Considerable portions of the *Union Prayerbook* have been set to choral music, some of it with orchestral accompaniments by Ernest Bloch, Arnold Schoenberg, Darius Milhaud and other distinguished modern composers.[20]

Music of the Mormons. In July 1830, about three months after the organization of the Church of Jesus Christ of Latter-day Saints in Fayette, New York,[21] Joseph Smith received his first revelation and call as a prophet. The message of the revelation was as follows:

> And verily I say unto thee that thou shalt lay aside the things of this world, and seek for the things of a better. And it shall be given thee, also, to make a selection of sacred hymns, as it shall be given thee, which is pleasing unto me, to be had in my church. For my soul delighteth in the song of the heart; yea the song of the righteous is a prayer unto me, and it shall be answered with a blessing upon their heads.[22]

This led to the compilation of the first Mormon hymnal titled, *Hymns of Jesus Christ of Latter-day Saints.*[23] It contained ninety hymns in four-part harmony set to well-known hymn texts by Isaac Watts, the Wesleys, Samuel Medley, Bishop Ken and others.

In 1948 a revised edition was published in Salt Lake City containing some original tunes by Mormon composers. Among the most appealing melodies are "In Remembrance of Thy Suffering" by Evans Stephens and "High on the Mountain Top" by Ebenezer Beesley. The Mormon melodies are cast mostly in the major keys. A few are gapped, that is, some are minus the sixth degree. Congregational hymn singing has always been an important part of the worship of the Mormons, not only in the actual services but in the homes of the Saints. The Mormon church has become known as a musical church through such performing groups as the Mormon Tabernacle Choir and the Mormon Choir of Southern California.

FOOTNOTES

[1]Ma-GlA, No. 34.
[2]Ma-GlA, Nos. 32 and 33.
[3]Ma-GlA, No. 36.
[4]Ma-GlA, No. 35.
[5]Ma-GlA, No. 37.
[6]Ma-GlA, No. 31.
[7]The full title reads *"Millennial Praises, containing A Collection of Gospel Hymns in Four Parts: Adapted to the Day of Christ's Second Appearing, Composed for the use of His people.* Hancock, Mass., 1813.

[8]AndG, p. 144.
[9]TudN, pp. 171-172.
[10]AndG, p. 91.
[11]Philadelphia.
[12]EllinR, p. 344.
[13]New York.
[14]Philadelphia, 1920.
[15]Boston.
[16]Cincinnati.
[17]Indiana.
[18]New York, 1887.
[19]New York, 1897.
[20]EllinR, p. 352.
[21]Popular opposition and continuous persecution forced the Mormons to move to Missouri, then to Mississippi and finally to Salt Lake City.
[22]Doctrine and Covenants, *Book of Commandments for the Government of the Church of Christ* 25:10-12 (1835).
[23]Kirtland, Ohio, 1835.

fasola, doremi and revivalism

Folksy Religious Songs. It is well-nigh impossible to pinpoint the time and area of the appearance of the folk element in our hymn tune books, but it is possible to enumerate the processes and events which brought it into being. It was above all a sociological phenomenon sparked by religious revivals which lasted intermittently from the end of the eighteenth century to the mid-nineteenth: the Wesleyan movement which brought into existence hundreds of "folksy religious songs," many based on well-known secular tunes;· the paraphrased hymns of Isaac Watts, which were greatly admired and used by southern folk hymn compilers; the diffusion of the singing school movement as a concommitant and logical outgrowth of mass meetings and great open-air assemblies which took place in the south, southeast and midwest. Irving Lowens states:

> It is reasonable to assume that the highly characteristic style of composition practiced by Daniel Read, the Lewis Edsons, Jacob French, Oliver Brownson, Timothy Swan, Justin Morgan, and many others active in Connecticut and central Massachusetts during the 1780s and 1790s was based on the music they heard around them; the semi-folk idiom they cultivated was in all likelihood based on the music ingrained in their consciousness — Anglo-Celtic folk-music and its religious offshoot, American folk-hymnody.[1]

The Tune Books. Much of this music found its way into southern hymnody. According to Lowens, John Wyeth's *Repository of Sacred Music Part Second,* 1813, was the source of the many tunes used in southern collections and first included in Ananias Davisson's *Kentucky*

Harmony in Harrisonburg, Virginia about 1815. There followed James M. Boyd's *The Virginia Sacred Musical Repository* (Winchester, Va., 1818); Allen D. Carden's *The Missouri Harmony,* (St. Louis, 1820); Joseph Funk's *Genuine Church Music,* (Mountain Valley, Va., 1832); William Walker's *The Southern Harmony* (Spartanburg, S.C., 1835); White and King's *The Sacred Harp,* (Philadelphia, 1844). Each borrowed tunes from earlier publications and added new ones, and all were notated in shape notes. Many of the collections contained tunes which George Pullen Jackson has classified as Spirituals;[2] he distinguishes three types among them: (1) *Religious ballads,* whose subject matter was usually drawn from the Bible and set to original or borrowed music;[3] (2) *Folk hymns,* whose texts are usually in praise of the Lord and are set frequently to known melodies;[4] (3) *Revival Spiritual songs,* which are akin to Negro spirituals, are musically very simple and because of their text repetition, were very popular in revival meetings.[5] The obsessive concern with the inevitability of death, the flames of hell and the rewards of repentance was the subject of most sermons. Similarly, the texts of countless hymns by Watts, John Cennick, John Newton and John Leland are indeed a sad and morbid lot. But curiously enough, they are set to some very appealing and stirring melodies.[6]

The Musical Contents. The melodies are principally diatonic and are cast in major and minor keys and in the Ionian, Aeolian, Mixolydian and Dorian modes. Many melodies are pentatonic in which the fourth and seventh degrees of the scale are omitted in major keys; whereas, the second and sixth degrees are omitted in minor. Hexatonic melodies omit the fourth or seventh degree in major and the sixth in minor. The melodies are principally diatonic, that is, nonchromatic, but in performance they are freely ornamented with added notes, portamenti, scoops and anticipations. The harmony is usually in three parts (minus the alto) with the melody in the tenor. Parallel fifths often occur and the third is frequently omitted in the last chord; however, it is the manner of performance which imparts to this music its primitive flavor. The upper parts were taken by both men and women. Instead of three or four voices with each part remaining within its prearranged ambit, intervals become inverted. Thus, a progression of parallel fourths would be sung as fourths by some singers and as fifths by others, who, finding the parts too high, would sing them an octave lower thus creating an organum-like sound.

The Four-Syllable Notation (Fasola). The quest to provide a kind of music notation that music illiterates could learn in the least amount of time was forever present in the minds of tune book compilers. It will

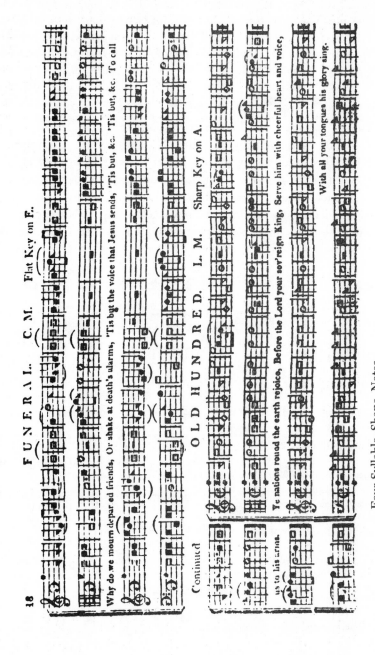

Four-Syllable Shape Notes
Wm. Little & Wm. Smith, *The Easy Instructor*, New York, 1802.

be remembered that John Tufts had already come to grips with this problem in 1721 (See p. 11). While conventional notation was in general use in the northeastern states, shape notes with their corresponding syllable names, *fa, sol, la, mi,* found favor in southern and midwestern states. The innovation of attaching solmization syllables to shape notes has been claimed by collaborators William Smith and William Little and by Andrew Law. The singing school teachers, Little and Smith used their system, *fa* ◀ , *sol* ◖ , *la* ◀ , *mi* ◆, in *The Easy Instructor,* the earliest known edition published in New York in 1802.[7] In Law's system, which first appeared in his *The Musical Primer* (Cambridge, Mass., 1803), the shape notes *la* and *fa* are reversed and the staff is dispensed with.[8] There followed a few modifications of this system, but despite such attempts all other hymn tune books adhered to the system pioneered by Little and Smith. The shape note system did indeed cater to the "meanest capacities." It was necessary for the

Chapin & Dickerson (Phila., 1810)							
David Sower, Jr. (Norristown, Pa., 1832)							
J.B. Aiken (Phila., 1846)							
A. Auld (Cincinnati, 1847)							
M.L. Swan (Nashville, 1848)							
J. Funk (Winchester, Va., 1851)							
A.W. Johnson (Nashville, 1853)							
W.B. Gilham (Columbia, Tenn., 1854)							
S. Wakefield (Cincinnati, 1854)							
J.J. Fast (Hudson, Ohio, 1854)							
E.D. M'Cauley (Fredericksburg, Pa., 1856)							
W. Walker (Spartanburg, S.C., 1866)							

Seven-Syllable Shapes

beginner to recognize the shape, position and value of the note and to understand that the progression *mi-fa, fa-mi,* and *fa-la, la-fa* always signified a half step. With this knowledge firmly entrenched, it was possible for him to sing a new tune at sight provided he could put into sound a leap or descent of a fourth or fifth when he saw one.

The Seven-Syllable Notation (Doremi). There were those compilers, however, who opposed the four-syllable system. Francis Hopkinson favored the seven-syllable system (Doremi) and explained it in his *A Collection of Psalm Tunes,*[9] perhaps for the first time in the United States. Chapin and Dickerson in their *The Musical Instructor* proposed the use of the following, namely, *do, na, mi, faw, sol, law, ba.*[10] David Sower, Jr., also preferred seven syllables admitting, however, that "there are various setts [sic] of syllables at option." He himself employed, *lo, sa, me, fa, sol, la, se* in his *Musical Teacher.*[11] Their use prompted Sower to introduce three new shapes (see chart), thus began a succession of publications using various modifications of the three new syllables. Lowell Mason, often called the "Father of American music education" also used seven syllables in his *Sacred Harp or Eclectic Harmony.*[12] He stated the reason for his preference in the introduction:

> The most correct method of solmization is to apply a distinct syllable to each note of the scale: viz, the syllable DO to one, RE (ray) to two, MI to three, FA to four, SOL to five, LA to six, and SI (see) to seven. Indeed, by pursuing the common method of only four syllables, singers are almost always superficial. It is therefore recommended to all who wish to be thorough, to pursue the system of seven syllables, disregarding the different forms of the notes.[13]

Other Notations. Numeral notation also had its adherents. There are two claimants having the honor of first substituting numbers for notes. These are H. W. Day and F. F. Beale's *Boston Numeral Harmony*[14] and Thomas Harrison's *The Sacred Harmonicon.*[15] In this system, which is claimed by the authors (Day and Beale) "to be the most comprehensive and simple Musical Notation ever published in the world," one line indicating key center replaced the staff and numbers replaced note heads. Clefs, bar lines, slurs and dots had the same function as in conventional notation. A short vertical line directly below the number indicated a quarter note, while a stem and flag indicated an eighth note. Harrison's publication has two lines and does not add stems and flags to the numbers. Excluding all conventional music symbols, Silas Leonard in his *The Christian Psalmist* relied exclusively on numbers and letters. That his system was well received is evidenced by the fact that "40,000 copies were sold in two years and a half."[16] There were other unortho-

GAINSBOROUGH. C. M.

TANSUR.

When I can read my title clear, To mansions in the skies, I'll bid farewell to every fear, And wipe my weeping eyes.

DUNDEE. C. M.

When I can read my title clear To mansions in the skies, I'll bid farewell to every fear, And wipe my weeping eyes.

2 Should earth against my soul engage,
  And fiery darts be hurled,
  Then I can smile at Satan's rage,
  And face a frowning world.

3 Let cares like a wild deluge come,
  Let storms of sorrow fall,
  So I but safely reach my home,
  My God, my heaven, my all.

4 There I shall bathe my weary soul
  In seas of heavenly rest,
  And not a wave of trouble roll
  Across my peaceful breast.

Numeral Notation

Thomas Harrison, *Sacred Harmonium*, Cincinnati, 1845.

dox notations such as T. Van Tassel's *The Phonographic Harmonist*,[17] which gives the appearance of a thirteenth-century manuscript with its breves, longs and maximas; one credited to J. J. Hood, who inserted a short line, cross, dot, or caret within the note head;[18] others used the letters of the alphabet alone or letters of the alphabet in lieu of note-heads.[19]

The Concern Over Musical Illiterates. The idea of providing a kind of music script which would enable the singer to read at sight with the utmost speed was of course first encountered in Guido d'Arezzo's *Micrologus de disciplina artis musicae* (c. 1040) in his discussion of the solmization system which since the eleventh century has been in continuous use in western culture. Guido was particularly eager to present a system that aided the "trained singer" of the *schola cantorum*. In brief, his efforts were directed to the professional singer. The American hymn tune composers and compilers were not so concerned with the professional, but rather with the musically illiterate churchgoer.

The experiment in the various music notations was undoubtedly the result of conditions created by the westward movement with its new settlements, towns and pioneer-type existence which left very little time to the cultivation of music. In their effort to reach the rural population, itinerant singing masters traveled on horseback to small communities where they taught congregations to sing by note. Each was prepared to remain several days if necessary to teach singing and the rudiments of music to the townsfolk. Indeed, it is no wonder that compilers, composers and publishers worked hand-in-hand in the belief that the most expeditious manner to improve singing and sight singing in the churches was through a simplified notation system. To determine whether or not they were successful, it suffices to state that over six hundred thousand copies of William Walker's *Southern Harmony*[20] were sold (first published in 1835 employing Fasola notation only) and his book was only one of many.

Revivalism. Revivalism underwent a major change after the Civil War. Eighteenth- and early nineteenth-century revivalism (see the Great Awakening) under the influence of Jonathan Edwards was a salvation-through-terror religious movement calling for a total rejection of worldly ways as a means of escaping the wrath of God. In contrast was the post-Civil war revivalism which was molded largely from socio-economic factors. The most salient of these factors were the influx of urban, non-protestant Europeans and the conflicts between the middle class masses and affluent big business and the exploitation of the middle class by big business.[21] The evangelists attempted to inculcate the immi-

God the Father.

112 Dundee. C. M.

Andro Hart's Psalter, 1615.

Key F.

:d	m :f	s :d	r :m	f :m	r :d	d :t_1	d :—	—
:d	d :d	t_1 :l_1	t_1 :d	d :d	t_1 :l_1	l_1 :s_1	s_1 :—	—
Mak-	er of	earth, to	Thee a -	lone Per -	pet - ual	rest be -	longs;	
:m	s :d	r :d .m	s :s	l :s	s :m	r :r	m :—	—
:d	d :l_1	s_1 :l_1	s_1 :d	f_1 :d	s_1 :l_1	f_1 :s_1	d :—	—

:s	d^1 :t	l :s	s :fe	s :m	r :d	d :t_1	d :—	—
:d	m :r	d :r	d :d	t_1 :d	t_1 :l_1	l_1 :s_1	s_1 :—	—
To	Thee bright	choirs a	round Thy	throne Pour	forth their	end - less	songs.	
:m	s :s	m :r	m :l	s :s	s :m	r :r	m :—	—
:d	d :s_1	l_1 :t_1	d :r	s_1 :d	s_1 :l_1	f_1 :s_1	d :—	—

2 But we, as sinless now no more,
Are doomed to toil and pain;
Yet exiles on a foreign shore
May sing the heavenly strain.

3 Father, whose promise binds Thee still
To make the captive free,
Grant us to mourn the deeds of ill
That banish us from Thee.

4 And, mourning, grant us faith to rest
Upon Thy love and care;
Till Thou restore us with the blest,
The joys of heaven to share.

Tr. *J. M. Neale*, 1850.

113

My God, my everlasting hope,
I live upon Thy truth:
Thy hands have held my childhood up,
And strengthened all my youth.

2 Still has my life new wonders seen
Repeated every year;
Behold, my days that yet remain,
I trust them to Thy care.

3 Cast me not off when strength declines,
When hoary hairs arise;
And round me let Thy glory shine,
Whene'er Thy servant dies.

Isaac Watts, 1719.

114 St. Frances. C. M.

G. A. Löhr, 1866.

Key E♭.

:d	f :m	r :d	s :f	m :m	r :s	l :l	s :—	—
:d	d :d	t_1 :d	r :r	d :d	r :t_1	m :r .d	t_1 :—	—
Lord!	when my	rapt - ured	thought sur -	veys Cre -	a - tion's	beau - ties	o'er,	
:m	l :s	f :m	s :s	s :s	s :r	m :fe	s :—	—
:d	d :d	s_1 :l_1	t_1 :t_1	d :d	t_1 :s_1	d :r	s_1 :—	—

Theodore Seward, *The Church Praise Book*, New York and Chicago, 1888.

grant masses with a common faith and value system. While the middle classes united in the struggle against social problems, the approach used by the evangelists to achieve audience conversion gradually changed. Led by Dwight L. Moody (1837-1899), the violent fervor of prewar revivalism was transformed into one of compassion, gentle persuasion and self-restraint. The "God of wrath and judgment" was replaced by a "God of love and mercy."[22]

Hymns by such composers as George Root (1820-1895), Ira Sankey (1840-1908) and Charles C. Converse (1832-1918) were often borrowed and refurbished with new texts. These, sung at revival meetings, were simple and attractive tunes in verse and refrain form, composed over simple tonic and dominant harmonies usually in major keys and often employing the dotted eighth and sixteenth note pattern of a marching song. Root's "Tramp, Tramp, Tramp, the Boys Are Marching" became "Jesus Loves the Little Children." Other hymns widely sung were The "Ninety and Nine," "A Soldier on a Cross," and "What a Friend We Have in Jesus."

FOOTNOTES

[1]LowM, p. 139.
[2]JacSF, p. 5.
[3]Ma-GlA, No. 97.
[4]Ma-GlA, No. 99.
[5]Ma-GlA, No. 101.
[6]Ma-GlA, Nos. 91, 95, 98, 100, and 103.
[7]See LowM, pp. 115-137.
[8]Andrew Law is credited with having initiated in the United States the practice of placing the melody in the soprano.
[9]Philadelphia, 1753.
[10]Philadelphia, 1810.
[11]Norristown, Penn., 1832.
[12]Cincinnati, 1835.
[13]*Ibid.*
[14]Boston, 1845.
[15]Cincinnati, 1845.
[16]Louisville, 1850.
[17]Syracuse, 1846.
[18]Used by R. A. Glenn in his *The Pleasant Hour*, Philadelphia, 1883.
[19]See plates, pp. 23 and 35.
[20]Spartanburg, S. C. For a discussion of the various kinds of music notation used in tune books in the United States from 1721 to 1901, see MarrN, pp. 136-42.
[21]DowR, p. 116.
[22]*Ibid.*, p. 116.

patriotic and national songs and our lighter side

In this genre we are again indebted to England for three of her fine melodies which we have appropriated for our own. "Yankee Doodle" and "To Anacreon in Heaven" found their way into our repertory during our war years with England, but "God Save the King" was annexed during peace time. All melodies were well known and sung on both sides of the Atlantic even before the wars. "Yankee Doodle" was borrowed by the Yankees when they routed the British at Concord.[1] "To Anacreon in Heaven" was the constitutional song of the Anacreontic Society of London. Its text, written by Ralph Tomlinson about 1775, is addressed to the Grecian poet, Anacreon, and celebrates the virtues of wine and song.[2] In 1798 Thomas Treat Paine adapted a new text to the English drinking song and titled it "Adams and Liberty.[3]" On September 14, 1814 Francis Scott Key, appointed to negotiate for the release of an American prisoner aboard a British man-of-war, found himself witnessing the bombardment of Fort McHenry. So overcome with joy when at the approach of dawn he saw the Stars and Stripes still flying over the fort, he penned the familiar words, and titled it "The Defence of Fort McHenry." It first appeared as a broadside with the indication that it was to be sung to the tune of "To Anacreon in Heaven." In the same year the words and music were published by Carr's Music Store in Baltimore. As if four stanzas were not enough, Oliver Wendell Holmes added a fifth in 1872.[4] The late Richard Hill compiled a list of eighty-five American parodies adapted to "To Anacreon in Heaven" between 1790 and 1818. Also see "The Star-Spangled

Banner in the United States Before 1820," in *Essays Honoring Lawrence C. Wroth,* Washington, 1951.

Perhaps embarrassed that the music which was chosen as our national anthem was sung in English pubs, and because of its wide range and awkward leaps, James Hewitt adapted Key's words to his own melody. His attempt was futile. The Anacreontic tune, refurbished with patriotic words, had already become an indissoluble part of our new nation; however, the "Star Spangled Banner" was not formally entered as our national anthem until 1931. The bill was signed by President Herbert Hoover. "God Save the King" was, of course, sung in the Colonies. In fact, it was included in James Lyon's *Urania*[5] in 1761 with a different text and titled "Whitefield's." At the suggestion of Lowell Mason who wanted attractive melodies suitable for children, the Reverend Samuel Francis Smith set a new text beginning with the words "My Country Tis of Thee" to the tune "God Save the King," and it was first performed by children in Park Street Church on July 4, 1831.[6] The words to "Hail! Columbia" were written by Joseph Hopkinson (son of Francis) and set to the tune "The President's March" composed by Phillip Phile in 1798.[7] Its patriotic text refers to our decision for neutrality during the hostilities between the French and English. The treaty of Alliance of 1778 pledged us to aid France in the defense of her possessions in the West Indies and to allow her the use of our ports. Washington maintained that the treaty made with the government of Louis XVI was not applicable to the new government of the first French republic, and therefore abrogated the treaty on April 22, 1793.

The period of the Civil War gave birth to several fine patriotic songs. "When Johnny Comes Marching Home" composed by the famous bandmaster, Patrick Gilmore under his nom-de-plume, Louis Lambert was enormously popular.[8] "Marching Through Georgia," composed by Henry Clay Work, refers to Sherman's famous march from Atlanta to the sea.[9] "Tenting on the Old Camp Ground," composed by Walter Kittredge, became so popular that it was sung by both belligerents.[10] "Glory, Hallelujah" was composed by William Steffe sometime before 1855. It became a camp-meeting song with a new text, "Say Brothers Will You Meet Us?" In 1861 Julia Ward Howe set a more dignified text to the tune and it was published in the *Atlantic Monthly*, February, 1862, with the title, "The Battle Hymn of the Republic."[11] "Dixie's Land" was composed by Dan Emmett in 1895 as a walk-around, the grand finale of a minstrel show. Its popularity was so widespread that it was adopted by the Confederacy as its battle song.[12]

Sentimental Ballads. Romanticism in European literature first appeared in the works of such poets as William Wordsworth and Samuel Taylor Coleridge and others and soon found its way to the continent and across the Atlantic at the turn of the century. The romantic vocabularly of love, death, wounds, tears, pain, night and so forth — the school of self-pity found many kindred spirits in the United States. Among those who came to our country in the 1830s and performed their own sentimental ballads were Charles Horn (1786-1849), Joseph Knight (1812-1887) and Henry Russell (1812-1900). Among their compositions that proved immensely popular are "Cherry Ripe," "The Grecian Daughter," "Rocked in the Cradle of the Deep," "Woodsman Spare that Tree," "The Old Arm Chair,"[13] "Who Will Care for Mother Now?," "Nobody's Darling." John Hill Hewitt (1801-1890), son of James, called the Father of American balladry, was perhaps our foremost exponent. His "The Minstrel's Return from the War" was composed in 1825. One of his most successful ballads was "All Quiet Along the Potomac Tonight" composed in 1861.[14] The popularity of these songs was so enormous that concerts of vocal music containing such songs drew large receptive audiences. Poignant words, a sentimental melody and an overly well-done performance were the ingredients that insured instant success.

FOOTNOTES

[1]Ma-GlA, No. 110.
[2]Ma-GlA, No. 113. For an exhaustive study of our national anthem see, MulB.
[3]Ma-GlA, No. 114.
[4]Ma-GlA, No. 115.
[5]Philadelphia.
[6]Ma-GlA, No. 116.
[7]Ma-GlA, No. 111.
[8]Ma-GlA, No. 120.
[9]Ma-GlA, No. 121.
[10]Ma-GlA, No. 119.
[11]Ma-GlA, No. 117.
[12]Ma-GlA, No. 109.
[13]Ma-GlA, No. 123.
[14]Ma-GlA, No. 118.

nineteenth-century musical sophistication

Political unrest, economic distress and the Industrial Revolution in nineteenth-century Europe had triggered another immigrational wave to America. There were, of course, some fine musicians in New York City, such as Henry Christian Timm (1811-1892), Daniel Schlesinger (1799-1839) and William Scharfenberg (1819-1895) who were active in the 30s, but the news of music-famished Americans was all that was needed for European orchestras, opera companies and soloists to fulfill concert engagements in our metropolitan cities as well as in Montreal, Quebec and Toronto.

Visiting Concert Artists and Orchestras. It is surprising to read that Ole Bull, the famous Norwegian violinist, concertized in America (reaching California) and realized $400,000 in two years. Jenny Lind, idolized in Europe, came to America in 1850 and, managed by Barnum and Bailey, netted $135,000 in two years. Sigismund Thalberg, a pianist, arrived in 1856 and barnstormed throughout the United States specializing in pyrotechnical variations on operatic themes. But these artistic luminaries, whose presence before American audiences merely served to demonstrate the calibre of their artistry, did not remain as did the Germania orchestra, to contribute to and nurture our musical growth. Their contractual obligations fulfilled, they returned to Europe with fattened purses. The Germania Musical Society orchestra first came in 1848 with a repertoire of mostly contemporary music; they created a profound impression. It was a fortunate decision for us when the Germanians, disbanding in 1854, settled in our country, thereby contributing

to the musical growth of our major cities through their excellent training and consummate artistry.

The widely heralded French conductor, Louis Antoine Jullien,
a truculant and master showman, presented his orchestra to American
audiences in 1853. Contemporary critics reported that the orchestra
performed with uncanny accuracy. Surprisingly, of the one hundred
and two musicians, only twenty-six accompanied him from Europe;
seventy-six were recruited from resident musicians of New York City.

Emulation of European Musical Styles. Of the various nationalities
who came to our shores, the Germans in particular became active in
our musical life. Their background of European music culture together
with the fame of the nineteenth-century German master-composers resulted in the emulation of their music as ideal models for our art-music.
The serious American student of music usually went to Europe to study
with some German teacher of repute. Hence, the typical styles of
European Romantic music were transplanted in America. But because
these styles had no organic relationship to the true cultural background
of American society, they proved sterile in the cultivation of an indigenous American expression. They did provide, however, well-developed
technical tools and proven forms with which eventually we could develop
our own musical language.

Romantic Tradition in General. The style that so dominated our
music of this period has been called "Romantic" by historians because
of its emphases on emotionalism, subjectivity and individualism. In
terms of musical expression, the forms are more freely constructed (exemplified in the symphonic poem) and abound in programmatic description; the textures are predominantly ornamented homophony; the melodies show a wide range, irregular phrase lengths and express warm,
personal feelings; on the whole, the rhythmic patterns are regular but
there are frequent mixtures with irregularity; the harmonies show much
use of altered chords including added nonchordal tones, seventh and
ninth chords on all scale degrees and chromaticism involving much use
of diminished seventh chords to effect unconventional and remote modulations (often obscuring the key feeling) for color effects.

William Henry Fry (1813-1864). Fry has the distinction of being
one of the first composers trained in Europe to continue its music
traditions in this country and help fight the battle of the American
composer. A Philadelphian by birth, he chose to pursue journalism as
a career, becoming music editor and critic on the *New York Tribune.* His
music compositions include four symphonies but it is his opera *Leonora*[1]
(1845) which best represents his style as well as achieving for him the

honor of being the first American to write an opera in his native tongue (although not on an American subject). Examination of the "Leonora" score reveals that although the arias have flowing lyrical melodies, they seem superficial with an overabundance of feminine cadences resembling the melodic treatment in the then current Italian operas by Vincenzo Bellini and Gaetano Donizetti.

The rhythmic grouping is foursquare and regular. The harmonies favor the tonic and dominant seventh chords with the material moving through a variety of keys. In contrast to the overuse of sentimental melodies in minor keys, Fry's arias are often in major modes; for intense emotional or dramatic expression, diminished seventh or augmented chords are used. Most reminiscent of the Italian operatic style is the use of the *da capo* aria with its obvious phrase repetition; particularly noticeable is the often monotonous recurrence of a rhythmic pattern which may be set to different interval groupings. Overall, the recitatives and choruses as well as the arias lack real dramatic characterization and integrated organization.

George Frederick Bristow (1825-1898). Born in New York, Bristow probably will be remembered as the first native-trained (although by immigrant pedagogues) American composer to successfully use the European traditional musical styles and larger forms. His career included playing the violin in the New York Philharmonic Symphony, but he made his reputation as director of the New York Harmonic Society, a choral group which was dedicated to the performance of works by native composers. Bristow wrote much music for orchestra, choral and chamber groups, instrumental and vocal solos but his outstanding work, as with his contemporary Fry, is the opera *Rip Van Winkle* (1855) which, unlike Fry's *Leonora,* is on a native subject.

Bristow's style resembles that of Mendelssohn's in its flowing melodies which often consist of small figural patterns and simple chord progressions, but it lacks the large conception of logical structural development and satisfying expressive warmth of the master. Specifically, Bristow's melodies are simple and straightforward with less ornamentation than in Fry's melodies; there is a predominance of simple rhythmic grouping with much beat and subdivided beat reiteration to realize a foursquare, solid effect. Tonic and dominant seventh chords prevail but with frequent modulations (often to distant keys) through diminished seventh chords. The phrase structure is even but with less use of repeated interval and rhythmic patterns than in Fry's music; on the other hand, the various dramatic tensions and feelings all show about the same musical treatment.[2]

William Mason (1829-1908). The son of the famous music educator, Lowell Mason, William completed his study of music in Germany and returned to America to become a prominent concert pianist, a successful teacher (evolving new methods of finger control), a sponsor of chamber music and a composer. His many compositions, mostly piano pieces, are in the typical Chopinesque style of rather free melodic figuration, regular rhythm and harmony but loosely knit forms; however, in attempting to avoid the conventional, hackneyed chord formulas of the German Romanticists, Mason's progressions often seem to lack goals as well as cumulative form.[3]

Dudley Buck (1839-1909). Another of the group of Americans who studied music in Germany, Buck returned to contribute to our musical development as a performer and composer. He was employed as a church organist in Hartford, Chicago, Boston and New York but was known primarily for his choral compositions. Although some of the compositions are in the larger form of the cantata, his reputation rests largely on small pieces of popular appeal, mainly, mixed quartets for church performance. His *Mottette Collection* marked an epoch in American church music since it was the first collection of appropriate vocal ensemble music published in America with independent organ accompaniment. Stylistically, his music in cantata form resembles Wagner's in the frequent use of leitmotifs to identify characters and emotions; the patterns though never protrude from an Italian-like declamation as well as *bel canto* melodic style. Harmonically, there are the usual conventional progressions enriched with a preponderance of diminished seventh chords. His smaller church pieces are in the simple, homophonic style so typical of mixed quartet music; the diatonic, foursquare melodies couched in dominant and diminished seventh-chord-saturated harmonies undoubtedly reflect the tastes of the church-goers of that era.

Sidney Lanier (1842-1881). Although leaving little music, Lanier is considered one of the most talented early American composers. He studied violin and flute, playing the latter professionally in the Peabody Symphony in Baltimore, but his main efforts were devoted to writing poetry and music. His goal was an art expression based on a synthesis of music and poetry. Unfortunately, Lanier died before attaining his full musical potential. His works include three unfinished symphonies, some instrumental pieces (mostly for flute) and some songs. Although Alice Fletcher, who later attained renown with her studies of American Indian music, felt that Lanier "was not only the founder of a school of music," but the founder of American music.[4] It would seem more reasonable to consider Lanier's meager musical output with less enthusiasm —

indicating considerable talent and possibilities but hardly showing the stylistic and technical constituents to inaugurate a new tradition.

John Knowles Paine (1839-1906). Paine was a New Englander who received his music training in Germany and returned to this country to give organ recitals and become the first director of music at Harvard College where he pioneered the establishment of courses in music form, harmony and counterpoint. Besides attaining prominence as an educator (his students included Arthur Foote, Frederick Converse, John Alden Carpenter and Daniel Gregory Mason), he was the first native composer in the larger musical forms to achieve some lasting fame both at home and abroad. His compositions include two symphonies, several symphonic poems, a number of large choral works, art songs, chamber music and an opera. The orchestral-choral composition *Oedipus Tyrannus* (1881) — a prelude, six choruses and postlude on a text by Sophocles — is his best work. One of the earlier historians of American music said, "There at last we find, and for the first time, an American composition that not only equalled but excelled European settings . . . the greatest composition which up to that time had been written in this country."[5]

Paine's workman-like style shows a strong Brahmsian influence, but there are also descriptive, programmatic aspects that suggest both Liszt and Wagner. His melodies move forward logically, often in short fragments suggesting Mendelssohn, and the rhythms show a firm, regular continuity. While considerable transient modulation within the conventional harmonic framework (an innovation in choral works) again shows the influence of Wagner, a regularity of phrase structure builds overall unity.

Frederick Grant Gleason (1848-1903). Another New Englander who studied music in Germany, Gleason returned to Chicago as a teacher and critic. His works include symphonic poems, choral cantatas and two operas, none of which stands out with any strength of expression. Gleason attempted to blend the intellectual workmanship of Brahms with the leitmotif treatment and diminished seventh-chord harmonies of Wagner. Unfortunately, the lyric quality of his melodies, reflecting the influence of Italian operatic arias, do not gracefully incorporate the leitmotif development, nor do the diminished seventh-chord progressions have the emotional impact of their prototypes, but instead end up as contrived clichés. Gleason, however, was a pioneer in the sense that he did not hesitate to occasionally break existing laws of partwriting (even to the extent of using parallel fifths)[6] to indicate a possible faint undercurrent of rebellion against the existing shackles of European musical domination. But many years (and composers) would pass before these bounds would be broken.

William Wallace Gilchrist (1846-1916). Receiving his music training in this country, Gilchrist became a church organist, teacher and choral and orchestra conductor in Philadelphia. His compositions include symphonies, choral and chamber music, and show the then conventional German styles in all aspects. His technique is adequate but never rises above a correct but contrived use of materials.

Silas Gamaliel Pratt (1846-1916) studied music in Germany and returned to teach at the Metropolitan School of Music in New York City; later, he founded the Pratt Institute of Music and Art in Pittsburgh. Symphonies, symphonic poems, cantatas and two operas are included in his music output. He had an affinity for using national events, past and present, as subjects for his works, but all are composed in the usual nineteenth-century German Romantic styles.

FOOTNOTES

[1]Ma-GlA, Nos. 128 and 129.
[2]Ma-GlA, Nos. 130 and 131.
[3]Ma-GlA, No. 126.
[4]StarL, p. 389.
[5]ElsH, p. 167.
[6]HowA, p. 322.

new england academicians

Combined Classic-Romantic Influence. In the last years of the nineteenth and the first decades of the twentieth centuries a group of composers centered around Boston continued to write in the traditional German Romantic styles, but with more refined structural techniques which, interestingly, often revert back to the Classical tradition of Haydn and Mozart. This tradition is exemplified by objectivity, use of restraint (no exaggeration), clarity of form (developed through short, regular phrases) and balance and proportion of all elements. Specifically, this ideal is realized in simple, folklike melodies, regular, obvious rhythmic patterns, many triadic harmonies and modulations to the nearest related keys, and two- and three-part and sonata-allegro forms favoring the obvious, often abrupt contrast of thematic material. Of course, none of this Boston group set up the Classic principles as their sole aspiration; rather, their goal was, as in the music of Brahms, some compatible fusion of certain Classic with Romantic elements. Unfortunately, this synthesis, as with the use of the Romantic style alone by the earlier American group, lacked conviction because the combined styles had little sympathetic relationship to the immediate environment of the composers — no real roots in the cultural traditions of our land. Nevertheless, the group did establish a school of American composition which attained professional dignity and artistic prestige at home and abroad.

Arthur W. Foote (1853-1937). One of the first of the new Boston group to gain prominence, Foote received his musical training from Paine at Harvard and eventually settled in Boston to become an organist, pianist and composer. His works are many and in varied forms, in-

cluding symphonic poems, chamber music and vocal music in large
forms as well as over one hundred fifty songs. Foote's style is not only
composite but changes in particular compositions; however, he favors
vertical harmonic writing over contrapuntal lines. A pre-Classic influence is manifest in the frequent use of such forms as the prelude, gavotte
and fugue; the use of church modes, especially in his chamber music,
harkens back to even earlier periods. The symphonic poem *Francesca
da Rimini* (1893), one of his better known works, is in the rhapsodical
style of Liszt, showing considerable descriptive effects. Two of his major
choral works with orchestra *The Wreck of the Hesperus* (1888) and *The
Skeleton in Armor* (1893) reveal much of Wagner's typical diminished
seventh-chord saturation. However, Louis C. Elson felt that Foote's
dramatic music reveals a narrow range of expression with different, even
opposite moods cast in the same musical settings.[1] Be that as it may,
his chamber music reflects the wide-range melodies, varied rhythms and
rich harmonies of Brahms; the leitmotif principle of Wagner is also
evident in some pieces. Although Foote was not hesitant to use the
Baroque structural principle of ever-changing variation, most of his
music shows the Classic treatment of thematic contrast.

   George W. Chadwick (1854-1931).   After study at the New England
Conservatory of Music and further training in Europe, Chadwick returned to the Conservatory as a teacher; he was also active as a church
organist and conductor of choral groups. Chadwick left over twenty
works for orchestra, many large choral numbers, several operas, some
chamber music and songs. Many of these show a preference for
legendary and mythological subjects expressed musically in a variety
of forms. A good example of his instrumental style is the *Symphonic
Sketches* (1895-1907) consisting of four movements titled, "Jubilee,"
"Noel," "Hobgoblin" and "A Vagrom Ballad," in which, incidentally,
we have a bit of real Americana in the rough vitality, freshness of spirit
and Yankee humor expressed so well in the music. In "A Vagrom Ballad" Philip Hale, a noted American music critic of Chadwick's era,
found "a certain jaunty irreverence, a snapping of the fingers at Fate
and at the Universe, that we do not recognize in music of foreign composers, great or humble."[2]

   Chadwick's larger choral works seem unimaginative, although the
part writing is correct and smooth in the traditional homophonic, German cantata idiom; his many ballads, however, effectively combine a
folklike simplicity with a dramatic expressiveness. He was at his best
in the instrumental works. Here, the textures combine homophony with
a virile counterpoint; his melodic treatment may show a Mendelssohnian

figural succession or an expansive freedom reminiscent of Liszt; his rhythms are regular and have strong forward movement and his conventional Romantic harmonies sometimes approach the richness of Brahms' progressions. Although a Classicist in the frequent and proper use of forms built of contrasting thematic material (the overture, sonata-allegro form), Chadwick imbued new life and freshness into these often stereotyped structural formats. In addition, a flair for colorful orchestration enhances the effectiveness of these works.

Horatio Parker (1863-1919). Parker studied with Chadwick and completed his training in Germany, returning to New York City as a church organist and teacher at the National Conservatory; he eventually became Professor of Music at Yale and active as a choral conductor. Although his works include much chamber music and pieces for piano and organ, it is with his choral cantatas that he made his reputation. Parker also composed two operas *Mona* (1912) and *Fairyland* (1913), both winning substantial prize money; the first won, as well, a performance at the Metropolitan Opera House in 1912. His sacred cantata *Hora Novissima* ("Day of Judgment," 1893) for mixed chorus and orchestra is considered his outstanding work.

Like all of his colleagues, Parker's musical style is also composite, reaching back to Baroque composers for inspiration. Most of his instrumental works reflect a Mendelssohnian melodic facility and rich Wagnerian harmonies in an ornamental homophonic structure typical of Handel, although his occasional fugal writing is proper and effective in the Baroque tradition of Bach. In his choral works, the heritage of Puritan hymn singing is evident in the straightforward melodies and massed chordal effects; however, because Parker abhorred the obvious, he consistently avoided literal repetition in his musical development, favoring instead some expression of the age-old principle of variation.[3] Hence, it is understandable why, in his day, Parker's music seemed austere and cerebral and never enjoyed the immediate appeal of the music of his contemporaries.

Charles Martin Loeffler (1861-1935). Born in Alsace and educated in Europe, Loeffler came to live in the United States in 1881 and joined the Boston Symphony as a first violinist. In 1903 he retired to devote full time to composition, mostly in the forms of solo instrument or voice with orchestra, chamber music and songs. Probably his best known work is *A Pagan Poem* (1901-1907) for orchestra and piano. Loeffler's style is a synthesis of an archaic element: modal, Gregorian chantlike melodies and French Impressionism which, together, seem to evoke a mystical spirit of past ages. His music shows refined and polished workmanship as well as many subtleties characteristic of Impressionism, such as free, rhapsodic melodies which develop gradually from a germ idea, frequent alternation of duple and triple meters in irregular rhythms, parallel movement of seventh and ninth chords, loosely knit forms and delicate nuances. A sensitiveness to subtle orchestration effects enhances the characteristic color of his compositions.

Hence, Loeffler is hardly an academician in the terms discussed at the beginning of this chapter. Nevertheless, he is included here because of his New England residence and communal sharing in the creativity of the other composers in this group. Besides, his penchant for reaching back to the church chants for inspiration might be considered academic to an extreme degree although, paradoxically, his strong leaning toward French Impressionism places him in the *avant-garde* of his day — the first composer in this country to consistently and successfully express himself in this idiom.

Daniel Gregory Mason (1873-1953). Mason studied with Paine, Chadwick and Percy Goetchius in this country and after advanced study in Paris, returned to join the faculty of Columbia University in 1910. Mason's avowed goal was to revive the musical ideals of the Classical symphonists — clarity of style, restraint of emotional expression, balance of form — exemplified in the music of Haydn and Mozart; however, he could not stifle inherent Romantic tendencies, particularly, emotional exaggeration. Although he incorporated some Anglo-American folk tunes and Negro spirituals in his compositions, he did not feel that their use would necessarily develop a native musical expression; rather, this could be achieved only by developing the distilled essense of folk melody in an ecclectic style through skillful organization in accepted forms: This was his artistic credo. Mason's works are mostly for orchestra and instrumental chamber groups; one of his best known orchestral pieces is the *Chanticleer Overture* (1928). His melodies tend toward a Classic clarity and regularity of rhythm; his harmonies suggest those of Mendelssohn and Schumann and, at times, the chromaticism of Wagner, although on occasion more modern effects of added sixths to triads and parallel movement of chords can be found. His emulation of Classical form is evident in the use of regular phrase succession in an overall balanced grouping of material and in the principle of thematic contrast. Besides enjoying a reputation as a composer and lecturer, Mason wrote several books on American music: *From Song to Symphony, The Dilemma of American Music, Tune in America* and *Music in My Time.*

Arthur Whiting (1861-1936), *Edward Burlingame Hill* (1872-1960). Both of these New Englanders studied music with Chadwick and after further study abroad, returned to this country to teach and compose — Whiting in Boston and Hill at Harvard. Both favored the orchestra and chamber groups as their media of expression and, like Daniel Gregory Mason, were academic traditionalists interested in the Classical clarity of balanced forms and symmetry of structural components. Their melodies show proper workmanship but seem cold and austere, lacking in musical interest; their rhythms are regular but of no particular distinction; their harmonies are weak imitations of the Romantic chord progressions with Hill's music now and then revealing some influence of French Impressionism (the two *Stevensoniana Suites,* 1917-1922, for orchestra).

Ethelbert Nevin (1862-1901), *H. H. A. Beach* (1867-1944). These two composers should be remembered not for a particular contribution to serious music but for many lyrical, sentimental songs for voice and piano. Nevin is best known for his songs "The Rosary" and "Mighty Lak' a Rose" and his pieces for piano, "A Day in Venice" and "Narcissus." Mrs. Beach, the most prominent American woman composer of her time, left over one hundred fifty songs including the well-known "The Year's at the Spring" and "Ah, Love but a Day."

Edward MacDowell (1861-1908). Although not considered one of the Boston group per se, MacDowell wrote in the same Classic-Romantic vein; however, he instilled more vitality in these worn-out musical traditions than any of his contemporaries and, at the same time, brought this phase of American music to its close. After the usual music study in this country and in Germany, MacDowell returned to Boston and in 1896 became Professor of Music at Columbia University, New York City, where he sought to teach music as part of a broad, liberal culture. In 1904 he resigned over disagreement with the University's educational policy and retired to Peterboro, New Hampshire to compose. His works include orchestra suites, many songs and piano pieces. The *Indian Suite* (1897) for orchestra and *Woodland Sketches* (1896) for piano remain his most popular compositions, but the Second Piano Concerto in D minor (1885) is the most impressive musically. Interestingly, although he rejected the idea of a music nationalism based on folk material, his pieces using Indian themes are some of his best music. In his lectures at Columbia University he further clarified his position on American music: ". . . nationalism, so-called, is merely an extraneous thing that has no part in pure art. . . . What we must arrive at is the youthful optimistic vitality and the undaunted tenacity of spirit that characterizes the American man. That is what I hope to see echoed in American music."[4]

Stylistically, MacDowell's larger works are rhapsodical, dramatic and programmatic in the tradition of Liszt; melodies with much configuration weave through a basic homophonic texture. His smaller pieces are exquisite vignettes which unashamedly express obvious sentimentality; the themes are characteristically short in strong, regular rhythms; the harmonies carry the conviction of Mendelssohn's with occasional Wagnerian chromaticism. Although MacDowell's music leans toward an oversentimentality, more so than is found in the traditional Romantic piece, his well-proportioned forms and clear, logical organization of material through thematic relationships and contrast reveal the true Classical approach. Also, his transparent orchestration which "achieves the fitness that characterizes Tschaikowsky" is not to be overlooked as contributing to the immediate effectiveness of his orchestra pieces. Although MacDowell's music may not stand the test of time as a profound, indigenous tonal expression, "he was the first of the Americans to speak consistently a musical speech that was definitely his own."[5]

FOOTNOTES

[1]ElsH, p. 189.
[2]EngC, p. 439.
[3]HowA, p. 338.
[4]HowA, pp. 382-83.
[5]*Ibid.*, p. 378.

music education

Lowell Mason. It would be no easy task to find a more influential personality in nineteenth-century United States music than Lowell Mason (1792-1872). It was he who first campaigned for and won the right for children to receive elementary music instruction at public expense. Although he had some lessons in music from Oliver Shaw, he was largely self-taught. He was a bank clerk when his collection, appropriately titled *The Boston Handel and Haydn Society Collection of Church Music*, was accepted for publication by the Handel and Haydn Society in 1821. Mason, however, hesitant that his activity in musical matters might create unfavorable reaction in banking circles and perhaps hinder his career, insisted that his name not appear as editor of the publication. Within the next thirty-five years the publication had gone into twenty-two editions and netted Mason and the Society $30,000 each. In 1827 he moved to Boston as church organist and president of the Handel and Haydn Society.

Mason composed over twelve hundred hymns and published many collections of sacred music, some in collaboration with George Webb or Thomas Hastings or even with his brother, Timothy. His most popular hymns are "Nearer My God to Thee," "My Faith Looks Up to Thee,"[1] and "From Greenland's Icy Mountains,"[2] which are still sung today. As a composer his talent and taste were mediocre; harmonically and rhythmically he remained a primitive. It is true that he succeeded in bringing music to the masses, but in so doing the artistic sights were lowered. In the words of Gilbert Chase, "Mason was instrumental in thrusting the native American musical tradition, as represented by our early New England music makers, into the background while opening the gates for a flood of colorless imitations of the 'European Masters.' "[3] The colorless imitations were actually arrangements made from parts of compositions by European composers. The level of his taste may be measured by his comments on Handel's and Haydn's oratorios in his *Lyra Sacra*. Some appalling statements are as follows:

> The choruses of Handel and Haydn are too difficult for choirs to perform or audiences to comprehend. These choruses are designed for the sole purpose of musical exhibition and display. . . . The anthems of the best English composers with a few exceptions, are designed to show the composer's skill in counterpoint, fugue and artificial conceits.[4]

Mason organized annual conventions which drew its members from New England to the Middle Atlantic states. With the publication of his *Manual of the Boston Academy of Music* (1834) Mason's position in the field of music education was absolute.

Our First Music Schools. With George Webb (1803-1887) Mason founded the Boston Academy of Music in 1832 for the purpose of elevating the standard of singing schools and to improve the quality of church music. Pupils were taught the art of singing, the rudiments of thorough bass and harmony, teaching methods and choral conducting. In 1838 he went to Zurich to study the Pestalozzi method and one year later he demonstrated the application of the Pestalozzi method by teaching music to children at the Hawes school. The approbation of the Boston public school board was immediate and music was allowed to join the other disciplines in the school curriculum. Between 1838 and 1845 he was superintendent in the Boston schools. In 1853 he organized the New York Musical Normal Institute and in 1855 he was awarded the honorary degree of Doctor of Music from New York University.

Followers in the Tradition of Mason. His work was carried on by such music educators as George Webb, who came to Boston from England in 1830 and taught in Boston, Orange, New Jersey and New York City. His best known hymns are "Stand Up, Stand Up for Jesus" and "T'is Dawn, the Lark Is Singing."[5] Webb introduced an unusual and practical way of making a keyboard score for the organist by adding the alto and tenor parts in small notes to the treble and bass parts. William Bradbury (1816-1868) worked with Mason and Webb at the Boston Academy and then became an organist and choirmaster in New York. A prolific composer and editor of over fifty music collections, Bradbury's most famous tunes are "Just As I Am" and "He Leadeth Me." Isaac Woodbury (1819-1858) was particularly successful in publishing tune books that found favor among glee clubs. His "The Song Crown" contains two compositions which still belong to the repertory of choral groups and glee clubs, "The Farmer's Daughter"[6] and "Stars of the Summer Night."[7]

George Frederick Root (1820-1895). A graduate of Dartmouth College and a minister in North Reading, Massachusetts, Root is remembered as a prolific writer of hymns and battle songs. He began the study of music comparatively late, but made such rapid progress that he was named to assist Lowell Mason in the Boston public schools. In 1859 he became a partner in the Root and Cady music publishing firm in Chicago. A year later he traveled to Europe and on his return was awarded a Doctor of Music degree by the University of Chicago. His best known compositions are "The Battle Cry of Freedom" (1861), "Just Before the Battle Mother" (1862), and "Tramp, Tramp, Tramp" (1864). In all, Root composed about thirty war songs.

The Growth of Music Schools. Schools and conservatories for the study of music in this country were established in close succession soon after the middle of the nineteenth century, although music education had been part of the curriculum at Oberlin College since 1835. In 1862 Harvard University offered its first courses in music. The first independent school of music was the Oberlin Conservatory established in 1865, although Eben Tourjée is credited with originating the conservatory system in this country in 1853. The New England Conservatory was established in Boston in 1867 mainly through the efforts of Lowell Mason.

The year 1867 saw the opening of the Cincinnati Conservatory and Chicago Musical College. The Peabody Institute was established in Baltimore the next year, followed a year later by the Philadelphia Musical Academy. Nine years later, 1878, the New York College of Music came into being and in 1886 the American Conservatory was founded in Chicago. These remained the important music institutions until 1904 when the Institute of Musical Art in New York City was organized by Frank Damrosch, later (1926) to merge with the Juilliard School. In 1920 both the Eastman School of Music in Rochester, New York and the Juilliard School of Music in New York City were founded and, with the Curtis Institute in Philadelphia established in 1924, became the first graduate schools in our country to offer study in music performance and theory equal, if not superior, to the best that Europe could offer.

Music Organizations. Along with the establishment of many first-class schools of music in the second half of the nineteenth century, efforts were initiated to improve the quality of teaching and teaching materials and to upgrade the professional status of the teacher through national organizations. The first of several such organizations, the Music Teachers National Association was established in 1876; in 1884 the American College of Musicians was formed.

In 1907 the Music Educator's National Conference was organized to promote the development of music in the public schools; national and more frequent sectional meetings have offered opportunities to share common problems and cooperate in their solutions. In recent years, the organization has been concerned with raising musical standards for teachers as well as establishing music as an academic discipline on an equal footing with other subjects in the general educational program.

Footnotes

[1]Ma-GlA, No. 84.

[2]Originally composed and published as a solo song and dedicated to Mary W. Howard of Savannah, Georgia. Later, the song was arranged for three and four parts. Ma-GlA, No. 83.

[3]ChaA, p. 160.

[4]*Lyra Sacra,* Boston, 1832, preface.

[5]Ma-GlA, No. 87.

[6]Ma-GlA, No. 89.

[7]Ma-GlA, No. 90.

native musical activity

Music, A Business. Unquestionably, music was an important, if not lucrative, commodity in our metropolitan centers. By 1829, Boston, New York and Philadelphia families accounted for almost twenty-five hundred pianos. Between 1765 and 1828 Boston boasted of fifteen music publishers; Philadelphia had fourteen between 1785 and 1818; New York had twenty-four between 1793 and 1827; Baltimore had six between 1794 and 1838. These statistics, while often boring, are extremely meaningful for they prove beyond a shadow of doubt, that music in its various manifestations — composition, publication, diffusion, performance and sales — had a large and receptive market.

Choral Societies. But Americans were participators as well as spectators in musical activity. Our interest as participators goes back to 1762 when the St. Cecilia Society was founded in Charleston. The Stoughton Musical Socity was founded by William Billings in 1786. It is still in existence and has a membership today of four hundred singers. The Euterpean Society was founded in New York City in 1799; the Handel and Haydn Society was founded in Boston in 1815 and presented ambitious works. In 1823 this society commissioned Beethoven for a choral work, but unfortunately the composition was never realized — Beethoven was apparently too busy on other commissions. Philadelphia had its Musical Fund Society since 1820 and presented both choral and orchestral concerts. In 1812 James Hewitt announced a circulating music library of several thousand compositions. Although the terms of borrowing were not specified, the rate was six dollars for annual subscribers.

At the mid-point of the nineteenth century, the number of organizations that met regularly for the performance of serious music of quality still remained small. The German Sängerbund were friendly groups who gathered for the communal enjoyment of choral singing, meeting for the first time in Cincinnati in 1849 and thereafter every two years. The Handel and Haydn Society of Boston continued to meet triannually throughout the nineteenth century, rehearsing and performing standard oratorios of the day. The two Peace Jubilees of 1869 and 1872 under the music supervision of Patrick S. Gilmore involved huge choruses of thousands of voices recruited from many parts of the country. The spectacles were impressive and the stimulus to music appreciation was significant, but the hopelessly unwieldy choruses resulted in poor performances.

New York Philharmonic Orchestra. By 1900 there were only some six orchestras of major importance in the United States; however, in the next fifty years, over thirty were established. The Philharmonic Society of New York, later renamed the New York Philharmonic, was the first orchestra to be organized on a professional basis. Originally a cooperative venture by the members of the orchestra, it owes its beginning to the enthusiastic efforts and guiding spirit of Ureli Corelli Hill (1802-1875). In 1842 the orchestra gave its first concert, becoming the third-oldest symphony orchestra in the world. The cooperative status continued until 1901 when the orchestra was reorganized with the musicians receiving guaranteed salaries. A distinguished series of conductors included Emil Pauer, Walter Damrosch, Willem Mengelberg and the great Arturo Toscanini who brought the orchestra's performance ability to near perfection. After Toscanini's resignation in 1936, conductors of the caliber of Sir John Barbirolli and Bruno Walter maintained the high quality of performance previously established. At present, the gifted Leonard Bernstein is instilling new life into the group.

Thomas Orchestra. The next important orchestra development resulted from the efforts of Theodore Thomas (1835-1905), a violinist and conductor, who persuaded New York businessmen to support a permanent orchestra which he organized and conducted in its first concert in 1862. Subsequently, he toured the country with the orchestra, giving concerts in the principal cities to develop large appreciative audiences for symphonic music. His programs were well balanced, each having selections from the Classics, serious American works and lighter, popular pieces.

Boston Symphony. This orchestra was the first in this country to result from the efforts and subsidy of one man — Henry Lee Higginson

(1834-1919). He contracted sixty orchestra musicians and a conductor by the year, with sufficient remuneration for them to devote full time to adequate rehearsals and concerts in Boston and the surrounding area. Their first concert was in 1881 in Boston Music Hall under George Henschel; in 1884 Wilhelm Gericke became conductor and in 1889 Arthur Nikisch brought the orchestra to a high level of attainment. In the new Symphony Hall, Karl Muck was to develop the orchestra to its greatest heights; he became conductor in 1906 for two years and after returning to Berlin's Royal Opera came back in 1912 to resume his leadership of the orchestra. In 1924 Serge Koussevitsky became one of the orchestra's most illustrious conductors; his encouragement to native composers by regular performances of new works did much to improve and develop American music. Erich Leinsdorf assumed the leadership in 1951 and is continuing the high tradition of his predecessors.

Chicago Symphony. Historically, the next orchestral development was in Chicago where a concert given by Theodore Thomas in 1869 eventually led to the establishment of the Chicago Symphony Orchestra with Thomas as its first conductor. The famous Orchestra Hall was dedicated in 1904, but Thomas' death in the same year dampened the festive spirits of the occasion. Frederick Stock, whom Thomas had nurtured as an assistant, took over the leadership to build one of the finest orchestras in the country with an extensive repertoire. Stock was very sympathetic to the development of American music, giving many first performances of native works. After Stock's death in 1942, a series of many conductors followed to maintain the quality of performances set by Stock.

Philadelphia Symphony. This orchestra gave its first concert in 1900 under the direction of Fritz Scheel with Ossip Gabrilowitsch (who later was to become one of its conductors) as piano soloist. The orchestra grew out of the combination of an amateur group, the Philadelphia Symphony Society led by W. W. Gilchrist, with a professional group, the Thunder Orchestra led by Henry Gordon Thunder. Subsequently, its array of famous conductors included Richard Strauss, Felix Weingartner and Leopold Stokowski. The last named took over in 1912 and experimented in the seating arrangement of the orchestra to produce a better-balanced, full-bodied tone quality; during his extended period as leader, he brought the performances to a degree of technical brilliance unknown before as well as sponsoring many new contemporary works. In 1936 Eugene Ormandy was called to lead the orchestra, maintaining its position as one of the world's best.

Other Orchestras. In 1903 the Minneapolis Symphony was founded with Emil Oberhoffer as its conductor; this was the orchestra that Eugene Ormandy took over in 1931 and developed to a high state of perfection before leaving to conduct the Philadelphia Symphony. In 1909 Leopold Stowkowski inaugurated the first season of the Cincinnati Symphony; in 1922 Fritz Reiner assumed its leadership; in 1931 Eugene Goosens was appointed director. In close succession, the Detroit Symphony made its debut in 1914 under Ossip Gabrilowitsch; the Baltimore Symphony followed in 1916 under Gustave Strube; in 1918 the Cleveland and Los Angeles orchestras followed with Nikolai Sokoloff and Walter Henry Rothwell, respectively, as conductors. Somewhat later, the Indianapolis orchestra was started (1930) then the National Symphony was begun in Washington, D. C. (1931).

Bands. One must not overlook two famous performance groups which quality-wise did little to further the cause of serious American music; yet the Gilmore and Sousa bands in their extensive concerts over the country did much to stimulate mass musical interest among the people. Patrick S. Gilmore (1829-1892) was a native of Dublin, Ireland who went to Canada and later Boston and organized the famous Gilmore's Band in 1859. He has earned a measure of immortality for his stirring march, "When Johnny Comes Marching Home." John Philip Sousa (1854-1932), after conducting the United States Marine Band from 1880 to 1892, formed his own band in 1892 to eventually tour this country and Europe and become world famous. A prolific composer of tuneful marches ("Stars and Stripes Forever" and "Semper Fideles"), he captured the rhythmic pulse of the nation and was dubbed the March King.

Early Opera: Louisiana. Perhaps the most important event in nineteenth-century America was the purchase in 1803 of the whole province of Louisiana for a mere $15,000. Fourteen states were created wholly or in part out of the Louisiana territory and it doubled the area of the United States. Owned by the Spanish, ceded to France and settled primarily by the French, it soon took on the appearance of a sophisticated and elegant French city. The earliest record of a theatrical entertainment was in 1791 in New Orlean's first theater, *Le Spectacle*, on St. Pierre Street. According to Ronald Davis, "historians agree that there can be little doubt that opera was given in the theater from at least 1793 on, for it seems unlikely that Louisiana-born Frenchmen, or Creoles as they were called, would have supported a theater with an orchestra unless the operas of their day were presented there."[1] In 1808

Le Spectacle was torn down and a new theatre was built in its place appropriately called Le Theatre de la Rue St. Pierre; to commemorate its gala opening *Le Prince Tekeli,* or *Le Siege de Mantgatz* was performed.

January 30, 1808 witnessed the opening of another theater, the St. Phillipe. In 1809 the Theatre d'Orleans was erected only to be completely gutted by fire in 1813. It was rebuilt in 1816 and was considered the most beautiful edifice in New Orleans. Davis tells us that "by the 1820s the companies and orchestras were large and of superior artistic caliber. The public, as well as the critics, growing more appreciative of the lyric theater, became exceptionally judicious in its musical tastes. The Creoles demanded the highest standards possible and tolerated no cutting or tampering with the score."[2] The repertoire, consisting of operas by Etienne N. Méhul, André Grétry, Christoph Gluck, Gioacchino Rossini, Gasparo Spontini and Wolfgang Mozart, attracted such famous singers as Jenny Lind and Adelina Patti, who were engaged year after year.

Giacomo Meyerbeer's opera *Les Huguenots* received its first American performance in New Orleans only a few months after it had been staged in Paris; however, this was an exception. At least two years elapsed between a first performance in Paris or Milan and one for the New Orleans *affizionados.* Toward the end of the nineteenth century visible signs of a waning interest in opera began to appear. The mounting cost of staging operas and the indifference of the younger generations toward opera, brought a glorious era to a close. With the end of World War I, opera in New Orleans became a memory.

Opera in New York. It is curious that opera, the aristocratic but expensive musical art, should have gotten such a comparatively early start. No doubt it was due to the appealing combination of the varied aspects of music, drama, scenery and, not the least in importance, the stellar casts of singers. In 1825 New York City had its first performance of Italian opera with Rossini's *Barber of Seville;* the performers were the then famous Manuel Garcia troupe from Italy. During the next quarter of a century, a number of entertainment-opera houses were built in New York City (the Academy of Music on 14th Street becoming the most important) in which a succession of opera companies produced both English ballad and Italian operas (the latter, often with librettos translated into English) with varying degrees of success. There were also occasional productions of proven German fare such as Carl Maria von Weber's *Der Freischütz* and *Oberon,* Mozart's *Magic Flute* and Beethoven's *Fidelio.*

From the very beginnings of opera it is interesting to note that the American public preferred its entertainment in an understandable language; operas in their native Italian, French and German were slow to capture the enthusiasm of the audiences.[3] Although this situation has changed considerably, there are many today who still would prefer to understand and follow the unfolding drama as it happens rather than from the recollection of a previously read translation. By 1859 Wagner's music, specifically *Lohengrin* and *Tannhäuser,* had been introduced in New York by traveling as well as local groups. By 1878 when James Henry Mapleson (1830-1901) brought a London company to the Academy of Music in New York to perform the popular Italian operas of the day, interest in opera had become widespread enough to assure its ever-increasing development. Mapleson's roster of singers, the best obtainable, included Adelina Patti (1843-1919), Christine Nilsson (1843-1921) and Lillian Nordica (1859-1914) and no doubt contributed to the growing popularity of opera.

Metropolitan Opera House. By the late nineteenth century, interest in opera had broadened to include the patronage of many socially ambitious people with financial means who were willing to subsidize it. The result was the construction of the Metropolitan Opera House which opened in 1883 with a performance of Charles Gounod's *Faust;* following closely, Donizetti's *Lucia di Lammermoor* was given with Marcella Sembrich (1858-1935) in the leading role. Unfortunately, New York City could not support this company and Mapleson's competing group at the Academy of Music; as a result, both suffered financial losses at the close of the season. But Leopold Damrosch and his son, Walter, stepped in to inaugurate a new era of German opera, including Wagner's greatest works sung by the best singers; they successfully kept opera alive at the Metropolitan and at the same time expanded the appreciation of the opera repertoire. Among the singers brought over from Europe at this time, Lilli Lehmann (1848-1929) stands out for her brilliant interpretations of Wagnerian roles. In the last decade of the century, the desire for German opera waned and the standard Italian repertoire was reinaugurated featuring such famous singers as Lillian Nordica, Ernestine Schumann-Heink (1861-1936), Emma Calvé (1858-1942) and Nellie Melba (1859-1931).

When Heinrich Conried became director of the Met in 1903, he intrduced Enrico Caruso (1873-1921) and in 1904, the first performance of *Parsifal* in this country. Geraldine Farrar (1882-1967) made her debut in the first performance of Giacomo Puccini's *Madame Butterfly* in 1906; Richard Strauss' *Salome* was performed in 1907. In 1908 Giulio

Gatti-Casazza from Italy became manager and, subsequently, brought over Arturo Toscanini; during Gatti-Casazza's regime the following famous singers were heard: Feodor Chaliapin (1873-1938), Frieda Hempel (1885-1955), Frances Alda (1883-1952), Maria Jeritza (1887-   ), Florence Easton (1884-1955), Giovanni Martinelli (1885-   ) and Giuseppe de Luca (1876-1950). Edward Johnson became manager in 1935 and continued the repertoire of standard operas featuring such singers as Lily Pons (1904-   ) and Kirsten Flagstad (1895-1962). In 1950 Rudolf Bing modernized the presentations by bringing the staging up to date and creating new sets and costuming. For many years the company has regularly toured the country, developing a widespread appreciation for this art form.

Manhattan Opera House. Oscar Hammerstein (c.1848-1919), theatrical entrepreneur and operatic impressario, opened the Manhattan Opera House in 1893, but after producing two operas was forced to close; in 1903 the House was reopened and remained so for four years. During this time it was a challenge to the Metropolitan Opera, producing a variety of interesting works including first performances of Claude Debussy's *Pelléas et Mélisande,* Gustave Charpentier's *Louise,* Jules Massenet's *Thaïs,* Jacques Offenbach's *The Tales of Hoffmann* and Strauss' *Electra.* Eventually, the company succumbed to its more wealthy and powerful rival.

Chicago Opera. Before 1889 opera in Chicago had been a hit-or-miss affair but in this year the new Auditorium was opened to provide an incentive for more and better performances. In 1910 the financier, Otto H. Kahn, took over Hammerstein's Manhattan Opera Company in New York City to establish it in Chicago on a firm basis. Mary Garden (1877-1967) made her reputation here and the quality of opera performances was equal to that of the Metropolitan. In 1928 the company took over headquarters in the new Civic Opera House.

Other Opera Companies. The Boston Opera Company opened in 1909 with Lillian Nordica and Louise Homer (1871-1947) in Amilcare Ponchielli's *La Gioconda;* heavy expenses forced the company to close five years later. The Cincinnati Opera Company has fared better; opening in 1921 with summer performances, it has served as a professional training ground for many singers. San Francisco showed its first interest in opera as far back as 1852, but it was not until 1923 that an opera company was organized. Gaetano Merola, the director, engaged the best available singers and in conjunction with the San Francisco Symphony, performed a varied repertoire. Today the organization remains a cultural symbol of the city.

Instrumental Virtuosi. The stellar system of great singers, nurtured in the development of opera during the early decades of the twentieth century, found an even more extensive expression in the instrumental virtuosi (mostly European) who toured the country presenting the best of the Classical and Romantic instrumental solo repertoire in masterful performances. Some of the outstanding violinists include Fritz Kreisler (1875-1962), Mischa Elman (1881-1967), Jascha Heifetz (1901-   ), Josef Szigeti (1892-   ), Yehudi Menuhin (1916-   ) and of recent acclaim, Isaac Stern (1920-   ) and Ruggiero Ricci (1920-   ); Pablo Casals (1876-   ), and Gregor Piatigorsky (1903-   ) are violoncello virtuosi of considerable fame. The pianists include Alfred Cortot (1877-1962), Josef Hofmann (1876-1957), Ignace Paderewski (1860-1941), Sergei Rachmaninoff (1873-1943), Vladimir Horowitz (1904-   ), Myra Hess (1890-1965), Rudolf Serkin (1903-   ), Artur Schnabel (1882-1951), Artur Rubinstein (1886-   ) and the young contemporary artists, Van Cliburn (1934-   ) and John Browning (1933-   ). Also during this era, chamber music groups consisting of virtuosi performers were organized to develop through country-wide tours an appreciation for what is considered the purest formal expression of music — the string quartet. Among the more prominent groups must be mentioned the Hungarian Budapest String Quartet founded in 1921, the Austrian Kolisch String Quartet organized in 1928, the Roth String Quartet which made its American debut also in 1928, and the Juilliard String Quartet founded in 1946.

Phonograph Records. The symphony orchestras, opera companies and traveling virtuosi did much to develop and satisfy the musical tastes of the people. But the invention of phonograph records had greater eventual influence in spreading the gospel of music on a mass basis than any other single event. In 1888 Josef Hofmann was the first to record on Edison's wax cylinder. The disc recording perfected by Emile Berliner enabled the Victor Company to solve the problem of mass production. In 1903 the Celebrity Discs of Columbia Records and the Red Labels of the Victor Talking Machine Company featured the great singing voices of the day. In 1906 the orchestra was first successfully recorded and in 1910 separate instrumentalists were reproduced. It was not until 1950, however, that much interest was shown in American music. Folkways Records has recorded considerable American folk material; a subscription organization, the American Recording Society has been regularly issuing works by serious contemporary American composers. Howard Hanson with the Eastman-Rochester Symphony has recorded many American orchestral works, the composers ranging from the early Boston academicians through the most contemporary. The Society for the Preservation of the American Musical Heritage, under the direction of its founder, Karl Krueger, has released thirty-seven long-playing records containing many eighteenth-and nineteenth-century compositions never before recorded.

Music Festivals. In recent years there has been a resurgence of interest in the festival idea, but fortunately not the colossal extrava-ganzas of Gilmore's Peace Jubilees of some one hundred years ago. Since 1925 the Eastman School of music has sponsored in the spring an annual series of concerts in which American compositions, new and otherwise, are performed. Following the lead of the Eastman School, many of the larger universities of the country, notably the University of Illinois, have established similar festivals. Of equal importance are the symposia in conjunction with the concerts in which enlightened discussions of the new music can help both composer and listener.

FOOTNOTES

[1]DavO, p. 2.
[2]*Ibid.*, p. 7.
[3]NYMC, pp. 10-17.

nationalistic elements I

INDIAN TRIBAL MUSIC

General Characteristics. American Indian tribal music of the West and Southwest is closely associated with both the mystical and the practical. Some melodies are attached to myths and legends handed down from one generation to another; others are related to realistic experiences of everyday living, in fact, some tribes have a melodic expression for nearly every important act of daily life. But every song had the purpose of helping the Indian attain something he felt was beyond his power as an individual to attain.[1] A primitive aspect of their melodies is the lack of importance attached to verbal expression. Few melodies have words which express a feeling or tell a story; rather, word syllables (those having the more singable vowel sounds) are used usually without meaning being the most effective way of presenting a melody vocally.[2] Another characteristic found in most primitive music is the use of a separate note for each word syllable.

Investigations. Although isolated inquiries into tribal music had occurred from time to time, it was not until 1880 that the first systematic investigation was undertaken by Theodore Baker. Some of the more reliable studies and collections of musical material are as follows: *Über die Musik der Nordamerikanischen Wilden* (1882) by Theodore Baker, *Indian Story and Song from North America* (1900) by Alice Cunningham Fletcher, studies published in *A Journal of American Ethnology and Archaeology* (1891, 1908) by Benjamin Ives Gilman, *American Primitive Music* (1909) by Frederick Burton, *The Indian's Book* (1907) by Natalie Curtis and many bulletins under the auspices of the Bureau of American Ethnology of Smithsonian Institution (1907 through 1942) by Frances Densmore. The latter bulletins constitute the most comprehensive treatment of Indian tribal music. The Library of Congress has a large collection of Indian tribal music on phonograph records as the result of a government-sponsored investigation in 1911.

Tonal Elements. Most of the tribal melodies utilize intervals of varying sizes which are not part of our tempered-interval system. There is some use of quarter tones but the intervals that predominate in both upward and downward movement approximate our major seconds and minor thirds. Various arbitrary tonal successions (scales) are used, many being the accidental result of the tones produced from the aesthetic habit of equispacing the holes in the flute instruments (pipes and whistles). Some tonal groupings contain only three or four tones, but most of them are pentatonic; the two most common may be approximated on our tempered scale as follows: (1) *cdega* (without the fourth and seventh and (2) *acdeg* (without the second and sixth). The span of a fourth, including a minor third and major second intervals, can be found with such frequency in tribal songs that it has become the most important and characteristic motivic (figural) grouping.[3]

Many songs are built around a framework of three tones that approximate our major triad. Harmony as such does not enter into the American Indian conception of music; however, the occasional practice of singing the same or different melodies by small groups of people but not always together often results in some unusual, unplanned vertical combinations of sounds.

Rhythm. Rhythmic expression combines regularity with irregularity and interestingly is often restricted to two time values, short and long, which tend to follow the metric patterns of words when they are used. Most of the melodies show a regular continuity of beats, but they are grouped by accents or motivic juxtaposition into units which may vary successively from two to five beats; a five beat grouping of three plus two is most common.[4] Some melodies show a small grouping of beats as a fixed unit which recurs many times with regularity, but within each unit there may be free rhythmic subdivision changing from measure to measure, in effect, resembling the ordered but free rhythm of Gregorian chant.

Organization. Many tribal melodies conform to a basic shape: From an initial low unaccented tone, a jump is made, as from a springboard, to a high tone of tension, which is followed by a gradual fall to tones in the lower register, relaxing the tension; one or several small motives may, in various successive juxtapositions, build this overall line, interspersed with long held notes and short repeated notes which provide some variety. After an overall descending pattern reaches a lower tone of rest, it is not uncommon for repetitions of this note, one to a word syllable, to continue the song through one or more phrases.[5] Other melodies have a much shorter descending pattern which is repeated many times, showing either no development or else slight changes in each recurrence. The balanced grouping of material into even-lengthened contrasting phrases and periods is never found in tribal songs. Rather, a succession of homogeneous irregular short units is the rule. In other words, the developmental principle is one of iteration — the progressive variation of a motive. Overall, downward moving intervals occur about twice as often as upward moving intervals. Although some melodies end on upper chord tones corresponding to our fifth or third, most come to a close on a low tonic tone of rest.

Conflicting Rhythms. A most important and characteristic aspect of their music is the counterpoint of conflicting rhythms. This texture is realized when a vocal or flute melody is accompanied by one or more drums. The accompanying rhythm may show the same regularity of beats as in the solo melody but be grouped in different, irregular units. Or the accompanying rhythm may have an entirely unrelated, independent pattern.[6] This opposition of rhythm seems to have been a most desirable goal; when several accompanying drums are used, sometimes three or four different intricate patterns are combined simultaneously.

Instruments. The instruments used are simple but adequate for the musical needs of the tribes. The basic rhythm instrument is the drum. It is made in many sizes with no planned pitches, but the usual size is that of the snare drum. Dried animal skin is stretched over a hollowed log or other rounded frame. Rattles of all sorts constitute the other most used rhythmic instrument. Pipes and whistles made of bone, clay or wood are the main melody instruments; the usual instrument has from three to five holes and can produce from five to seven shrill tones. Although solo singing is common, it is just as common for several singers to join in group performance. Often, a kind of verse-chorus relationship occurs in the performance of a song; the chorus may begin singing some vowel syllables followed by a solo singer using meaningful words in the verse.[7] Or a leader may sing an introduction to be joined by the group in the body of the song. The typical singer strives for what we would consider unusual tone production: a tense, tight nasal quality or a light, clear falsetto — both with a fast, narrow vibrato. There is usually much slurring from one tone to another. According to the spontaneous emotional feeling of the singer, a melody might be interrupted at any point by sharp, shrill cries.

FOLK MUSIC

Definition. Folk music is the expression in melody and rhythm of the racial feelings, characteristics and interests of a people without benefit of musical training; this is exemplified in simplicity of melody and form, spontaneity of individual performance and oral transmission from generation to generation. Some authorities believe folk songs were originally composed by individuals, but have been and will continue to be changed through the cumulative expression of "communal re-creation."[8]

English-Scottish-Irish Influences. During the seventeenth and eighteenth centuries, settlers from England, Scotland and Ireland brought their folk music to our country, first to the Atlantic seaboard and as the population migrated westward, to the interior settlements. The Old World songs have retained their original characteristics best in areas such as the Appalachian highlands were geographical location has tended to isolate them from outside influences. Although the original poems have been altered to conform to the new locales, usually resulting in lower quality verse, the melodies have retained their original freshness and unique qualities.

Other Influences. Because of the close ties in language, religion and literature, the English-Scottish-Irish tradition has dominated most of our folk music development, but some French influence has occurred in the North through the folk songs brought to Canada by French immigrants and in the South, particularly Louisiana, through the songs of the French Creoles and Creole Negroes. Also, in the Southwest there has been some Spanish and Mexican influence. Other European immigrant settlements scattered over the country have affected our folk music to a lesser degree.

Investigations. Although field trips to remote areas of our country are still being made to collect folk music (usually new versions of traditional songs), most of the investigations now are concerned with the comparative study of the already collected folk songs to determine which are originals, which are variants and the many ways the variants differ from the originals. A monumental piece of research into all aspects of the English ballad texts has been done by the Englishman, Francis James Childs (1825-1896). A similar study of the tunes of the same ballads has just been completed by the American, Bertrand Harris Bronson (1902-   ). There is need for similar intensive analyses of both the texts and tunes in other folk song categories. Outstanding research and collections have been made by the following: George L. Kittredge, (1860-1941), Francis B. Gummere, (1855-1919), Louise Pound, (1872-1958), Philip Barry, (1880-1937), C. Alphonso Smith, (1864-1924), Cecil J. Sharp, (1859-1924), R. W. Gordon, (1888-1961), John Powell, (1882-1963), Annabel M. Buchanan, (1889-   ), Carl Sandburg, (1878-1967), John A. Lomax, (1872-1948), George Pullen Jackson, (1874-1953), and D. K. Wilgus, (1918-   ).

Scales. The commonly used pentatonic scale combines three whole steps with the two minor thirds of D to F and A to C; any one of the five tones may be used as a tonic.

The hexatonic (six-tone) and heptatonic (seven-tone) scales are more recent, having evolved from filling in one or both of the minor third gaps with E-flat or E-natural and B-flat or B-natural, respectively.

These added tones usually have a weak status, being used only sparingly as embellishing tones. In actual performance they vacillate somewhere between the major and minor third and the lowered and raised seventh (reckoned from the tonic C) often within the same tune; as a result, they are called neutral intervals.

Transposition. Any of the scalar groupings of the above tones can be transposed to other pitch levels. Curiously, the gamut of tonal combinations used in American folk tunes approximates the six ancient diatonic modes: Ionian (c to c'), Dorian (d to d'), Phrygian (e to e'), Lydian (f to f'), Mixolydian (g to g') and Aeolian (a to a'). Our modern "artificial" minor scale with the minor third and raised seventh degrees seldom occurs in folk tunes.[9] In order to utilize the best range of the human voice, the following three modes constitute the scalar material most often used in our folk tunes:

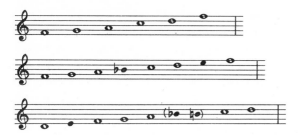

Harmony. Although accompanying harmonies are not considered an integral part of the inherited folk melody tradition, most tunes seem to lend themselves to a simple succession of tonic, dominant and subdominant chords (probably another reason for the widespread and enduring popularity of folk music); however, peculiar to the musical background (or lack of it) of the individual performer, out-of-key chord insertions, parallel chord movement and modal cadences are not uncommon. (Notice that scale 2a is the transposed Ionian or our common C major scale and 2b is, in one version, our natural D minor scale.)

Rhythm. Generally, the meter of the poem sets the rhythm of the tune. Duple and triple meters, the latter inherited from the lilting dance tunes of England, show about equal use. The Scotch snap (♪♫.) is found frequently as well as the Irish influence of irregular-lengthened rhythmic groupings (measures having from five to seven beats). A common characteristic is to add one or more beats at the ends of phrases outside of the prevailing metrical grouping. Depending on the particular European cultural influence, a folk tune may show a variety of dance patterns.

Stages of Development. The folk music of Western European countries is usually direct and simple because the languages of the people lack excessive ornamentation and accent; American folk tunes have inherited these qualities from their prototypes. Most musical cultures show that the higher the degree of civilization, the more symmetrical the musical forms, the less monotonous the use of repetition and the more use of contrasting figures and contrasting longer phrases. One can trace five stages in the development of folk tunes: (1) the savage yell, (2) the monotonous repetition of a small figure or part of a phrase, (3) the use of contrast versus repetition to effect a balance of phrases, (4) the creation of a focal point (climax) to unify material, (5) the creation of a closed formal grouping of repetition-contrast-repetition. All of the American folk tune heritage can be grouped in the last three developmental stages.

Old World Ballads. Our folk songs can be grouped according to form type and functional purpose: The traditional Old World ballads adopted in our country are impersonal narrative songs about historical and timely events and people. Because of the exhaustive study of the texts of the English-Scottish-Irish songs by Francis James Child, this category has been named the Child's ballads. There are about one hundred seventeen basic song texts, but many more variants have been found in America. In Bertrand Harris Bronson's similar intensive study of the tunes of the same ballads, many melodic variants were also found. A similar but heterogeneous category from the Old World includes humorous songs, sea chanteys, hunting and drinking songs and nursery songs; as the titles imply, the texts are mostly descriptive of moods or situations, although a few in the ballad style relate sequential stories. Mention must be made here of the English broadside ballads — professionally composed pieces dealing with timely events and people which were printed on large sheets of paper and sold in the streets. Some of these passed into the English and eventually American tradition, becoming absorbed and recreated often to the point of losing their original professionally conceived characteristics.[10]

Native Songs. Another category of some size is that of the strictly native songs having both new texts and melodies. Most of these songs are subjective and are concerned with specific emotions or points of view. Included are the woodsman-shantyboy songs, love songs, prison-convict songs and cowboy-western songs. The majority of these seem crude, showing little literary or musical value; however, because many of the cowboy songs are parodies of old ballads or are altered versions of outdated American popular songs, they show a higher quality of both texts and music. As the cowboys rode range on their horses, they sang to alleviate the loneliness of herding the cattle; the characteristic rhythms of the songs naturally approximate the walk, trot or lope of the horses. The day-herding songs are often based on cattle calls and are sung loudly to keep the cattle moving, but the night-herding songs are invariably in a quiet, restful mood to lull the cattle to sleep or to prevent stampedes. The texts are in the first person and grouped in a simple verse-refrain form; the tunes may have large interval progressions assimilating yells or shouts or may flow smoothly in diatonic movement.

Composite Category. The songs of this grouping have characteristics of both the two main groupings just discussed: Some of the songs have new tunes with traditional texts; others have traditional tunes with new texts. This category is growing constantly as texts or melodies which heretofore were thought to be original have been found to be variants of other songs. There are strong indications that further intensive, scholarly research will result in an ever-decreasing wellspring of folk songs that have both original texts and tunes.[11]

Spanish-Mexican-American Songs. In the third category must be included the Spanish-American, Mexican-American songs. During the sixteenth century, in the migration of the Spanish to the lower West coast areas of America (California, Mexico), many of their traditional songs were transplanted to the New World, but the texts were altered to deal with the many new aspects of the locale and way of life. In border areas the songs were further enriched with elements of native Mexican songs. Some of the oldest songs are the *alavados* which are traditional hymns sung during Holy Week; other songs used in the nativity play *Los Pastores* are over three hundred years old. A few of the older songs show Moorish traits of unusual scalar formations and intricate rhythmic patterns. The majority of the everyday songs are love songs: plaintive melodies of unrequited love. The narrative type ballad is seldom found. The *dicho* is a song having a short, spontaneous verse of four lines and a usually improvised melody similar to the impromptu songs of our modern-day folk singers; the topics are concerned with the affairs of local people and timely events. A prominent rhythmic characteristic, especially of dance tunes, is the abrupt interruption of a smooth flowing 6/8 pattern by a slower 3/4 pattern to create intriguing syncopation.

Creole Songs. Also in the third category are the Creole songs of Louisiana in which the melodic interval progressions show definite French and Spanish origins while the rhythms are from Africa. The texts are concerned with all aspects of Negro life, emphasizing the elemental emotions of love, hate, fear, jealousy and so forth. The songs are also used for dancing. The predominant meter of the tunes is 2/4 with syncopation characterizing most of the dance patterns; French influence is seen in the *contredanse* figure (♫♩♫), Spanish influence in the *habanera* figure (♪.♩ ♫♩) and African influence in the cakewalk figure (♫♫ ♫♩), an added accent is usual on the last eighth note (weak half beat) of any of the above patterns. Many songs begin with a quick syncopated figure called a catch (like the Scotch snap) and then continue with the main patterns.[12] The *calinda,* in earlier times one of the most common dances, has satirical texts with music of French origin; the *bamboula* and *congo* are unique as wild, primitive dances.

Organization. More specifically, the texts of the majority of folk songs have four lines to a verse with from six to ten syllables per line. The iambic grouping of feet is common with four stresses to the first line, three to the second followed by a beat rest, four to the third line and three to the fourth line followed by a beat rest; the last words of the second and fourth lines rhyme. The end of the second line, the halfway point, is important structurally in the music, usually falling on the dominant chord; the final cadence at the close on the tonic chord satisfyingly resolves the mid-pause dominant cadence.[13] The pauses at the end of the first and third lines, poetically, are usually negligible and hence are accompanied by weak musical cadences. The above grouping may be repeated for many verses. The newer songs sometimes have a verse-refrain arrangement with some evidence of rhyme, but most songs show some kind of verse repetition or extension: (1) Accumulative songs add a new line in each succeeding verse, each time repeating back from the beginning; (2) incremental repetition songs repeat the substance of each verse in the following verse but with some changes to advance the narrative or to clarify the meaning; (3) relative sequence songs deal with different individual family members or friends in each successive verse. In the music structure, besides the cadential grouping mentioned above, there generally are two contrasting parts (phrases) which are juxtaposed successively in different ways. The most common phrase combinations are as follows, in order of prevalence: (1) AABA, (2) ABBA, (3) ABCA. Most tunes are unified by a reverting back type of construction in which earlier-used intervallic motives are repeated after intermediate contrast, or through a rhythmic formula of a half or full phrase pattern which recurs successively throughout, recalling the early use of isorythmic patterns in Medieval music (and for the same purpose of unification).[14] Usually, tunes begin and end on the tonic tone but a few conclude on the fifth or third.

Instruments. The outstanding characteristic of folk song performance is the freedom allowed and expected in adding, omitting and changing words as well as in varying the intervals and rhythms of the tunes. The third and seventh degrees of the scale are the common variable tones. Individual singers are often identified by certain figural embellishments or glissandos. A rather archaic, rural effect results from the rhythmic tendency to stress unimportant word syllables as well as to freely change the meter of songs to fit the words. A related peculiarity is the irregular sustaining of the last note of some phrases an extra beat or two, according to the whim of the singer. The guitar and related strumming instruments of the zither type are, by far, the most used for accompanying Anglo-American ballads and cowboy songs. One popular instrument of this type, the dulcimer, is an oblong, shallow wooden box with sound holes; three strings are stretched over the top, two used as drones and the third for plucking or occasionally bowing the melody. Incidentally, whatever the instrument used, the almost continual reiteration of one or more tones in the manner of a drone, remains a common performance practice. The four-string banjo is the favorite instrument used with Creole songs. For folk dance songs, violin and accordion-type instruments are commonly used.

THE MUSIC OF THE NEGROES

A Deep-Rooted Expression. When the first Negro slaves arrived in Jamestown in 1619, they brought with them their love of music and bodily rhythm. Most of them came from the Gold Coast, western Congo, Dahomey and what is now Nigeria. The Afro-Americans sang songs to provide for material comforts, to accompany repetitive manual labor, to learn facts and to sell commodities. According to Ernest Borneman: "The impact of Christianity on the Afro-Americans was, of course, the origin of the spiritual, owing to the fact that practically all of the missionary work was done by nonconformist ministers, their evangelical hymns set the style and flavor of the spiritual as we know it today."[15] But Miles Fisher tells us, "There is more, far more that the ordinary Christian zeal embedded in Negro spirituals. They are not merely religious hymns written or recited to sweeten the service or improve the ritual. They are the aching, poignant cry of an entire people."[16] The large body of spirituals is indeed the documented history of the Negro in the United States. The interchange of slaves among plantation owners, their common destiny, their introduction to Christianity and the solace obtained through the singing of spirituals welded them into a homogeneous group. It should be noted that slaves were encouraged to embrace Christianity, not only to keep them peace loving and amenable, but also for the slaveowner's peace of mind.

It was not until 1867 that *The Nation* announced the publication of the first book of Negro songs bearing the title: *Slave Songs of the United States, One Hundred and Thirty-Six Songs from all parts of the South, Never before published or brought together, historically of the greatest possible value.*

Types of Songs. The true spiritual was performed in a call-and-response manner. A contemporary report, which mentions this respon-

sorial singing, points expressly to "the way in which the chorus strikes
in with the burden, between each phrase of the melody chanted by a
single voice, is very curious and effective."[17] Some spirituals are fast
moving with short phrases and syncopated rhythms, such as "Shout All
Over God's Heaven" and "Little David Play on Your Harp;" others are
slow, with sustained and long-phrased melodies, such as "Nobody
Knows De Trouble I've Seen" and "Huntin' For a City." Work songs
conjure up scenes of Negro life during the restoration period as well
as those sung in penal institutions, for such songs served to coordinate
the manual tasks and to alleviate mental fatigue, such as "Long John"
and "Long Hot Summer Days." Blues, a later manifestation and the
secular counterpart of the spiritual, is the solo song of the thoroughly
disillusioned individual who has lost interest in heaven and earth, such
as "Sometimes I Feel Like Nothin'." Ballads are directed to the stoicism
of the Negro. Adversity, hopelessness and the continuous battle for sheer
survival are always present in the texts. The ballad of the "Grey Goose"
is an example of the Negroes' indestructibility, for, after having been
shot, the goose was "six weeks a-fallin', six weeks a-findin', six weeks
a-pickin', six months a-parboil;" he was so tough that he was inedible.
Among other examples on this theme are "Ella Speed," "Duncan and
Brady," "Railroad Bill," and "Stackalee." The Music Division of the
Library of Congress issued in 1942 several albums of *Folk Music of the
United States* edited by Alan Lomax. Volumes III and IV contain examples of the above-mentioned types.

Melodic Structure. From an examination of over two hundred
examples of Negro melodies drawn from the southeastern area of the
United States, the following observations may be of interest: (1) All
melodies are unharmonized, (2) there are as many hexatonic as there
are completely diatonic melodies, (3) in hexatonic melodies, major or
minor, either the fourth, sixth or seventh degree is most likely omitted,
(4) in pentatonic melodies, the fourth and seventh degrees are usually
omitted, rarely the sixth and second, (5) a few melodies fall into modal
structures such as the Aeolian and Mixolydian, (6) most of the melodies
are in duple meter (2/4 or 4/4) rarely 3/4.

Recognition of the artistic value of Negro songs is comparatively
recent, although one of the first pronouncements was made in 1883 by
Frederic Louis Ritter, an Alsatian emigrant to America, who stated,
"The people's song is not to be found among the American people." But
he acknowledged the fact echoed later by Antonin Dvorak that "the
songs of the colored race had merit."[18] Sidney Finkelstein goes one
step further by declaring, "The greatest creative contribution to United
States folk music was made by the Negro people."[19]

Musical Heritage. It is quite evident that the traditional folk songs of other countries have enriched our musical heritage in many ways. Besides the contribution of a wealth of "tried and proven" melodic material which includes new, intriguing rhythms, there are also the structural features of interesting scales pregnant with developmental possibilities as well as basic formal groupings of repetition and contrast that have weathered the tests of centuries of experimentation. Certainly this nuclear material that has taken root and flourished in our native soil will continue to mold our musical art expression, directly and indirectly, for some time to come. The following views of Roy Harris, one of our most respected native composers, may well reflect the attitude of many other composers concerning the value of folk music:

> . . . folk songs stimulate him [the composer] to his best creative ingenuities. . . . He may find the material an esthetic chart which leads him to new riches. He may even enhance the beauty and scope of natural folk tunes, and in so doing learn to sense the inherent values of musical materials, follow the natural flow of creative form, to gather his creative thoughts into a homogeneous stream of musical continuity. For this is the basic creative process which all folk-song singers have achieved in short simple forms, and which all composers must master in more extended complex forms.[20]

FOOTNOTES

[1]DenA, p. 77.
[2]FleO, p. 12.
[3]BurA, pp. 89-90.
[4]DenA, p. 60.
[5]McAlI, p. 10.
[6]BurA, pp. 44-66.
[7]McAlI, p. 10.
[8]BarP, p. 59.
[9]BucA, p. 707.
[10]NetI, pp. 44-45.
[11]BayP, p. 105.
[12]McMC, pp. 715-716.
[13]BroI, p. 78-79.
[14]NetI, pp. 13, 15.
[15]BorR, p. 17.
[16]FisN, p. 25.
[17]KemJ as quoted by ChaA, p. 233.
[18]RitM, p. 385.
[19]FinH, p. 107.
[20]EweM, p. 249.

nationalistic elements II

RAGTIME

A Style, Not a Form. About 1890 a new style of musical expression called ragtime evolved from the earlier minstrel, vaudeville and variety shows which combined elements of Negro dance songs with white minstrel songs. Ragtime and to a degree, jazz are unique in the development of musical forms since neither is a new structure but rather a new way of embellishing in performance standard popular melodies. This new style was nourished in the jam sessions of the Negro workers in the river towns of the South as well as in the Negro bands of the cities. It mattered little whether the music played was a current popular hit, a folk song or a favorite march, it could receive the same rag treatment. Only a few of the songs composed specifically in ragtime style have words; this is due to the many-noted figurative style, often with awkward melodic irregularities which do not lend themselves to intelligible word continuity. Hence, ragtime is essentially an art of piano performance; even in instrumental combinations the piano dominates.

Tonal-rhythmic Elements. Ragtime pieces show almost entirely the simple tonic, dominant and subdominant triads nearly always in the major modes. Using the standard meters of 4/4 and 2/4, rhythmic syncopation is one of the most important elements. The cakewalk figure (♪♫♪) dominates most of the melodic phrases; originally a plantation dance, the cakewalk featured the above rhythmic figure in melodies having a smooth succession of intervals (diatonic progressions with some thirds). Improvisation in the minstrel and vaudeville shows eventually evolved the application of the characteristic rhythmic figure to more angular melodies having the frequent alternation of interval direction, that resulted in the style of ragtime.

Organization. The use of two or more different rhythmic patterns simultaneously (polyrhythms) stemming from Afro-American music is the most characteristic element of ragtime. Specifically, over a regularly accented pattern in the bass in 4/4 or 2/4 meter a syncopated melody is played in what may be called a conflict of rhythmic counterpoint. The melody consists of short, angular motives of from three to six notes which are repeated to form small structural groups; throughout the melody these are contrasted with other similar groups; but the emphasis is always on the rhythmic interplay rather than the interval successions. Usually a simple, conventional popular tune of sixteen or thirty-two measures serves as the skeleton around which the syncopated figuration weaves its course; however, the embellishment can easily obscure recognition of the underlying melody.

Instruments: Performers. Because the banjo had such an important role in the early minstrel and vaudeville shows, it became an intimate partner in the development of the cakewalk into ragtime. When ragtime moved into the dance halls of the cities, the piano took over as the important performance vehicle. Scott Joplin (1869-1917) was one of the first as well as most famous exponents of the piano style; his "Maple Leaf Rag" (1899) received wide acclaim. Other outstanding composers and performers in the style were Thomas M. Turpin (1873?-1922), James S. Scott (1886-1938), Ben R. Harney (1871-1938), Alex Christensen, (1881-   ) who also wrote a most successful ragtime textbook, Anthony Jackson (1876-1921), Ferdinand "Jelly Roll" Morton (1885-1941), James P. Johnson (1894-1955) and Thomas "Fats" Waller (1904-1943). During the first decade of this century commercial over-exploitation as well as the characteristic inherent monotony of repeated formulas contributed to the decline of ragtime. By the time Irving Berlin's "Alexander's Ragtime Band" came out in 1911, ragtime had all but disappeared.[1]

BLUES

Afro-American Influences. Around 1915, after ragtime had run its course, a new popular musical form as well as style took over in this country. This form known as the blues, is rooted in the Afro-American folk expression of spirituals and work songs which has flourished in the South since the beginning of Negro slavery. Unlike these earlier group expressions, the blues are solo songs with words and music that create an all-pervading feeling of lament; yet by combining everyday events with flights of the imagination, the texts are not without an undertone of humor.

Tonal Elements. Both pentatonic and major scales are used, but the characteristic that most identifies the blues scale is the consistent flatting, often microtonally, of the third and seventh degrees of the major diatonic scale; these notes have come to be known as blue notes. According to the whim or emotional fervor of the singer, their pitches vary as much as a half step below. As a result, the seventh degree seldom functions as a leading tone. The most used chords are the tonic, dominant and subdominant, as in ragtime; in the blues, though, sevenths and ninths are added to the chords and are used thus more frequently than the simple triads. It is interesting to note that the dominant seventh chords on the subdominant and tonic tones (which are used freely in the blues) are seldom found in the European conventional song accompaniments.

Rhythm. As in ragtime, the cakewalk syncopated figure is used, but the blue notes of the melody and the prevalence of seventh chords stand out rather than the rhythmic emphasis; moreover, the usual slow tempos do not lend themselves to much rhythmic emphasis and the nature of the texts (bewailing the loss of a lover, etc.) influences a style of declamation in smooth, flowing rhythms and leisurely tempos. The most common meter is 4/4.

Organization. The typical melody is basically diatonic in the manner of the popular tune of the day. Its form, however, is different, having three lines of words with four measures of music to each line. Although the second line of words is different from the first, the music is the same for both lines; the third line is new both in words and music. This form of statement, repetition and response has remained a standard format for the blues. Each four-measure melodic phrase ends on some tone of the tonic chord, but, as typical of the form, the last word syllable of each line falls on the first beat of the third measure. It is in the remaining beats of each phrase that a characteristic element of the melody takes place: The final note of the phrase is sustained through the remainder of the phrase or the note is short with added rests, either of which gives the singer time to plan the following phrase, or as more often happens, the singer takes off in an improvised interpolation known as a break. According to the skill of the singer, the break will be simple or elaborate.

The harmonic form is based on a four-measure chord progression which begins and ends on the tonic chord. Between these extremities typical chord progressions favor dominant harmonies moving rootwise by fourths and fifths through several consecutive dominant seventh chords, with the melody and some of the inner voices moving chromatically. In effect, we have an early and probably original version of barbershop harmony. Following is the standard chordal sequence for a blues harmonization (with one chord to a measure):

I I I^{7b} I^{7b} IV^{7b} IV^{7b} I I   V^7 V^7 I I

First phrase   Second phrase   Third phrase

Notice in the following typical progression of barbershop harmony the cyclic sequence of dominant seventh chords (not really effecting modulations); the chromatic and parallel movement of upper voices (some theorists suggest this is a direct carry-over from the finger patterns used on the banjo and guitar accompaniments in the early minstrel and vaudeville shows); the absence of the key's leading tone in the penultimate chord.

One other typical harmonic characteristic of the blues is the use of the lowered (or neutral) third of the scale in the melody either sung or played against the major third in the harmonic accompaniment.

When the blues formula is taken over by instrumental groups which also feature singing, a more refined combination of blues scales, harmony and improvisation usually results. For instance, after an appropriate short introduction, the voice sings the first four measures with the instruments filling in the harmony and providing a smooth background rhythm; in the next four measures the voice rests while one or more instruments answer in improvisations on the theme; this procedure is repeated for each four-measure phrase, the form now being extended to four phrases (16 measures). Occasionally, interesting contrapuntal effects result when a solo instrument weaves an obbligato along with the solo voice.

Boogie-woogie. This characteristic style is a piano offshoot of the blues. Within the twelve-bar harmonic structure of the blues, the left hand plays a persistent broken-octave figuration in dotted rhythm; against this ostinato-like background the right hand plays a somewhat smoother melody conceived to be at cross rhythms with the bass figuration.

Performers. William C. Handy (1873-1958) is given the credit for introducing this style with his "Memphis Blues" (1909) and "St. Louis Blues" (1914). Some of the famous blues singers of the period were Gertrude "Ma" Rainey (1886-1939), Bessie Smith (1895-1937), Huddie Leadbetter (1885-1949) and Bertha "Chippie" Hill (1905-1950). Jimmy Yancey (1898-1951) and Clarence "Pinetop" Smith (1900-1928) were well-known exponents of boogie-woogie for the piano.

Musical Innovations. The blues have enriched our musical vocabulary in several ways: Melodically, they continued the freedom of improvisation introduced in ragtime, but refined and smoothed out the more violent eruptions of this prototype; harmonically, they contributed colorful consecutive dominant seventh chord progressions which in turn produced a new linear-chromatic movement; formally, the characteristic odd-numbered, three-phrase grouping was a pleasant change from the traditional multiplies-of-two grouping. These fresh, new innovations affected both American popular and serious composers. But, like ragtime, the blues era was just another intermediate step in the transition to jazz. Actually, it coexisted with jazz, gradually being absorbed by the latter in the early decades of this century.

JAZZ

A Composite Improvisational Style. Like the blues, jazz is a combination of stylistic improvisation and new formal elements. Derivation of the word itself remains obscure; it was a synonym for music having much rhythmic excitement and is thought to have appeared about 1916 among Negro bands of the South. Embodying the attributes of ragtime and the blues (in particular the influences of Afro-American spirituals and worksongs and white minstrel and vaudeville tunes), jazz also includes influences of the Irish-Scotch-British tradition of folk melody. In essence, a conventional, popular tune is recreated by the performer through improvisation (which varies with each performance) within a predetermined format. Many jazz enthusiasts feel that the ability and adroitness of the performer are more responsible for a successful performance than the musical worth of the original tune.

Periods of Development. Because jazz includes the rhythmic intricacies of ragtime as well as the emotional expressiveness of the blues, it is capable of creating a variety of moods from simple, personal sadness through expansive, dramatic imagination to angry, vicious protest. Historians have labeled the various periods of jazz development as follows: (1) archaic jazz (1870-1890), one of the earliest expressions, developed in the hot music of the New Orleans Negro street bands which initiated improvisations on the march tunes performed in parades and funerals; (2) classic jazz (1890-1910) showed the first large scale emphasis of improvisation on popular tunes by the New Orleans Negro bands which had now moved into the dance halls; (3) Dixieland jazz (1900-1920) was the performance of the New Orleans style classic jazz by white musicians in northern and western cities as well as in the South; (4) sweet jazz (1910-1930) was jazz music carefully arranged and rehearsed with a minimum of improvisation; (5) swing jazz (1920-1940) returned to the classic hot jazz style of improvisation but with smoother melodic contours and more refined rhythmic patterns. Around 1940 many jazz enthusiasts felt that the New Orleans and swing styles had exhausted their potential of development. Hence, radically new expressions were introduced in bebop (or bop), progressive jazz and cool jazz. Characteristic of all these are the use of more subtle and irregular rhythmic patterns than in previous styles and new harmonic elements outside traditional tonalities.

Tonal Elements. To the tonic, dominant and subdominant chords of ragtime the secondary chords, especially the supertonic (II) and submediant (VI), have been added; a free, almost promiscuous addition of thirds to these chords results in a prevalence of seventh and ninth chords. The custom of adding a color tone to any chord (a 6th, 2nd or 4th) when it is sustained is another characteristic. Bebop and cool jazz, on the other hand, extend the harmonic limits with the use of eleventh, thirteenth and polytonal chords often to the point of atonality.

Rhythm. The earliest jazz took over the 2/4 meter of the marches on which they improvised; later 4/4 became the standard meter. Jazz retains the syncopation so characteristic of ragtime but smooths it out by lengthening its patterns to extend over bar lines; these broader patterns often consist of many repetitions of a dotted rhythmic figure. In essence, against a basic 4/4 meter with strong regular pulsation, a melody develops different rhythms in opposition to the fundamental beat; the most common polyrhythm is a three-beat dotted pattern in the melody set against an underlying chordal accompaniment pattern of regular recurring, four beats.

This syncopation should be distinguished from the occasional European use in which a fundamental 4/4 or 2/4 meter always predominates against some rhythmic grouping of three which is set off momentarily and with less emphasis. What seems to be a distinct contribution of jazz is the longer progressions (several or more measures) of the two antagonistic rhythms, each having equal emphasis — a true polyrhythmic process. According to Winthrop Sargeant, "Syncopation may thus be used as a means of rhythmic distortion — as a method of achieving surprise."[2] He feels that the process of tension (unrest) created by the offbeat syncopations and their resolutions (relief) on the main beats is the basic underlying principle of jazz structure. What seems strange is that jazz seldom shows a two-over-a-basic-three pattern, probably because fundamental jazz meters are always in some multiples of two. In bebop the strong beats are subdued with many unexpected, shifting offbeat accents. Cool jazz continues to deemphasize the basic beat, adding frequent changes of tempo.

Organization: General. Most jazz melodies are basically diatonic with frequent use of ascending and descending minor thirds; retained from the blues are the unstable third and seventh degrees of the scale which continue to be flatted microtonally in performance. It must be mentioned that the multitoned improvisations are all built around a core of two tetrachords; the lower one comprises the nucleus of most blues tunes while the more expansive jazz tunes use both equally. The usual movement tendencies of each tone are also indicated:[3]

(key of C)

All of the classical embellishments of passing tones, appoggiaturas and so forth are used profusely. Common progressions, almost to the point of being clichés, are the chromatically raised second and sixth degrees of a key, each resolving a half step upward; strangely, other accidentals besides the blue third and seventh seldom appear in melodies, although

they are common enough in accompanying harmony. Of all the melodic
devices the most characteristic and prevalent are the microtonal variation in pitch and the glissando.

The more expert jazz performers have evolved a varied treatment
of rhythm in organizing and articulating tonal material. With the usual
mixture of dotted notes and triplets, there is always a subtle rhythmic
freedom of anticipation or retardation of the main beat, most often too
slight to be notated. With this all-pervading characteristic may be used
the more obvious devices of a simple syncopation of a few beats, a polyrhythmic pattern of several or more measures, a phrase distortion of
successive, unequal rhythmic segments and a rhythmic-melodic device
of alternately accenting and unaccenting an appoggiatura or repeated
melodic figure. The following few bars of a simple tune will illustrate
several of the devices just described:

original

jazz version

Harmonically, as in the blues, consecutive seventh chords often
create melodic segments which move downward chromatically. Cadences
are unique in that seldom does the leading tone of a key move directly
upward to the tonic; instead, the tonic is approached usually through a
descending or ascending minor third (in the inner parts as well as
melodically). The simple, conventional dominant seventh-to-tonic cadence is not too common. Rather, this progression as well as the plagal,
subdominant-to-tonic chord progression is colored with added tones of
a fourth, sixth or ninth in the penultimate chord, or the penultimate chord
may be constructed of fourths chromatically altered to create augmented
or diminished chords.

common cadences

Some of the most recent expressions of jazz, particularly bebop, have lowered the fifth of the dominant chord, creating what many enthusiasts consider a new blue note. It seems logical to attribute the alteration of this tone to bebop performers in their search for new tonal frontiers; because of the tone's strong tendency to move to the tonic, flatting it is an effective means of nullifying traditional harmonic tonality. In the earlier jazz styles there were no modulations, but in the more sophisticated, arranged jazz, modulations are common in one or more choruses to closely related keys. In bebop and cool jazz unusual shifts in tonality and polytonality are frequently found.

The formal structure of most jazz styles is rooted in the Baroque chaconne, ostinato form. Usually, a set harmonic progression of sixteen or thirty-two measures is repeated many times, over which a different melodic-rhythmic variation is devised each time. Fortunately, the usual simplicity of chord progressions allows almost unlimited improvisational freedom in the melody, but at the same time prevents the improvisation from ending up in any formal chaos. Cool jazz is noted for its use of Baroque counterpoint and such forms as the fugue, which are preplanned to include unifying climaxes. Occasionally in more sophisticated arrangements, the traditional folk tune form of AABA is found — the B component serving as a bridge between statements of the main phrase. Also, a result of popular musical comedy tunes is the verse-refrain format in which several phrases introduce the main tune which then may be repeated a number of times. The construction of phrases may show a simple statement of the melody in regular four-measure phrases, or profuse ornamentation but with the original melody still recognizable (typical of most jazz styles up to 1940) or a completely new melody with the original harmonies (typical of bebop and cool jazz). In the latter category the phrases are irregular in length, each consisting of short melodic fragments in jerky, disjointed successions.

Organization: Classic Style. Specifically, this style emphasizes improvisation. The usual texture shows three lines in polyphony over an underlying, regular ostinato-type base line. The melody is broken up into two- or four-measure segments which are embellished with much freedom in an antiphonal, call-and-response format (a higher development of its first elemental occurrence in the blues form); as each line (instrumental part) in turn improvises on the subject, the other lines sustain three-part harmony. A blues singer often participates in the antiphonal improvisation.

Organization: Sweet Style. Jazz in this style is deliberately arranged and rehearsed, incorporating the traditional European techniques.

The large size of the bands which perform this music makes improvisation impractical; the loss of spontaneity, however, is compensated for by the clever, sophisticated arrangements in many-voiced textures. A typical jazz melody is used, but the rhapsodical figurations and syncopated rhythmic patterns are now subdued and controlled; these are set against a rhythmic background of several different ostinato patterns. When such a background rhythmic pattern is repeated incessantly to build up tension, it is called a riff. There is no antiphonal alternation of small melodic segments as in classic jazz; rather, fewer textures are established and each is maintained longer. A complete performance usually shows a juxtaposition of melody and harmony for the introduction or verse and at least two other different arrangements for the refrain. Throughout, there are occasional obbligatos and varied figuration in the accompaniment. The frequent doubling of the melody in thirds and sixths as well as the compounding of intricate rhythmic patterns makes for "sweet" sounds but tends to lose the spontaneity and freshness of real classic jazz.

Organization: Bebob, Cool, Progressive Jazz. The most recent manifestations of jazz can be characterized by an over-intellectualized approach which seems too contrived and lacking in emotion to perpetuate the originally simple feelings of jazz. Melody is fragmented, broken into staccato-like figures often in top registers and in distorted timbres; tones are attacked with so much vibrato that such melody bears little resemblance to its generating inspiration. Furthermore, melody is developed not from the original tunes but from the harmonies in an ever-continuous development-without-repeat structure. Rhythm is subdued with deemphasis of the main beats by having them (the main beats) performed on the cymbal rather than on the bass drum, and by frequent shifting of the meter and subtle accentuation of unaccented portions of the beat. Harmony is pushed to the frontiers of atonality with the use of all kinds of chordal combinations and successions. A typical performance will involve a succession of solos by different members of a group; each performer must be technically competent to devise not just accompanying harmonies but intricate counterpoint. Cool jazz differs from bebop mainly in attempting to soften the harmonic harshness and smooth out the angular, jerky lines of the latter. As a reaction against the excesses of bebop, cool jazz also is interested in understatement, with no sharp or loud attacks and very little vibrato in the production of tones. But as Sheldon Meyer has so aptly put it, "In avoiding the frantic excesses of bop, it [cool jazz] became somewhat uncommunicative in its aloofness and soporific in its lack of excitement."[4] Cool jazz involves listeners intellectually but leaves them cold emotionally. Progressive jazz is a less-used name for both bebop and cool jazz.

Instruments: *Classic Jazz*. The typical early New Orleans band that performed classic jazz contained from five to seven instruments: cornet or trumpet, clarinet, trombone, guitar, string bass or tuba, drums and piano. The cornet, clarinet and trombone were considered the most expressive, flexible and hence the most capable of carrying the melody; the guitar, string bass or tuba and drums comprised the rhythm section. Sometimes the bass saxophone replaced the string bass or tuba. The piano was used primarily for rhythm, but usually took its turn in the breaks of improvisation. In general, the overall tone quality of such a band was raucous and coarse. It was typical for a blues singer and cornet or clarinet and trombone to alternate antiphonally in improvising sections of the melody. In three-part sustained harmonies the usual arrangement was to put the clarinet on top, the cornet in the middle and the trombone on the bottom; since accompanying harmonies were generally more subdued, it was assumed that the higher but weaker clarinet could hold its own in balance with the two brass instruments. In most of the early bands the cornet or trumpet player was the leader.

Instruments: *Sweet and Swing Jazz*. Today as in its earlier days, the sweet band is large, featuring sections of violins and saxophones as well as doubling and tripling the number of instruments in the usual sections. Most of the bands attempt to keep a balanced three-group division of reeds (clarinets and saxophones) and violins, brasses (trumpets or cornets and trombones) and rhythm (guitar or banjo, string or brass bass, drums and piano). The number of instruments in each section allows ample doubling of octaves, unisons, thirds and sixths especially in the melodic parts. Instead of ever-changing improvisation, display of originality and competence of individual performers, each band attempts to develop a characteristic melodic style, unusual harmonies and rhythmic intricacies which often become identifying trademarks. The swing bands have maintained the instrumental grouping and characteristic style of the sweet bands, but generally with reduced numbers of instruments in each section, often omitting the violins.

Instruments: *Bebop and Cool Jazz*. Recent tendencies are to reduce the size of bands to quartets or quintets to, in effect, approximate the texture of classic chamber music. A typical group contains one instrument of a kind (piano, vibraphone or xylophone, drums or string bass, clarinet or saxophone, trumpet and trombone); however, the demands on each performer are much greater than in the larger bands. Not only must each performer have a fluent technical facility on his instrument, but the new far-out harmonies require a thorough theoretical knowledge.

Performers. Some outstanding Negro performers in the early classic style were Charles "Buddy" Bolden (1868-1931), Freddie Keppard (1883-1932), Joseph "King" Oliver (1885-1938) and Ferdinand "Jelly Roll" Morton. Jack "Papa" Laine (1873-   ) is considered the father of white or Dixieland jazz. Paul Whiteman (1890-   ) with his symphonic jazz band helped considerably to popularize the large-band sweet style. The following have made reputations primarily in the swing style, although all have used large bands in the sweet style as well: Louis Armstrong (1900-   ), Fletcher Henderson (1898-1952), Edward "Duke" Ellington (1899-   ), William "Count" Basie (1904-   ), Benny Goodman (1909-   ), known as the "King of Swing," Harry James (1916-   ), Gene Krupa (1909-   ), Tommy Dorsey (1905-1956), Woody Herman (1913-   ), Glenn Miller (1909-1944), Artie Shaw (1910-   ) and Lionel Hampton (1914-   ). "Dizzy" Gillespie (1917-   ) and Charlie Parker (1920-1955) have been responsible for establishing the bebop trend. Lennie Tristano (1919-   ), Stan Getz (1924-   ) and Miles Davis (1926-   ) have developed the cool jazz style. Stan Kenton (1912-   ) has successfully adapted these recent styles in arrangements for the large band.

Influences of Jazz. The contemporary American composer, Roger Sessions, contends that the very elements defining jazz — certain overused harmonic and rhythmic formulas as well as the basic square phrase structure — restrict its emergence as a flexible, wide-ranged medium that could effect a national musical style: "While immobility of these bases [the cliché formulas] makes a play of rhythmic detail and of melodic figuration possible, this always is a question of lively detail rather than of extended organic development."[5] However, although jazz per se will probably never attain the status of American art-music, its characteristic tonal configurations as well as its intricate polyrhythmic fabric have undoubtedly influenced the development of our serious music. And even if one minimizes the structural contributions of jazz, the fresh spontaneity of its improvisational styles alone has done much to counter the academic conventions which by the beginning of the century had stifled much of the originality our serious native composers might have had. But an eminent authority on jazz, André Hodeir, contends that jazz indeed created a structural format that is a unique contribution to melodic development, ". . . the chorus phrase does not have an exact equivalent in European music. It behaves and looks like a variation, but it does not arise directly from any melodic theme. . . . It exploits no given figure. It includes no repeats. The only things it sticks to are the basic construction and the harmonic foundation from which it springs."[6] One might question Hodeir's contention somewhat as it is not uncommon in Baroque music to find a melody within a set of variations constructed out of the ostinato harmonic progression; however, in bebop and cool jazz where melodic development seems totally unrelated (tonally or rhythmically) to the accompanying material, one can agree with the jazz historian.

Footnotes

[1]SarJ, p. 141.
[2]SarJ, p. 56.
[3]SarJ, p. 167.
[4]MeyM, p. 261.
[5]SesR, pp. 158-159.
[6]HodJ, p. 152.

nationalistic composers I

Indigenous Musical Inspiration. In the preceding chapter our concern was with the particular musical elements which through localized development or adoption may be considered indigenous to our country. In this chapter we will endeavor to show how these elements have been used directly or indirectly in serious music having workmanship and artistic quality. With this heritage of material made more readily available, our native composers could express themselves with musical inspiration of vital substance not borrowed from other countries. This period of nationalism in music includes roughly the last decades of the nineteenth to the middle of the twentieth centuries. Many musical elements are blended to create this music — Indian, Negro, Creole, Spanish-Mexican, cowboy tunes and jazz. For the most part, unfortunately, these native elements are couched in typical European Romantic music styles. Only in recent years have our composers developed new, often boldly dissonant idioms that may be more compatible with the virility of our indigenous musical material (we must not confuse the often outward simplicity of our native tunes with their inherent developmental possibilities). Or there are those who feel that the natural tuneful qualities of our musical heritage could quite advantageously instill some semblance of logic and intelligibility into much of the far-out contemporary American music.

USE OF INDIAN TRIBAL THEMES

Anton Philip Heinrich, Our First National Enthusiast (1781-1861). Historically we must begin with Heinrich, although he did not truly participate in the wellspring of our musical heritage. An amateur musician, Heinrich came from Bohemia to finally settle in New York City. He sought to create an American music inspired by Indian tribal life and our natural scenery and history. His many compositions, mostly for orchestra, voice and piano, show the noblest of intentions, but his lack of original creative talent is evident in the monotonous use of hackneyed clichés of the German Romanticists; he particularly emulated the styles of Beethoven and Mendelssohn. A detailed study of his music reveals a preference for ornamented melodies having considerable chord figuration and chromatic movement; his basic rhythmic grouping is uncompromisingly regular; most of the harmonic progressions involve the tonic, dominant seventh and diminished seventh chords (use of the latter is often reminiscent of Wagner).[1] In formal style the even-lengthed, regular recurring phrases emphasize the antecedent-consequent phrase relationship; one frequently feels that the lengthy developments are too drawn out for the interest potential of the material. Heinrich's Indian pieces show no actual tribal tunes but only his characteristic tonal-rhythmic impressions. Nevertheless, Heinrich was one of the first composers to believe in and strive for a native musical expression.

Charles Sanford Skilton (1868-1941). One of the first native composers to use Indian tribal tunes in serious music composition, Skilton studied at Yale University and in Berlin. While teaching at the University of Kansas, he became interested in Indian music and learned many tribal tunes from students of the nearby Indian school, Haskell Institute. His works include two operas and several orchestral suites; "Two Indian Dances" from *Suite Primeval* (1920) is his best known piece. Skilton uses many tribal melodies in his compositions and although the rhythms are regularized and the melodies conventionally harmonized, enough Indian characteristics remain to effectively achieve the composer's intent.

Arthur Farwell (1872-1952). Farwell was one of the first American composers to ignore the German Romantic tradition and strive for an indigenous idiom. He felt the interplay and assimulation of the various native musical elements would create an individual artistic expression of our own. Farwell studied in Boston as well as in Germany and Paris, returning in 1899 to teach at several colleges and pursue the study of Indian tribal music. His compositions for orchestra, voice and piano and piano solo are, for the most part, concerned with the American Indian and are based on Indian tunes, but his broad interest in folk material is evident in several works in which Negro, cowboy and Spanish-California tunes are utilized. His folk curiosity also led to some experimentation with Oriental scales. Although Farwell tends to mold the irregular rhythmic grouping of the Indian tunes into regular, symmetrical patterns, he does keep the use of harmonies to a minimum to preserve most of the primitive quality.

Wa-Wan Press. Alhough it is doubtful whether or not Farwell achieved his goal of a characteristic, native musical expression, he was responsible for much practical help to the native contemporary composer of that time. He founded the Wa-Wan Press for the publication of music by American composers who were concerned either with the expression of indigenous elements or showed talent or progress along traditional musical paths. Although few of the thirty-seven composers represented in the catalogue attained much eminence, the Press contributed to the upgrading of the status of our composers as well as advancing the cause of American music.

Other Indian Theme Composers. Arthur Nevin (1871-1943), Frederick Jacobi (1891-1952) and Charles Wakefield Cadman (1881-1947) all used Indian tribal themes, but the primitive qualities were diluted by regular rhythmic patterns and conventional harmonies. The latter composer was better known by his songs "At Dawning" and "The Land of the Sky Blue Water." In this category of romanticized Indian music, Henry Franklin Belknap Gilbert (1868-1928) must be included, although his collaboration with Farwell in promoting a national music movement was perhaps more beneficial to the cause than his five *Indian Scenes* for piano.

USE OF FOLK MATERIAL

Minstrel Show Music. An avid devotee of the minstrel show, Mark Twain considered the Jubilee Singers, "The perfect flower of the ages; and I wish it were a foreign product so that she [America] would worship it and lavish money on it, and go properly crazy over it. . . . If I could have the minstrel show back again in its pristine purity and perfection, I should have but little use for opera."[2] The minstrel show had its beginnings about 1820. Its subject matter centered around the impersonation of the southern Negro by northern whites and of northern Negroes who tried to imitate the white man. Often called Ethiopian opera, the minstrel show had much in common with the ballad opera; the most binding feature was its use of borrowed music, much of it reflecting strong influences of Negro folk expression. Designed to ridicule and to exaggerate, the white performers with black-

ened faces, dressed in striped trousers, swallow-tailed coats, over-
sized collars and white gloves, are often pictured seated in a semicircle,
singing to the accompaniment of a banjo, violin, tambourines and bones
(castanets). Some of the performances by such entertainers as George
Washington Dixon, Daddy (Thomas Dartmouth) Rice, (1808-1860)
and Dan Emmet (1815-1904) achieved such popularity that librettos
were published.[3] These do not give the actual format, perhaps because
there was none. But they do inform us that the proceedings on the
stage were interspersed with comic repartees, stump speeches and jokes
(in Negro dialect) and dances. Without music, the reader was informed
that the dance or the lyrics were to be sung to a particular tune mentioned by title.

Among the most popular tunes of the 30s were "Long-tailed Blue,"
"Jim Crow,"[4] "Zip Coon,"[5] "Virginny Neber Tire," and "Settin' on the
Rail." In his "Fun in Black," Charles Day, a member of the Arlington
Minstrels between 1868 and 1869, tells us that "Rice first jumped Jim
Crow in Louisville, Kentucky about the year 1829 and made a great
hit."[6] The original text to Jim Crow was as follows:

> I went down to creek, I went down a fishing,
> I axked the old miller to gimmy chaw tobacker
> To treat old Aunt Hanner.
>
> Chorus: First on the heel tap, den on de toe,
>   Ebery time I wheel about I jump Jim Crow
>
> I goes down to de branch to pester old miller,
> I wants a little light wood;
> I belongs to Capt. Hawkins, and I don't care a d——n.
>
> Chorus: repeat.[7]

Later it was published with another text, its second stanza containing
a reference to Massa Pagganninny.[8] Inasmuch as Paganini made his
first appearance in London in 1830, it is extremely doubtful that his
fame could have reached our shores earlier than 1831. According to
Day, George Nichols composed "Zip Coon" in 1834 and wrote that it
was taken from a rough jig dance called "Natchez Under the Hill."[9]

A show was customarily divided into three parts; the first containing mostly songs and instrumental pieces drawn from the repertory of
whites; the second and third parts were devoted mainly to Negro imper-
sonations and situations which included jokes, dances and speeches.
Female roles were played by men. Typical of a minstrel song is the solo-

chorus formula with repeated refrains sung in unison or in three or four parts over a simple accompaniment. The song, in a major key, is preceded by an introduction or vamp and ends with a tag, the melody of which may or may not have been drawn from the song. The walk-around was the grand finale of the minstrel show. The entire troupe assembled on the stage in a semicircle; a few members stepped forward and sang a stanza, during which they were interrupted by endmen. Then the whole company joined in the final chorus as some danced, some sang and others clapped or stamped in time with the music. Originally the walk-around was only a dance; later (about 1858) it was a dance and a song.

Stephen Collins Foster (1826-1864). The most widely known early American composer, Foster was almost entirely self-taught as a musician; he composed his first song, "Open Thy Lattice, Love," at the age of eighteen. There followed a number of other songs, but his reputation as a song writer was immediately established when his "Oh, Susanna!"[10] was sung at Andrew's Ice Cream Saloon in Pittsburgh in 1848 and soon afterward taken over by Christy's Minstrels. During the next decade he wrote many songs including their lyrics, the most popular being "My Old Kentucky Home," "Massa's in the Cold Ground," "Old Black Joe," "Old Folks at Home,"[11] "Jeanie With the Light Brown Hair," "Ring, Ring, de Banjo," "Beautiful Dreamer"and "Camptown Races." He had become deeply interested in Negro songs and often attended Negro camp meetings to listen to and study their manner of singing. As a result many of his songs are written in Negro dialect and like the minstrel show music reflect the spirit and traits of Negro life on the plantation. Despite the royalties from his songs, his addiction to liquor and his domestic problems (his wife left him twice) kept him in poverty. He died in Bellevue Hospital, New York. Foster was primarily a melodist. The range of his melodies do not exceed an eleventh, most all of his two hundred and one compositions are in major keys and his harmonies are simple — using a basic harmonic background consisting of tonic, dominant, subdominant chords with an occasional secondary chord.

Our First "Serious" American Composer. An indigenous American idiom was first detected in late eighteenth-century New England in the works of our hymn tune composers. Unfortunately, the ingredients which we consider American in our hymn tunes (see p. 13) were not nurtured and were left to die on the vine. One also expected to see a budding Americanism in the music of the second and third generation Moravians in Salem and Bethlehem. But here, too, for some inexplicable reason, the promise failed to materialize and by 1850 the Moravian force was spent. It seems incongruous to us that New Orleans, a city so far removed in culture and distance from the main stream of music, became the birthplace of our first American composer to gain international repute. He was Louis Moreau Gottschalk, born in New Orleans in 1829. A precocious child, he was taken to Paris and studied piano and composition from 1841 to 1846. After his debut he toured France, Switzerland and Spain and remained in the West Indies six years.

Upon his return to the United States he gave his first concert in the ballroom of Niblo's Gardens on February 11, 1853. With this concert Gottschalk had fully confirmed the great anticipation which Hector Berlioz, the great French composer, had predicted. Dwight's *Musical Journal* carried the translation of Berlioz's prediction:

> Gottschalk is one of the very small number who possess all the different elements of a consummate pianist. . . . He is an accomplished musician — he knows just how far fancy may be indulged in expression. He knows the limits beyond which any liberties taken with the rhythm produce only confusion and disorder, and upon these limits he never encroaches. There is an exquisite grace in his manner of phrasing sweet melodies and throwing light touches from the higher keys. The boldness, the brilliancy, and the originality of his playing at once dazzles and astonishes. . . .[12]

After his New York debut, a critic wrote, "Gottschalk belongs clearly to the most modern school, but he is essentially an artist. . . he has a colossal syle that surprised us. Best of all was the profound sense of a musical enthusiasm and devotion which pervaded all the performances and removed it from the merely 'astonishing' and 'sublime' . . . into the realm of pure music and the highest art."[13] Gottschalk's dazzling technique and romantic compositions made him a stellar attraction. An idea of his immense popularity, especially with the fairer sex can be had from a letter contained in the *Diary* of Amy Fay, an American piano pupil of Franz Liszt. It read: "I was dreadfully sorry to hear of poor Gottschalk's death . . . . If any more is in the papers about him you must send it to me, for the infatuation that I and 99,999 other American girls once felt for him still lingers in my breast."[14]

Gottschalk composed in two distinct idioms — the so-called salon style which includes such works as "The Dying Poet," "The Last Hope,"[15] and "The Maiden's Blush" and the second style in which he imbues the spirit and flavor of Creole songs and Latin-American dance rhythms in his music. One does not apologize for these compositions, for they are genuine works of art. Such compositions as "The Banjo"[16] (in which he used a snatch of "Camptown Races" and "Roll, Jordon, Roll"), *Le*

Bannanier,[17]   *La Bamboula,*[18] *Ojos Criollos, La Savana, Souvenir de Porto Rico* are excellent examples of the new music. Gottschalk's favorite medium was the piano, but he left us two symphonic works, *La Noche de los Tropicos* and *Escenas Campestres Cubanas* and two operas. It is believed an attack of acute appendicitus led to his untimely death on December 18, 1869 in Tijuca, Buenos Aires.

Dvorak's Influence. Some historians feel the visiting Bohemian composer, Antonin Dvorak, who taught at the National Conservatory of Music in New York City from 1892 to 1895, was the first composer of recognized fame to encourage the use of American folk music in serious composition.[19] He advocated either the attractive arrangement of actual folk songs in the prevailing Romantic tradition or the assimilation of folk song characteristics in the distinctive idiom of a composer. The latter way, more specifically, would involve exploring characteristic melodic intervals and rhythmic patterns of folk tunes for elements to inspire serious formal development. Although the Largo from his *New World Symphony* was thought to be an unaltered Negro spiritual, Dvorak insisted that it represents only the spirit and feeling of such a song.[20] Through influence on his students, Williams Arms Fisher (1861-1948), Harvey W. Loomis (1865-1930) and Henry T. Burleigh (1866-1949), Dvorak's stimulus to an indigenous American music expression was far-reaching. Burleigh in particular, a Negro, made a reputation as a singer and arranger of Negro spirituals, "Deep River" being one of the best known.

Henry Franklin Belknap Gilbert. Although mentioned earlier as using Indian themes, Gilbert is probably better known for his works which use Afro-American tunes: *Negro Rhapsody* (1913) for piano and *Comedy Overture on Negro Themes* (1905). His symphonic poem *The Dance in Place Congo* (1906) draws specifically on Creole music such as the *bamboula* dance. Stylistically, although Gilbert decried the German Romantic influence, he was not able to free himself from it. Only occasionally in his derivative music is there some chordal progression, technical development or particular orchestration effect in which he strikes out toward originality.

John Powell (1882-1963). A composer of the South, Powell was concerned at first with cultivating the Negro tunes of Virginia and later the Anglo-American folk music found in the Appalachian Mountains. The *Negro Rhapsody* (1919) for orchestra and piano is his most popular work, although Symphony in A (1947) based on Anglo-American folk tunes is his best work. Again, the traditional Romantic treatment is evident, but the modal nature of the tunes is retained and the developing rhythms and harmonies are made to conform to the spirit of the tunes. One feels a sincere attempt has been made to capture the peculiar essence of the melodies without the superficial dressing of contrived harmonic progressions, particularly chromaticism.

William Grant Still (1895-   ). Still has been one of the most successful Negro composers in using the moods and characteristic figural elements of the Negro folk expression in serious music composition. Actual tunes are not used literally, only their inspirational essence. In several symphonies and ballets the Negro folk tune characteristics are combined with popular vernacular idioms. His *Afro-American Symphony* (1931), one of his better known works, exemplifies this treatment. Inasmuch as the popular idioms inherit the offbeat, syncopated cakewalk patterns of early jazz and the Negro work songs and spirituals have these same rhythmic characteristics, the blend seems a natural one. By the same reasoning, the two component expressions are so much alike that their amalgamation does not really create a new definitive style; rather, both components are raised to the level of serious, symphonic development.

Ernest Bloch (1880-1959). Born in Switzerland, Bloch lived in the United States from 1916 to 1930 and again from 1939 until his death. He contributed a single but impressive work toward the development of our national music, although his main musical expression was in a different direction. Most of Bloch's works are religious in text and musical feeling; biblical texts served as inspiration. The music is cast in large molds, usually for orchestra with instrumental solo. Among many compositions, his *Psalms* (1914) and rhapsody, *Schelomo* (1915) stand out. But our concern here is with his epic rhapsody *America* (1927) which, in three parts, attempts to express musically in a basic chronology some important events in American history. Bloch avoids detailed descriptions or specific emotions, using only broad musical effects and moods. Indian tribal melodies, Civil War and Negro folk songs are woven into the basic homophonic texture which uniquely unfolds from a germ idea in the beginning to its consummate, climactic, fully developed form at the end. Again we find this variation developmental technique which harkens back to its embryonic, much cruder use in Indian tribal tunes; hence, aside from his use of native tunes, an indigenous structural characteristic is present in this work. However, Bloch's musical style is so obviously German Romantic with some added enriched harmonies and touches of Impressionism that no real, authentic American spirit is ever evoked in the epic rhapsody. A person unacquainted with the folk material used would be much impressed by the workmanship, strength and high quality of the music, but would just as likely conjure up European historical events as American.

Footnotes

[1]Ma-GlA, No. 127.
[2]As quoted by JohR, p. 44.
[3]ChriS, p. 94.
[4]Ma-GlA, No. 104.
[5]Ma-GlA, No. 105.
[6]DayF, p. 5.
[7]*Ibid.*, p. 6.
[8]Ma-GlA, No. 104.
[9]*Op. cit.*, p. 6. See Ma-GlA, No. 105.
[10]Ma-GlA, No. 107.
[11]Ma-GlA, No. 108.
[12]DwiJ, p. 143.
[13]PutM, p. 350.
[14]FayG, p. 42.
[15]BehP, p. 48.
[16]Ma-GlA, No. 128.
[17]BehP, p. 34.
[18]*Ibid.*, p. 15.
[19]How-BelM, p. 165.
[20]ChaA, p. 389.

nationalistic composers II

Douglas Moore (1893-   ). Moore is unique as one of the few American composers using traditional European styles in such a clever manner that through subtle musical innuendo he recreates much of the early American spirit. After study at Yale University with Horatio Parker and David Stanley Smith, Moore went to Paris for further study with Vincent d'Indy and Boulanger, finally returning to work with Bloch in this country. Moore's compositions are mostly of large dimensions including symphonies, orchestral suites and operas. His two operas, *The Devil and Daniel Webster* (1939) and *The Ballad of Baby Doe* (1956), are outstanding American landmarks in this form, containing a variety of moods and expressions from the lyric to the dramatic; of equal importance, the music is always wedded appropriately to the mood or action of the story. His writing for voices shows a sensitive adjustment of musical rhythm to the inflections of English prose and poetry.

For the most part, Moore's music shows simple melodies, regular rhythms, conventional Romantic harmonies and symmetrical phrase construction. But there is a freshness of melodic turn, a folkish irregularity of pattern, an unexpected out-of-key chord to imbue the music with vitality and continued interest. Although Moore does not hesitate to use an occasional country dance or fiddle tune, his music is American primarily because of its inspiration from native legend and literature and because of his talent for expressing these in such a compatible, homespun musical language. Otto Luening, composer-critic, has described Moore's talent in different but similar words: "He possesses the one quality that can't be learned, that is, the desire to sing . . . tried and well-known harmonic progressions take on new life, a rhythmic pattern is animated and counterpoint becomes counter-melody through the magic of his song."[1] Moore's literary contributions include the books, *Listening to Music* (1932, revised and enlarged, 1937) and *From Madrigal to Modern Music: A Guide to Musical Styles* (1942).

Virgil Thomson (1896-   ). Thomson has succeeded, like Moore, in stamping a native quality on his music through the smallest musical suggestion. After study at Harvard, Thomson continued with Boulanger in Paris but soon came under the spell of the radical Les Six which included Georges Auric, Arthur Honegger, Darius Milhaud and Francis Poulenc. Their dissonant idioms, however, soon became repulsive, causing Thomson to revert back to a simple, direct musical expression. Writing in a variety of forms including symphonies, chamber music, choral works and movie scores, Thomson, like Moore, is best known for two operas, *Four Saints in Three Acts* (1934) with a libretto by Gertrude Stein and *The Mother of Us All* (1943). Both stand out as monuments in the development of native opera through clear, faithful expression in music and words of the true American vernacular. Again like Moore, Thomson had the knack of musically pointing up prosody to enhance word accentuation and fluent word continuity.

Actually, although Thomson described himself as a Neo-romanticist, his style is more Classic than Romantic; his melodies, rhythms, harmonies and formal groupings are simple and direct, devoid of extraneous frills and affectations. As a revolt against the modern use of dissonances, he deliberately uses conventional, cliché effects, but at the proper psychological moments he manages to offset them with the unexpected — a sudden change of melodic direction, a bit of dissonant counterpoint or a chord out of its traditional context. Thomson does not hesitate to incorporate a variety of seemingly disparate elements in his music, including modal melodies, vernacular popular tunes and gospel hymns, in fact, he is one of the few contemporary composers to explore to any extent the possibilities of American hymnody. As an author, Thomson has lucidly described the many aspects of contemporary music in *The State of Music* (1939), *The Musical Scene* (1945), *The Art of Judging Music* (1948) and *Music Right and Left* (1951).

Ross Lee Finney (1906-   ). Finney is another of the few American composers interested in our early hymns as material for serious composition. His work with Roger Sessions and, in Europe, Alban Berg, Boulanger and Gian Francesco Malipiero resulted in, at first, a traditional Romantic style of melody and harmony mixed with a Classic emphasis on formal structure; later, he changed to a twelve-tone technique. Although there are only a few works in his early style, they are impressive. In the *Pilgrim Psalms* (1945), a cantata for mixed chorus, soloists and organ, Finney utilizes fourteen tunes from the *Ainsworth Psalter,* not literally but changed to impart his own emotional feelings. His *Variations, Fugueing and Rondo* (1943) uses as a unifying theme, Billing's hymn tune "Berlin"; here, the craftsman-like structure blending Baroque contrapuntal elements with Romantic but occasionally more dissonant harmonies is another example of the effective and artistic blend of traditional techniques with indigenous musical inspiration. In other early works Finney has used American folk tunes as nuclear material for the development of polished musical structures.

   Roy Harris (1898-   ). Like Moore and Virgil Thompson, Harris uses basically traditional musical material but in a large-scale structural framework that unfolds slowly and builds up masses of sound favoring the open quality of fifth and fourth intervals. The resulting structural strength, largeness of formal dimensions and folksy harmonic qualities have been interpreted by many as a most natural expression of the American spirit. After study with Arthur Farwell and Boulanger in Paris, Harris determinedly set out to develop his own musical idiom that would be, at the same time, representative of his country; he felt a sense of destiny as well as a moral responsibility to achieve this goal. In keeping with his penchant for large-scale forms, most of his works are symphonies, but there are many other pieces for chorus, chamber groups, voice, piano and solo instruments. Most critics feel that the Third Symphony (1939) is one of his most impressive works and typical of his style; strong emotional effects are generated, but they are always of a general, nondescriptive nature. However, Harris is not above the obvious use of folk tunes: The fourth symphony, the *Folk Song Symphony* (1941) for chorus and orchestra, exploits a Civil War song, cowboy songs, Anglo-American folk songs and a Negro camp-meeting hymn.

   Harris is a Classicist in his objective, nonprogrammatic approach to music. The texture of his music recalls the early Flemish and Baroque contrapuntal styles, but there is an underlying core of harmonic progression; the counterpoint is a secondary result of the harmonic writing. This goal of harmonic counterpoint is basic to Harris' musical credo.[2] His melodies show long flowing lines but are usually simple, consisting of diatonic movement mixed with thirds, ascending fourths and descending fifths (many of the latter two); there is little chromatic movement. Asymmetric rhythmic grouping is typical; a favorite device is to use regular meters but to subdivide the beats within each measure irregularly so a melodic pattern may consist of a mixed succession of two-, three-, four- and five-unit rhythmic figures. Harmonically, Harris favors using the church modes or a fluctuation between a major and its parallel minor key through a free interchange of the major and minor third. Although most always he uses only triads (seldom ever the dominant seventh chord) his typical treatment is to combine them bitonally — the simultaneous use of two different groups of triads, each group in a different key. Frequent parallel chord motion with emphasis on consecutive fourths and fifths adds to the folksy effect of much of his music. Practically all of the cadences are plagal.

Harris' structural technique harkens back to the Baroque era: A melodic idea is developed gradually through an organic, ever-changing unfoldment; the literal repetition or sequence of a melodic or harmonic segment is never found (possibly because in Harris' credo it indicated a retardation or even cessation of musical development). Again, this basic variation technique is the same universal principle used in the primitive Indian tribal music, suggesting another indigenous element in Harris' style. Many pieces and movements begin in unison and in a low register; irregular-lengthened phrases and indistinct cadences enhance the unbroken forward drive that is so characteristic. Although writing primarily symphonies, Harris does not use the traditional sonata-allegro form, in fact he seldom uses any of the forms that recapitulate but only those that unfold through continual change. Unfortunately, one is occasionally conscious of an overall imbalance or incompleteness of parts in a composition. This has also been recognized by one of Harris' contemporaries, Aaron Copland: "The composer's greatest weakness has proved . . . [to be] an apparent incapacity for shaping a long composition so that the form of the whole is truly logical and inevitable."[3]

John Vincent (1902-   ). Like Harris, Vincent has succeeded in instilling a unique, indigenous quality in his music, not through the literal use of folk material but through characteristic melodic movement, chord progressions and a clear, effective style. After study at the New England Conservatory, George Peabody College in Nashville and Harvard University, Vincent went to Paris to study with Boulanger. He has held several college teaching posts and is now Professor of Music at the University of California, Los Angeles. His compositions include symphonies, symphonic poems, chamber music, pieces for voice, chorus and orchestra and some songs. To date, the Symphony in D seems to be one of his most representative works; it has received numerous performances by major symphony orchestras over the country.

Stylistically, Vincent's music favors a contrapuntal build-up of melodic lines, although the texture always remains transparent and fluid. His melodies are basically diatonic, which is brought more in relief by the occasional, abrupt insertion of large intervals. Rhythmic regularity seems to predominate, but frequent asymmetrical groupings of mixed meters, and patterns are all the more set in relief by the underlying regularity. An interchange and fusion of modality and major-minor tonality runs throughout his music. Open, incomplete chords move in parallel motion or are inserted out of context of the mode or tonal key. Vincent has chosen to use the proven Classic-Romantic forms, but his structural technique is expansive, developing motivic patterns slowly over entire movements to create effective, forceful climaxes. His book, *The Diatonic Modes in Modern Music* (1951), is a definitive treatment of the modes, including their historical development and influence in modern musical expression.

USE OF JAZZ

John Alden Carpenter (1876-1951). Carpenter was one of the first native American composers to use elements of jazz in serious music composition. After music study with Paine at Harvard, Carpenter forsook music as a career for business, but remained an amateur composer, writing symphonies, choral works, chamber music and songs. *Skyscrapers* (1926), a ballet of modern American life and *Adventures in a Perambulator* (1941) are his most characteristic works. In a style that is harmonically European Romantic with considerable French Impressionism, jazz elements (mostly syncopated rhythmic patterns) are superposed on simple melodic lines. According to a then contemporary music critic, Oscar Thomson, *Skyscrapers* contains "not literal jazz, but jazz as it has filtered through the mind of a musician who thinks in terms of art, and whose purpose was to write an art work, not merely to add to America's store of popular music."[4] In additional praise the composer-critic, Felix Borowski, stated:

> . . . the Creator of *Skyscrapers* is of all our composers the most typically American . . . . There is not in Carpenter's music the racial tang which set the Russian Borodin apart from his colleagues in Germany or France or brought an ephemeral popularity to Grieg; but the essence of our highly vitalized American life, our febrile activity, our somewhat superficial emotion, our boundless energy are deeply implanted in the Chicago master's style.[5]

In its day one can understand how the novelty of *Skyscrapers* might have created the above impression. Today the effects are dated and have lost their tang; the jazz elements seem synthetic and foreign against the refined, atmospheric harmonies and loosely constructed forms of the piece.

Louis Gruenberg (1884-1964). Gruenberg has used jazz elements as well as Afro-American material blended in a Neo-romantic style. Gruenberg is remembered mostly for three operas, one of which, *Emperor Jones* (1933), is considered another landmark in American opera development because the music so aptly enhances the dramatic tensions of the story. The music is not tuneful in the obvious sense; rather, the melodies tend toward angularity and are loosely knit in irregular groupings; the rhythmic patterns are likewise not regular and dissonant counterpoint and harmonies are common. But these abtruse elements, rather than drawing attention to themselves, make the music even more effective as a strong support for the drama.

George Gershwin (1898-1937). In one of his few verbal expressions about music, Gershwin stated:

> Jazz I regard as an American folk-music; not the only one, but a very powerful one which is probably in the blood and feeling of the American people more than any other style of folk-music. I believe that it can be made the basis of serious symphonic works of lasting value, in the hands of a composer with talent for both jazz and symphonic music.[6]

Of all the American composers, Gershwin himself stands out as the most successful in this fusion of popular with art-music. Born in Brooklyn, he studied piano and composition, took a job as a song plugger and soon began writing scores for musical comedies. His serious career began when Paul Whiteman commissioned him to write a jazz piece in symphonic form. The result was "Rhapsody in Blue" which, orchestrated by Ferde Grofé, received its first performance in Carnegie Hall in 1924. In 1925, his Concerto in F for piano and orchestra was commissioned by Walter Damrosch who performed it with the New York Philharmonic with Gershwin as soloist. Other symphonic-jazz works followed: *An American in Paris* (1928), *Second Rhapsody* (1932) and the *Cuban Overture* (1934), but his most significant work is the opera *Porgy and Bess* (1935) which blends Negro-like work songs and spirituals with popular jazz idioms to create an American folk opera unsurpassed for its dramatic vitality and validity of musical expression.

Gershwin is unique in not only creating a style in popular music of sufficient quality to remain fertile and fresh in one musical comedy after another, but he also was the first and, to date, only composer to develop these popular elements in a way that made them fit and belong in the larger, serious musical forms. The lasting appeal of his tunes is due first of all to a characteristic rhythmic treatment: Often, he takes a simple, ragtime-like syncopated figure and through its regular repetition achieves a catchy momentum that vitalizes the tune; second, his melodies are basically diatonic, but broken-chord figures afford unexpected contrasts; third, the chordal progressions are the conventional ones of jazz, but Impressionistic groupings of seventh and ninth chords are used frequently in parallel movement, down or up a half or whole step, for piquant harmonic emphasis. The combination of all these results in a flavor that is Gershwin's alone and has not been imitated. Formally, he favored the juxtaposition of the more obvious elements of repetition and contrast in developing his ideas in the larger forms usually of the three-part, recapitulative genre.

Aaron Copland (1900-   ). A most remarkable composer, Copland's works, all of high quality, show such varied styles to afford a "compendium of 20th century trends"[7] in the use of native material as well as in the overall development of American music. His use of jazz elements and folk material in serious composition has given these indigenous, often naive musical expressions a high inspirational quality and dignity heretofore unattained. Copland, like Gershwin, was born in Brooklyn and studied composition with Rubin Goldmark and eventually with Boulanger in Paris. Copland's chief interest in jazz was its polyrhythmic effects; he felt the clash of two or more different rhythmic patterns used simultaneously was new in western music and was the only element in jazz of lasting value that could be applied to serious musical styles. His early works, *Music for the Theatre* (1925) for orchestra and piano and *Concerto for Piano and Orchestra* (1926), emphasize this rhythmic treatment, but with melodies and harmonies that still reflect German-Romantic influence.

Soon he found jazz rhythms too limiting and abandoned them for a rhythmic complexity resulting from contrapuntal texture — the coincidence of separate melodic lines, each complex in itself; to this, he added a Stravinsky-like Neo-classicism of economy of material, extreme melodic angularity and short, irregular groupings as well as Debussy-like Impressionistic effects of unresolved dissonances and parallel chordal movement. During this second period of forceful, concise, intellectually conceived music, the *Dance Symphony* (1925), *Symphonic Ode* (1928-1929), *Piano Variations* (1930) and *Short Symphony* (1933) stand out.

Feeling that in the works of his second period he had lost contact with the general public, Copland again changed his style, this time toward simplification. His main interest became American folk music which he used in an obvious enough manner, yet always cleverly dressed-up in complex, irregular rhythmic patterns; harmonically, simple triads are much in evidence but they usually occur out of context of conventional chord successions. The orchestral suite *El Salón México* (1936) makes use of Mexican folk songs and the ballets *Billy the Kid* (1938), *Rodeo* (1942) and *Appalachian Spring* (1944) comprise his most impressive works of this period.

In his fourth period, Copland returned to the abstract, austere style of his second period. The Third Symphony (1946) is typical with its wide-range melodies, irregular rhythmic patterns and dissonant counterpoint and harmonies; formally, one senses an overall Classic symmetry that unifies his lengthy developments. Relative to structural prowess which stands out in all of his works, Theodore Chandler has written: "In all questions of balancing tonalities, of negotiating transitions, of building up climaxes, and preparing cadences, Copland generally shows a flawless ear and sense of proportion."[8] There are many who feel that Copland's music is unique among contemporary American composers in effecting a balanced fusion of melodic-rhythmic inspiration, harmonic color and variety, and formal workmanship and proportion. Like Virgil Thomson, Copland has also contributed to the music literature of our times: *What to Listen for in Music* (1939), *Our New Music* (1941) and *Music and Imagination* (1952).

Other Folk Music Composers. Boris Kremenliev (1911-), born in Bulgaria, has since 1947 been Professor of Music at the University of California, Los Angeles. His music, typified in *Balkan Rhapsody* for orchestra (1965), blends Slavic folk elements with the prevalent contemporary American Neo-classic sound of asymmetric rhythms, polytonal harmonies and dissonances. David Guion (1895-), George F. McKay (1899-), Lamar Stringfield (1897-1959), Charles G. Vardell (1893-), Ernest Bacon (1898-), Elie Siegmeister (1909-), and Don Gillis (1912-) are composers or arrangers who have used American folk music in some combinations with popular dance idioms. Morton Gould (1913-) in particular has welded together the two styles in brilliant orchestral arrangements which explore music from spirituals through jazz. The fusion has been beneficial to both elements since the quality of popular music has been improved while at the same time, some of the stodgy pedantry of serious music has been eliminated.

Are Indigenous Musical Elements Really Definable? According to George Gershwin: "The great music of the past in other countries has always been built on folk-music. This is the strongest source of musical fecundity. America is no exception among the countries."[9] There are others who feel that the use of indigenous music material — Indian,

Negro and Anglo-American tunes and jazz — is not compatible with serious, intellectualized art-music since the cultural levels of the two expressions are too far removed to be satisfactorily combined. Furthermore, no less an authority on American music than John Tasker Howard has stated:

> Americanism is a more subtle thing than a mere question of geographic origin. As in spoken or written language, there are certain habits of speceh, and certain points of view, that are peculiar to us. Not mere reference to local events and scenes, but the manner of referring to them and looking at them. So, in music, it is a question of association and traits inherent in the music itself.[10]

Roger Sessions, a respected representative of our *avant-garde* group of composers has put it this way: "What is lacking . . . is awareness of the fact that genuine national character comes from within and must develop and grow of itself, that it cannot be imposed from without, and that in the last analysis, it is a by-product, not an aim of artistic expression."[11]

One cannot ignore the fact, however, that our often naive but forthright native melodies have instilled a comparable freshness and vitality into the serious music of many of our composers. When these influences become part of an unself-conscious background on which American composers of talent may germinate and develop their individual musical language, then we truly will produce a genuine, native musical expression. Some feel that, to date, the intellectualized, abstruse style of Copland's Third Symphony, or the rugged, virile, sense-of-destiny qualities of Harris' symphonies come closest to reflecting the pulse — the essence of a native idiom. Only the lapse of time will tell.

FOOTNOTES

[1]LueM, p. 248.
[2]CowH, p. 66.
[3]CopO, pp. 167-168.
[4]BorC, pp. 464-465.
[5]*Ibid.*, p. 466.
[6]GerJ, p. 187.
[7]ChaA, p. 502.
[8]ChaC, p. 49.
[9]GerJ, p. 186.
[10]HowA, p. 436.
[11]SesR, p. 151.

contemporary development of traditional styles

Modernization of Traditional Musical Style. In the preceding chapter our focus was attuned to those composers who emphasized nationalistic aspects in their music. Although most of this music is expressed in the usual Romantic or Classic traditions, it must have been evident from the detailed descriptions of the techniques of the more recent nationalists that exciting new musical styles are also involved in their idioms. These styles will now be briefly described. In the first decades of the twentieth century, a reaction against the traditional European Romantic style became increasingly pronounced, at first in Europe and then in America. The cliché melodic and harmonic progressions (particularly the Wagner-like chromaticism) became overripe from overuse; the intended subjective emotions and imagination were no longer aroused by the formerly sure-fire musical formulas. The reaction developed in the creation of new musical styles which reached forward into new unchartered paths as well as backward a hundred years into music history for inspiration. One of the styles contained the Romantic tradition, but with increasing refinement and dilution of its former characteristics.

Neo-romanticism. This style extended the old German Romantic tradition primarily in its tonal and formal aspects. The former typical chromaticism which, because of its frequent transient modulations, had already weakened the underpinnings of Classic tonality, was dealt a further blow by the addition of seventh and ninth intervals as well as nonchordal tones to many secondary triads. The result was that the enriched harmonies further obscured modulation to the point where it was necessary to use more and more remote modulations to achieve tonal contrasts. Also, the older formal dimensions were increased proportionally throughout a structure; melodies, their development and the movements themselves were extended and the orchestra was increased in size. Richard Strauss, Gustav Mahler and Anton Bruckner typify this style; not only did they bring it to its consummate development but, in so doing, contributed much toward its demise. In effect, the exaggerated emphasis of self-expression to the sacrifice of its formal containment led (as in any art expression) to its disintegration as a pure art form.

Impressionism. When the enriched chordal progressions of Neo-romanticism were carried a step further to disregard the accepted chordal movements basic to harmonic tonality, a new tonal concept — a new musical medium — was created. Impressionism is like Romanticism in revolting against Realism; it seeks to express not objects themselves but the effects of the objects in tone — the thoughts or emotions aroused by the images. Hence, the subjective, veiled, mystic musical impressions are a logical culmination of the Romantic style.

Musically, the three most important aspects of Impressionism are concerned with nullifying the tendencies of harmonic tonality: (1) The diatonic scale with added chromatic (but less important) auxiliary tones is no longer the main tonal skeleton; now, the chromatic twelve-tone scale is the basis, with each semitone having equal status melodically and as a root of its own triad. (2) New chord combinations foreign to a given key are used consisting of ninth, eleventh and thirteenth intervals as well as various added tones, not as appoggiaturas but as integral parts of the chords; furthermore, the dissonant intervals of these new chordal combinations that formerly required resolution are now used unresolved. (3) In defiance of the conventional part movement by contrary motion, now it became common for all tones of a chord to move in parallel motion, usually by half of whole steps or by augmented fourths.

Other characteristics of Impressionism are the avoidance of the leading tone and the use of whole tone scales and chords, medieval modes, exotic scales and triads with open fifths (no thirds). Structurally, the components of form are just as vague and indistinct as the musical material: Melodies are often fragmentary in irregular or free rhythms (bar-line pulsation is less pronounced), phrase lengths are irregular and the overall structure is loosely knit. The works of Claude Debussy and Maurice Ravel exemplify the atmospheric, delicate, refined music of this style.

Neo-classicism. In the revolt against the unrestrained emotionalism of Romanticism, some composers have returned to the eighteenth-century Classical point of view in which a modern objectivity replaces the Romantic subjectivity. The resulting impersonal, intellectual, abstract musical language is devoid of or at least minimizes the expression of emotional feeling and imagination. The emphasis changes from the content and significance of the music to the perfection of technique and form of its expression. The watchword is the elimination of unessentials and the condensation of materials. As a result, textures are simplified and reduced in density; eighteenth-century counterpoint is brought back because of its lucid transparency. But the obvious, naïve eighteenth-century harmonic progressions are missing, although a vague sense of tonality often underlies much of the music. Instead, there is usually dissonant counterpoint which most often avoids the old consonant intervals.

The separate lines show considerable angularity and rhythmic complexity. In the coincidence of the lines, polytonal or atonal effects may result. The former device uses two (bitonal) or more keys simultaneously to usually cancel out or considerably weaken any feeling of tonality; the latter device, as the name implies, completely negates any implication of keys. Occasionally, polychordal effects are found which combine two or more chords in different keys. Adding to the interest (and complexity) of the style, polyrhythms are common which combine two or more separate and distinct rhythmic patterns. Structurally, the forms and their component parts are comparatively brief. Phrases are irregular in length and, what is most characteristic of the style, show a minimum of repetition; actually, most composers avoid obvious repetition as being foreign to the style. Rather, an ever-changing development of material is evident, once again corroborating the musical validity of this age-old device.

However, although the ideal of the style stresses directness, clarity and simplification, the resulting musical language is often quite the contrary due to tonal dissonance and rhythmic complexity. Actually, what has occurred is that the eighteenth-century forms and structural techniques serve as familiar molds in which to unfold the bold, new unfamiliar tonal and rhythmic idioms, thereby creating some semblance of order and organization for easier comprehension of the music. Igor Stravinsky, Paul Hindemith and Béla Bartók are typical composers in this style.

NEO-ROMANTIC STYLE

Transition Composers.   Since there is no clear line of demarcation, it is difficult to separate American composers whose styles represent the older European Romantic tradition more than the newer extension and refinement of that tradition in Neo-romanticism. Some of the Romantic composers considered in previous chapters could with almost equal justification be included here. Frederick Shepherd Converse (1871-1940) is in this category. His *Fliver Ten Million* (1927) for orchestra is a humorous period piece reflecting a bit of America; *The Pipe of Desire* (1910) is the first opera by an American to be produced at the Metropolitan. Ernest Schelling (1876-1939) is best represented by *A Victory Ball* (1923) for orchestra. David Stanley Smith (1877-1949), although writing a number of orchestral works, is best known for his chamber music. The musical output of Arthur Shepherd (1880-) has been varied, including excursions in the folklore movement, but his most serious efforts have been in the absolute categories of symphonies and chamber music.

Howard Hanson (1896-). Hanson stands out as one of the most representative of the Neo-romanticists; his music carries a deep conviction, sincerity and broad emotional expression to give new profound meaning and prestige to this style. After study at the Institute of Musical Art in New York City and at the American Academy in Rome, Hanson soon became director of the Eastman School of Music at Rochester, New York. His symphonies, particularly the early ones, are the most popular and, many feel, his most characteristic works. There is also considerable choral and chamber music; his opera *Merry Mount* was performed at the Metropolitan in 1934. Hanson's orchestra music shows a basic homophonic texture, but in his choral writing he has developed a new, unique method: The individual choral parts are conceived together with and integrated in the orchestral parts; as a result, the chorus may, at times, sing in unison, in incomplete harmony or in a many-voiced division (usually at climaxes). Burnet C. Tuthill in his lucid article about Hanson suggests this use of the chorus as one of the chief contributions to modern music expression.[1]

Hanson's melodies are often modal and frequently unabashedly sentimental in spirit; basically diatonic in movement, fourths and fifths occur often enough to suggest the influence of Jean Sibelius; another melodic characteristic is the use of the minor seventh interval either as a skip or as the including compass of a melodic figure. The rhythmic patterns are regular with a penchant for syncopation; occasionally, polyrhythmic effects are used. Harmonically, seventh, ninth, eleventh and thirteenth chords predominate and are often spread out in superimposed fourth positions. Although the progressions are basically tonal, the dissonant chords built of added thirds are not always resolved conventionally, but characteristic of his idiom, move to other similar chords. There is little obvious use of the conventional dominant-to-tonic progressions or of conventional modulations. Although Hanson's music emphasizes emotional content (the widely spread intervals often suggesting stark bleakness or rugged strength), the structures are the Classic ones; the phrase lengths are regular, there is much use of a pedal point or pedal figure and overall balanced proportions are always evident. Edward Royce has summarily appraised Hanson's position as a composer: "Whether one judges Hanson's composing from the standpoint of vitality, that of originality, that of interesting content, that of appropriateness, or that of emotional intensity, he challenges attention."[2] Hanson's *Harmonic Materials of Modern Music* (1960) is unique as the first thorough analysis of the harmonic possibilities in the twelve-tone scale.

Gian-Carlo Menotti (1911-). Coming to the United States in 1928 from Italy, Menotti studied at the Curtis Insitute in Philadelphia and eventually has become one of the most prolific American opera composers. His operas include *Amelia Goes to the Ball* (1937) *The Old Maid and the Thief* (1939), *The Medium* (1946), *The Counsul* (1950) and *Amahl and the Night Visitors* (1951). Menotti cleverly blends the German Romantic trait of ripe emotionalism with the Italian flair for dramatic expression. Homophony predominates, but there are frequent contrapuntal passages; the melodies show larger intervals, more angularity and wider range than is typical of the pure Romantic style; rhythmic patterns are irregular enough to offer effective contrast to the predominantly regular patterns. The harmonies are basically the enriched Romantic ones, but like the rhythmic expression, are strikingly set off by unexpected dissonant chords. The operatic forms show all the customary tricks of the trade that are expected in this medium.

Samuel Barber (1910-). After study at the Curtis Institute of Music in Philadelphia and the American Academy in Rome, Barber has become another of the contemporary American composers who has infused new vitality into the Romantic style. Most of his works are for orchestra, the more popular being *Adagio for Strings* (1936), *Essay for Orchestra* (1937) and the overture, *The School for Scandal* (1932). *Medea's Meditation and Dance of Vengeance* op. 23a (1956) illustrates his most advanced dissonant style. Barber's style, like Menotti's, blends contemporary melodic, rhythmic and harmonic effects with the traditional Romantic style to achieve a strong and at times harsh musical expression. The texture of Barber's music shows a mixture of dissonant counterpoint and homophony, often also dissonant, but in which an underlying tonality can usually be ascertained. The melodies are lyrical and dramatic, encompassing a wide range. All sizes of intervals can be found and, peculiar to Barber's style, certain intervals often predominate in melodies to serve as focal tonal centers in place of tonalities. Some melodies are short, angular and jagged; others are rounded in long, smooth lines.

The rhythmic patterns are often complex and irregular in length; the harmonies show much use of dissonant chord combinations and some polyharmony. Robert Horan, in his esoteric survey of Barber's music attests by innuendo to Barber's use of dissonance and consonance:

> Barber has never contested the theory that dissonance introduces tension and consonance relaxation. Many contemporary works employing extreme dissonance manage to close on a consonant chord, which arrives rather like a death-bed confession. The importance of consonance would seem to be in the value and variety of relaxations it makes possible within any given work. Things must become *tense* and *attain* repose. This tightening and relaxing of elements is the essential nature of movement.[3]

Although Barber's melodies, rhythms and harmonies are boldly contemporary, his strongest link with the past is found in his larger works, which are firmly rooted in the principles of sonata-allegro form.

Leonard Bernstein (1918-   ). Bernstein may be remembered as one of the few American composers to have successfully fused a serious, intellectualized, technical approach with obvious popular melodic and rhythmic elements of jazz. After work at Harvard with Walter Piston and Hill, Bernstein's talents soon became evident in conducting as well as in composition. A protégé of Serge Koussevitsky, he has recently assumed the leadership of the New York Philharmonic Symphony. His compositional talent has successfully expressed itself in such divergent mediums as the serious symphony and popular musical comedy. His serious larger works include the *Jeremiah Symphony* (1944) for mezzo-soprano and orchestra, *The Age of Anxiety* (1949) for piano and orchestra, a satirical opera, *Trouble in Tahiti* (1952) and some ballets and incidental music for orchestra.

Bernstein's music shows a homophonic texture (specifically, mono-thematic with accompanying harmonies) and simple diatonic melodies that betray a strong popular influence. Rhythmically, the jazz element of syncopation is prominent while harmonically, the Neo-romantic chord progressions favoring simple triads with added tones and secondary seventh and ninth chords are characteristic. It is in the formal organization that Bernstein's competent craftsmanship cleverly welds together the divergent elements; while his phrases are regular in length, his developments are truly symphonic in proportions approaching at times the cerebral treatment of Brahms.

Other Neo-romantic Composers. It would be impractical to mention all of the American composers who continue to use the late Romantic style as a base structural medium on which each builds his own individual musical expression. Edgar Stillman Kelly (1857-1944) leaves an impressive oratorio, *The Pilgrims Progress* (1918) and a symphony entitled *Gulliver* (1937). Harl McDonald (1891-1955) is known for his Symphony No. 1, *The Santa Fe Trail,* (1934) and Symphony No. 2, *Rhumba* (1935). Deems Taylor (1885-1966)) is best represented by his two operas, *The King's Henchman* (1927) and *Peter Ibbetson* (1931) and the orchestral suite *Through the Looking Glass* (1923). Marc Blitzstein (1905-1964) leaves two operas concerned with class struggle and social justice: *The Cradle Will Rock* (1937) and *No For an Answer* (1941). *Leroy J. Robertson* (1896-   ), one of the foremost serious Mormon composers, won the $25,000 Reichhold Awards with his *Trilogy.* Leo Sowerby (1895-   ), Howard Swanson (1909-   ), Roger Goeb (1914-   ), Vincent Persichetti (1915-   ), Robert Ward (1917-   ), Harold Shapero (1920-   ), Lukas Foss (1922-   ) and Peter Mennin (1923-   ) have all written effectively in this style.

Operetta and Musical Comedy: General Characteristics. Continuing in the Neo-romantic category, we must include the lighter expressions of musical entertainment which often have highly refined structures and spicingly piquant harmonies. The usual standard format of proven clichés in the operetta and musical comedy involves some combination of popular melodies with spoken dialogue and the added visual attractions of lavish costumes, beautiful girls and some ballet. Musically, the usual texture is a monothematic homophony (a melody line with more or less chordal accompaniment); the melodies are obvious, diatonic and foursquare; the rhythms are simple and regular. The harmonies are the conventional, simple Romantic progressions with occasional out-of-key chords for color and special effects; it is in this element that the various composers stamp their individual characteristics on the standard format. The forms of the songs show successions of even-lengthed phrases in the standard popular tune, sixteen-measure or thirty-two measure groupings which are developed by obvious repetition and contrast. Transitional or connecting passages usually work over one or more phrases of selected tunes; the composer's technical ability (or lack of it) is often evident in these interludes.

Early Operetta Composers. This group continued the tradition established in Europe; most of the music emulates the light Romantic styles of Franz Lehar and Johann Strauss. Reginald De Koven (1859-1920) was one of the first American composers to write impressively in this form; his Viennese operetta, *Robin Hood* (1890) was most successful in its day, but is now remembered only by the song "Oh Promise Me" which has become indispensable to American weddings. Victor Herbert (1859-1924) has been called the "most significant creator since Stephen Foster"[4] of American popular music; a rival of De Koven, he attained greater eminence than the latter because of the wide range of emotions expressed in his songs and his superior technical competence; Some of his best known operettas are *The Fortune Teller* (1898), *Babes in Toyland* (1903), *Mlle. Modiste* (1905) and *Naughty Marietta* (1910). Rudolph Friml (1881-   ), continuing in the Herbert tradition, will long be remembered for *The Firefly* (1912), *Rose Marie* (1924) and *The Vagabond King* (1925). Sigmund Romberg (1887-1951) was the last American composer to write in the European operetta tradition, achieving music immortality with such works as *Blossom Time* (1921), *The Student Prince* (1924) and *The Desert Song* (1926).

Musical Comedy Composers. The popularity of operetta soon faded because the settings were usually foreign, the plots were unrealistic and historical, and the situations and character-types were stereotyped and overused. The new musical comedy, on the other hand, was completely American in background, situations, character-types and in lively, vernacular melodies typical of the Tin-Pan Alley variety. Many of the musical comedy composers saw fit to loosen the bounds of the heretofore rigid thirty-two bar song-chorus format by inserting measures or phrases to better fit the mood or unfolding narrative of the lyrics. George M. Cohan (1878-1942) was one of the first to use ragtime rhythms in his shows. Besides composing many songs, he produced, acted and sang his own songs as well; "I'm a Yankee Doodle Dandy," "Give My Regards to Broadway" and "Mary" are his best known songs and are still sung today. Irving Berlin (1888-) wrote many hit songs, including both words and music, in a fresh, new style for such musical comedies as *Louisiana Purchase* (1940) and *Annie Get Your Gun* (1946). Jerome Kern (1885-1945) not only enriched the medium with a clever sophistication, but deepened characterizations and stressed colorful, realistic backgrounds; his fame rests primarily on *Showboat* (1927) and *Roberta* (1933).

Vincent Youmans (1898-1946), like Irving Berlin, excelled in writing popular songs with warm, appealing melodies; his outstanding musical comedies include *No! No! Nanette* (1923) and *Hit the Deck* (1927). Cole Porter (1893-1964) wrote popular songs for shows that, in both words and music, have an air of sophistication and refinement not usually found in the typical popular songs; *The Gay Divorcée* (1932), *Anything Goes* (1934), *Panama Hattie* (1940) and *Kiss Me Kate* (1948) stand out among many musical comedies. Kurt Weill (1900-1950) is unique as a highly competent technical composer who combined a refined European light opera style with the jazz idiom and the blues; besides writing serious music for the stage, which includes *The Three-penny Opera* (1928), *Lost in the Stars* (1949) and *Down in the Valley* (1948), his musical comedies of a lighter vein, *Knickerbocker Holiday* (1938) and *Lady in the Dark* (1941), have been most successful.

George Gershwin, although achieving fame as a successful blender of popular and serious musical elements, is probably better known for his musical comedy songs for which his brother, Ira, wrote many of the lyrics. But Gershwin was also an innovator in the use of recitative, lengthy choral passages and instrumental interludes which point up a mood or situation; the shows, *George White Scandals* (1920-1925), *Lady Be Good* (1924), *Strike Up the Band* (1927), *Girl Crazy* (1930) and *Of Thee I Sing* (1931) are some of his most successful. Like George Gershwin, Leonard Bernstein has also written successfully in the popular vein; the shows, *On the Town* (1944-1945) and *West Side Story* (1957) most effectively portray facets of true America in strong, emotional, fast-moving melodies having lively, jazz rhythms. Richard Rodgers (1902-) combined his musical talents with the lyricists Lorenz Hart and, later, Oscar Hammerstein to produce some of the finest American musicals; Rodgers not only "adapted himself to the new demands of a folk drama by creating music with the overtones of a folk art,"[5] but he welded the music ever closer to the story, making it "an inextricable part of the dramatic action."[6] *Oklahoma* (1943), *Carousel* (1945), *South Pacific* (1949) and *The King and I* (1951) are some of the shows long to be remembered. *Sound of Music* (1959), one of his most recent shows, again reveals musically his warm sympathetic attunement with the common folk. Frederick Loewe (1904-) collaborated with the librettest, Alan Lerner, to write among other shows, *Brigadoon* (1947) and *My Fair Lady* (1956); the latter, from all indications, will be one of the greatest American musical comedies yet created. Loewe has the talent for a most sympathetic expression through music of a great variety of emotions and moods that range from the irony or sting of a Bernard Shaw quip to an obvious, warm Romantic sentiment.

IMPRESSIONISTIC TENDENCIES

Charles Tomlinson Griffes (1884-1920). Besides Loeffler, Griffes stands out as the only other American composer of some reputation to adopt French Impressionistic elements to a considerable degree in his music. After the study of piano and composition in Europe, Griffes returned to the United States in 1907 to teach. Although writing many songs and piano pieces, it is his orchestral works for which he is best known: *The Pleasure Dome of Kubla Kahn* (1916) and the *White Peacock*, an orchestra arrangement of a piece from *Roman Sketches* (1918), a four-piece piano composition. With free, fanciful melodies and atmospheric harmonies of Impressionism, Griffes blends the descriptive approach, the rhapsodic forms and the lush chord progressions of the Neo-romantics with the rhythmic complexities of the Neo-classics; there is also an exotic influence in his melodies. More specifically, the texture of his music is mostly homophonic; his melodies have small intervals but cover a wide range and favor unusual scales (pentatonic, whole tone and Oriental). There are many cross rhythms (different simultaneous patterns) each, simple in itself but when together, producing complexity; the chords favor the seventh, ninth and eleventh categories and besides much parallel progression, typical of Impressionism, they also occur in relationships of bitonality. Formally, Griffes' music tends toward free grouping of material with irregular-lengthed phrases.

NEO-CLASSIC TENDENCIES

Randall Thompson (1899-   ). In many ways this composer is like his near namesake and contemporary, Virgil Thomson, in that both favor the Classic harmonic idiom of triads and their traditional tonal progressions, and both draw on American folk and popular tunes for inspiration. Randall Thompson, however, has assimilated a wide range of styles, including French Impressionism and obvious jazz elements, all of which he expresses in a consistent Neo-classic style which shows an objective, impersonal approach, restraint, economy of means and sonata-like development of materials. Thompson studied with Hill and Walter Raymond Spalding at Harvard and with Ernest Bloch; later he taught at Harvard, the University of Virginia and Princeton. He has written a variety of significant works in the choral, symphonic and chamber music categories. His Second Symphony (1931) stands out as having deft craftsmanship and objective and emotional expression on a high plain; *The Peaceable Kingdom* (1936) and *Alleluia* (1940), both for mixed voices a cappella, particularly reveal his adeptness as a master of choral writing in setting words to musical rhythm. A close scrutiny of his choral settings will further reveal a subtle graded organization of phrases by cadential structure to give finesse to musical punctuation.

Thompson's musical texture is a sympathetic blend of sixteenth-and seventeenth-century contrapuntal techniques with homophony; a typical treatment shows the dissonance (tension) of contrapuntal movement resolved into chordal cadences. But there is never any feeling of complexity, regardless of the kind of texture. His melodies are simple, mostly diatonic and often impart a folksy quality through the use of the church modes and the avoidance of the leading tone. His rhythmic patterns, like his melodies, are obvious, often lively and regular, reflecting folk and popular (jazz) influences. Harmonically, Thompson unashamedly uses the triad and all its tonal involvements; structurally, he builds with regular phrase groupings, usually in some proven formula of repetition versus contrast.

Walter Piston (1894-). A true representative of the Neo-classic style in his objective approach to musical expression, Piston stresses intellectualized workmanship over emotional content. He has assimilated many contemporary "trade-marks," including Impressionism, dissonant counterpoint and the twelve-tone technique (but used tonally). Piston has, however, ingeniously incorporated these often disparate elements within a fairly strict sonata principle. After study at Harvard and with Boulanger in Paris, he returned to become Professor of Music at Harvard. Piston's compositions are numerous, including mostly symphonies and chamber music; his ballet, *The Incredible Flutist* (1938) and the Second Symphony (1943) are typical of his style and are the best known.

Piston's music favors a contrapuntal texture which is predominantly dissonant; his melodies combine a basic diatonic movement with bits of twelve-tone chromaticism, but the shapes are always rounded, never angular. The usual asymmetrical rhythmic grouping is clear enough in each line but produces complexity in the full texture of several combined lines. Harmonically, dissonant tonal combinations seem to prevail, but they are never too extreme and on closer examination, most often reveal an underlying skeletal movement of tonality. Piston uses almost exclusively the Classic forms of the sonata and the symphony; frequent use of fugal and canonic devices reflect Baroque influences. His phrases are usually irregular in length and become indistinct in the typical expanding motivic development which never emphasizes any devices to extremes. It is the Classic, formal grouping of larger sections that unifies this vigorous musical language rather than smaller, obvious referential elements of repetition and contract which are not emphasized here.

A contemporary American composer has remarked concerning Piston's eclecticism: He has "stood firmly on his own chosen ground, building up a style that is a synthesis of most of the important characteristics of contemporary music and assimilating into his own manner the various changes as they came along . . . his works have a uniform excellence that seems destined to give them an important position in the musical repertory."[7] As a progressive teacher Piston has been most influential in espousing American musical expression through the organization and clarification of contemporary musical materials and techniques; the publications of *Principles of Harmonic Analysis* (1933), *Harmony* (1941, revised edition, 1948) and *Counterpoint* (1947) attest to his clear and logical treatment of these musical fundamentals.

David Diamond (1915-   ). Diamond is another of the Neo-classic group who seeks expression through the actual musical material and its development per se, rather than through any programmatic effects they might conjure up; he does not, however, deny an emotional aspect in his music but specifies only that it is an "objectified" emotion. A product of the Cleveland Institute of Music and the Eastman School of Music, Diamond continued advance study with Sessions in New York City and Boulanger in Paris. His works comprise mostly symphonies, overtures and some vocal pieces; the *Rounds for String Orchestra* (1944) is one of his most popular works.

Diamond's style has assimilated elements, primarily the dissonant contrapuntal textures of the styles of Bartók, Copland, Sessions and Stravinsky. His melodies favor modal scales and are expansive and angular, combining diatonic and chromatic (12 equal half steps) movement; his rhythms, unlike that of the aforementioned composers, are not usually as complicated, with the result that the textures are more transparent. Harmonically, Diamond seems to be groping for some organization of dissonance; the listener often strives (with varying degrees of success) for a logical order of succession among the dissonant vertical tonal combinations. Fortunately, he is a Neo-classic in the economy of musical means; while his phrase structure is irregular, use of the traditional forms helps to group the material comprehensively and to unify it, although obvious repetition and contrast are antithetic to his idiom.

Norman Dello Joio (1913-   ). This composer is typical of a sizable group who combine modal themes, dissonant harmonies and Classic structure and forms. Dello Joio studied with Bernard Wagenaar and Paul Hindemith; besides music composition, his career has included organ performance, choir conducting and teaching. To date he has composed much choral, orchestral and chamber music; *The Mystic Trumpeter* (1943) for mixed chorus and symphony, and the opera, *The Triumph of St. Joan* (1951) are impressive examples of his ability.

Dello Joio's style shows a predominance of dissonant counterpoint; his melodies are often expansive and angular, mixing intervals of all sizes but step-wise modal progressions dominate. Rhythmically, complexity prevails in both the irregular patterns of the individual lines and in their combination. His vertical tonal groupings, whether in homophony or counterpoint, are generally dissonant; however, closer analysis will usually reveal a refined differentiation among them and what appears to be a well-planned logic in their succession. Structurally, Dello Joio is also typical of many of this group in combining the ever-changing variation technique with the Classic sonata-allegro development. This amalgamation seems to be a favorite one of modern composers; the proponents of both techniques seem to be satisfied with the compromise. The use of time-proven Baroque and Classic forms imparts further unity to Dello Joio's works.

Other Neo-classic Composers. Bernard Rogers (1893-   ) and Paul Creston (1906-   ) are alike in a subjective approach of instilling mood and emotion in their music but through the abstract, Classic development of musical ideas. Neither hesitates to use dissonance, although harmonic tonality predominates. Roger's best known work, *Soliloquy* (1938) for flute and strings, shows his typical treatment of expansive, rhythmically free, irregular-phrased melodies. Creston's *Choric Dances* (1938) reveals his penchant for structurally conservative but modal melodies. Following, are a few of the better known composers who have used in varying degrees elements of the Neo-classic style blended with elements of other styles: Burrill Phillips (1907-   ), Gardner Read (1913-   ), Paul Bowles (1910-   ), Alan Hovhaness (1911-   ), Arthur Berger (1912-   ), Elliott Carter (1908-   ), Irving Fine (1914-1962), Harold Shapero (1920-   ), Ingolf Dahl (1912-   ), Halsey Stevens (1908-   ) and Vladimir Dukelsky, also known as Vernon Duke, (1903-   ), who also has achieved fame as a composer of popular songs.

FOOTNOTES

[1]TutH, p. 148.
[2]RoyH, p. 97.
[3]HorB, p. 166.
[4]EweP, p. 90.
[5]EweP, p. 126.
[6]*Ibid.*, p. 127.
[7]CarP, p. 354.

on new paths

Extreme Uses of Traditional Elements. Three elements of music — melody, rhythm and harmony — are developed to extreme limits of comprehensibility by the following category of composers. Melody becomes exceedingly fragmentary, disjointed and angular; rhythm attains a complexity which most of the time cancels out any organizing, regular pulsations or recognizable, recurring patterns; harmony, in the conventional sense of chord progressions of consonance-to-dissonance and vice versa, is for the most part nonexistent, but instead is expressed in successions of highly refined, relative degrees of dissonance. Vertical tone clusters are now the harmonic units; they may contain several or many nonchordal tones which need not be prepared or resolved as before. Some composers, emulating the techniques exemplified in the music of Paul Hindemith and Ernst Toch, attempt to relate these dissonant tone clusters to one or several focal tones or areas in place of a tonal tonic; others use the clusters to point up emotional or programmatic aspects of their compositions; a few *avant-garde* composers completely disregard any vertical relationships and concentrate on melody and rhythm in highly developed linear contrapuntal textures.

Combining the New With the Old. Most of these composers have found Baroque-like counterpoint, Neo-classic economy of materials and brevity of forms as the most effective means of expressing their particular idioms. Each composer is an experimentalist, striking out on new paths with new combinations of sounds and new rhythmic complexities; however, the developmental techniques and overall forms are usually the traditional ones of proven effectiveness. Because we are

now in the midst of this experimentation, it is impossible to
which specific styles might point the way or indicate trends
development. Some feel that the twelve-tone serialists and
composers (to be discussed) have exceeded the boundaries ι
musical expression and that the future direction must rest witι.
posers such as those discussed in this chapter who have not compleς
disowned the past, but have through personalized creativity, reap-
praised, rearranged and rejuxtaposed the traditional musical values,
elements and techniques.

Charles Edward Ives (1874-1954). One of the most interesting of
all American composers, Ives' music ranges from the simplest, most
obvious Romantic clichés to idioms of extreme tonal dissonance and
rhythmic complexity. Only Ives' inventive genius could instill vital
continuity into such diverse musical elements and styles and unify them
into homogeneous compositions showing sincerity and depth of expression. Ives received his early training in music from his father and continued the study of the "conventional rules" with Parker at Yale. Because
he wanted to be creatively independent, Ives made business his means
of earning a livelihood and became very successful in the field of insur-
ance. His works include four symphonies and some orchestral sets, much
chamber music for unusual instrumental combinations, piano sonatas
and many songs; the *Concord Sonata* (1919) for piano stands out as one
of his most profound works.

Stylistically, Ives is a true eclectic: His music fuses the Romantic
European musical tradition with various indigenous expressions of
American music as well as with experimentations far ahead of his time.
Specifically, the monothematic homophony of American folk and popular music (including hymns, spirituals, minstrel tunes, country dances,
patriotic songs and jazz) is ingeniously combined with complex contrapuntal textures (often several different textures are maintained in a
contrapuntal relationship, each against the other). Ives' characteristic
incongruities are shown in the use of simple, diatonic melodies of small
range alongside angular fragments having large intervals and wide
range. His rhythms likewise may vary from even, hymnlike regularity
through obvious ragtime syncopation to complex irregularity and free,
ad libitum grouping, often with bar lines omitted; most characteristic
in his polyphonic writing is the use of several different meters simultaneously (polymeters), as well as multiple cross rhythms (polyrhythms)
which emphasize off-beat patterns.

Conventional nineteenth-century chords comprise much of Ives'
harmony, but they are not always used traditionally; rather, they often

move in unorthodox, theoretically incorrect progressions or are combined into tone clusters to create polytonality or extreme, atonal dissonance. In some places Ives even experiments with fractional tones and deviations from standard pitch. Formally, Ives stresses asymmetry in phrase lengths and in general grouping of material. He controls the overall design of each piece through the organic unfoldment (variation) of one or several motives or themes — another verification of this seemingly inevitable developmental phenomenon. Ives' independence of the then conventional music standards made most of his music too difficult for musicians of his time to perform or understand. Only in recent years, with the increasing frequency of performances, have critics begun to observe and appreciate the masterful way Ives fused such divergent styles into a unified and, of more importance, typical expression of New England America. According to Sessions, "He [Ives] certainly is one of the significant men in American music, and at the same time one of the most complex and problematical."[1] Henry Bellamann, a longtime close acquaintance of Ives, eulogizes him thus:

> One may differ profoundly with the aesthetic premises of this composer, but concerning his sincerity, the loftiness of his aims, the human sympathy, the consummate mastery of technique, and the prodigious musical erudition back of it there can be no question. . . [His music] is rooted, whether for good or evil, in the region and the thought of that part of America which may claim to be 'pure' in a national and a traditional sense.[2]

Carl Ruggles (1876-   ). Like Ives, Ruggles is another rugged individualist who wrote music ahead of his time. In an extremely dissonant idiom of free counterpoint, he uncompromisingly sought for a sublime quality of beauty through a highly intellectualized, meticulous development of materials. After music study at Harvard, Ruggles devoted himself to composing, painting and working at manual crafts. His output of music, not large, is mostly for orchestra and chamber groups; the published works include *Toys* (1919) for soprano and piano; *Angeles* (1921), one arrangement for chamber brass, one for chamber strings; *Men and Mountains* (1924) for chamber orchestra; *Portals* (1926) for string ensemble; *Sun-Treader* (1933) for large orchestra; *Evocations* (1937-1945) for piano solo.

His contrapuntal texture reflects back to the Baroque period of Bach and Handel. Interestingly, independent of Schoenberg, Ruggles worked out his own twelve-tone system of composition in which there is no repetition of a tone until after the tenth progression; this rule applies mostly to the main melody, less often to the subordinate melodies.

This structural technique characterizes most of his music although not all. Unlike Schoenberg, Ruggles' melodies are basically of small intervals, although diatonic movement is often mixed with trimmings of chromaticism. In the counterpoint each line is a real independent melody having no filler material in support of other lines. Definitive of Ruggles' style, there is little if any vertical relationship between the lines; like Schoenberg, the individual lines are of prime importance. Rhythmically, there is often a succession of many different meters and like the interval successions in the melodies, each line has its own succession of rhythmic patterns (usually irregular) which because they are independent of each other result in polyrhythms. The vertical simultaneous sounds of the contrapuntal lines are predominantly dissonant and unplanned (accidental); occasionally, there is some chordal writing aimed toward achieving large, vertical sonorities (tone clusters).

The phrases tend toward irregular-lengthed successions; their contrapuntal combination results in a continuous rhapsodic flow organized only in larger sectional groupings similar to sixteenth-century pieces. The developmental technique is the favored gradual motive unfoldment with no obvious repetition or sudden contrasts, but there is often a strange quality in the developments of avoiding any figuration, suggesting the austerity and economy of Neo-classicism. Considering the abstruse, intellectualized complexity and the wide imaginative inspiration in Ruggles' music, Charles Seeger summarizes his style in the ingenious understatement: "The technique as a whole shows a curious ratio between organization and fantasy . . . it would appear that in Ruggles' work there is a vast preponderance of fantasy."[3]

Edgar Varèse (1885-1965). The music of Varèse is like that of Ives and Ruggles in containing uncompromising dissonance, but unlike them in favoring the movement of abstract vertical sonorities rather than the horizonal development of melodic lines. Added to these sonorities are percussive rhythmic complexities of primitive music. But in spite of a wide gamut of expressive musical colors, there are no descriptive connotations in Varèse's music. Born in Paris, after study with Albert Roussel, Vincent d'Indy, Charles Widor and Ferruccio Busoni, Varèse came to the United States in 1916. His works are mostly for mixed chamber groups; the pieces that have aroused the most interest are *Density* (1936), *Octandre* (1924), *Ionisation* (1924) and *Integrales* (1926).

As suggested in the preceding paragraph, the ultimate textural effect of Varèse's music is homophonic, although the technical approach is through building up sonorities in horizontal layers of sounds. Even in his orchestrations, each instrument has its own melodic line and rhythmic patterns. The use of melody in the usual sense is deemphasized with the vertical sounds predominating; when a melody is made prominent, it is extremely angular and fragmentary, or in the other extreme, consists of a single tone repeated a number of times, each time with a different dynamic. Complex meters and patterns are generally pointed up by percussive instruments resulting in continuous polyrhythms; at times such rhythmic emphasis dominates all the other elements.

Complete dissonance to maintain constant tension is a primary goal in his music; consonant intervals are carefully avoided as Varèse felt they would break the continuity of tension. Henry Cowell amplifies this reasoning: "To introduce a consonant harmony would remove the sense of implacable, resilient hardness, and create a weak link in the chain; the let-down would be so great that the whole composition might fall to pieces."[4] The dissonances are carefully built up through overtones, through exploring the fractional tones between whole and half steps and through blending and contrasting instrumental timbres. There is little thematic development as such, but only continual kaleidescopic change of material. There is no overall design except the seemingly rhapsodic succession of changing senorities peculiar to each piece. Probably Varèse's unique musical contributions are (1) a highly refined use of dynamic nuances — a device which he uses constantly and which assumes equal importance to the other structural elements; (2) an equally constant awareness of the timbre of orchestral instruments; blending their subtle and unusual tone colors is likewise a prime creative goal.

William Schuman (1910-). Typical of a considerable group of "new-path" composers, Schuman accepts the older Neo-classic techniques and forms, but rejects the conventional harmonies in favor of a tonal palette consisting of varying degrees of dissonance. After studying with Roy Harris at Columbia University and in Salzburg, Schuman taught at Sarah Lawrence College and in 1945 became President of the Juilliard School of Music; since 1961 he has been director of the new Lincoln Center in New York City. His works include a number of symphonies, much choral music, scores for ballets, a one-act opera and instrumental concertos; besides his symphonies, two overtures, *American Festival Overture* (1939) and *William Billings Overture* (1943), have received frequent performances.

Schuman's style blends polyphony with homophony in a Neo-classic, objective approach, but linear aspects prevail. His melodies are expansive, often angular and rhapsodic with frequent skips of fourths and larger intervals, but a climax tone can usually be found in each melody to unify the interval successions. Although using regular meters, there is a constant shifting of accents to produce irregular rhythmic patterns which are strong but not necessarily complex; syncopation and jazzlike patterns are also found frequently. Usually there is an overall strong rhythmic drive with tension that generates slowly over long expanses of material. The ever-present dissonances that characterize his homophony as well as his counterpoint, while not showing any clear, graded relationships to a tonal center, do seem to gravitate toward certain focal areas that help organize the material. There is also a characteristic use of open parallel fourths and fifths and some polytonality.

Schuman leans toward the time-tested technique of developing material from a germ idea. His phrases are irregular in length and show little obvious repetition from measure to measure; however, in place of the traditional organizing factor of key relationships, he achieves overall coherence through large-scale thematic recurrence and the occasional use of imitation, sometimes in augmentation or diminution. The standard forms of the Classicist — the symphony, overture, concerto, fugue and so forth — conveniently provide built-in unification through recapitulation. Schuman groups his material in large sections and peculiarly unifies and articulates it by concluding on a simple triad or unison cadence. The dynamic energy and intensity that his music generates bespeaks favorably of this kind of expressive music in which melodic and rhythmic elements are, of necessity, emphasized and brought into sharper focus because of the dissonant and therefore, in an organizational sense, often neutral harmonic background.

Roger Sessions (1896-   ). Another composer of the dissonant group, Sessions' music exemplifies similar characteristics of Schuman's music, but to even more extreme limits. Interestingly, a highly intellectual, serious approach with the utmost emphasis on craftsmanship seems to strengthen rather than weaken a deep emotional feeling that pervades all of his music. His highly objective attitude reflects the Neo-classic influence of Stravinsky, and to Bloch and Richard Strauss he probably owes much of the deep emotional expression in his music although there is never any of the programmatic aspects often found in the music of the latter two composers. After study at Harvard and with Parker at Yale and Bloch in Cleveland, Sessions went to Europe, subsequently returning to the United States to teach at the University of California, Berkeley and at Princeton. Sessions' output includes several symphonies, much chamber music, a one-act opera and pieces for solo instruments; however, their difficulty of performance as well as comprehension by the listener has kept most of his music from the ears of the public. One of his earlier works, *The Black Maskers* (1923), is probably the best known of his compositions.

Most of Sessions' music shows a highly dissonant contrapuntal texture which becomes richer and more dramatic in his brilliant orchestrations. His melodies span the gamut from simple diatonic progressions through chromatic (nontonal) movement to wide, angular skips. His rhythmic patterns, especially in contrapuntal texture, attain extreme irregularity and complexity; as in Schuman's music, there is a strong rhythmic drive which builds up momentum over long sections of a piece. Sessions' treatment of harmonic dissonance as a highly colored background on which to unfold his melodies and rhythms is also similar to Schuman's technique, but with Sessions the dissonances are more acute. However, although there appears to be little use of graded degrees of harmonic dissonance, repeated hearings of his compositions suggest a vague, underlying sense of tonality built around focal centers that control the overall harmonic material.

Formally, the phrases are irregular in length, unfolding the material through constant change, although occasional suggestions of figural repetition run through the development to provide some cohesion; however, frequent use of the Neo-classic forms with their characteristics of coherence and unification afford most of the organization and containment of this highly abstruse but impressive musical language. Speaking of his *Concerto for Violin and Orchestra* (1932), Mark Brunswick states: "Sessions has achieved the complete identification of form with content which is the mark of the truly classic in its broadest sense."[5] Sessions has also helped the cause of modern music and composers in a literary way in his books, *The Musical Experience of Composer, Performer, Listener* (1950) and *Harmonic Practice* (1951).

Other New Techniques. John J. Becker (1886-1961) was interested in creating new sounds primarily through orchestration. Writing in a Palestrinian polyphonic but completely dissonant texture, he set off one dissonant line against another by scoring each for a contrasting, non-related instrument. He also used intervals of seconds sustained for related instruments (of the same color) as a background for a contrasting line scored for a contrasting instrument. Henry Dixon Cowell (1897-   ) was one of the pioneers in exploiting the use of tone clusters (usually, vertical superimposed groups of seconds) in place of traditional chords for piano and orchestra. Cowell also engaged in much acoustical experimentation at the New School for Social Research in New York; he collaborated with L. Theremin on the Rhythmicon: a machine designed to reproduce accurately all kinds of rhythmic patterns; he was founder and editor of the quarterly, *New Music,* which published new provocative works by both American and European composers of the nonconformist type; he authored the book, *New Musical Resources* (1930) which is concerned with problems of rhythmic complexity and notation; he also edited a collection of articles, *American Composers on American Music* (1933). In recent years, Cowell's experimental style has given way to a more conventional expression having definite folk music influences.

Ruth Crawford Seeger (1901-1953) explored the juxtaposition of two or more different textures in horizontal planes (heterophony), resulting in a counterpiont of independent multitoned textures rather than of separate lines. She also superimposed different meters (polymeters) and was one of the early experimenters with dynamics in which each contrapuntal line or texture is given a different dynamic scheme. Henry Brant (1913-) is another experimenter with contrapuntal aspects of tonal and metrical relationships. In his early works harmonic chords are built up and progress in oblique rather than the usual vertical relationships of the individual tones. In his later works Brant favored the placing of different instrumental and vocal groups in various parts of the concert hall with each group to perform music in a different succession of meters and tempos. This antiphony of polymeters and tempos results in a basically dissonant harmonic succession of sounds that must vary with each performance as the many simultaneous tempos (as many as twenty-one in one composition) can never be executed the same in successive performances.

George Antheil (1900-1959) was one of the first of the abstract group to explore the nonmusical sound media and he anticipated the new "concrete" expressions of music by mechanical means rather than by conventional musical instruments. His *Ballet Mechanique* (1927) scored for ten pianos and an assortment of percussion and noisemakers established him as a true experimenter in the use of abstract musical sounds. Revolutionary for its time, the weird sounds and strong primitive-like rhythms are more or less organized through contrasting rhythmic patterns. Antheil also wrote considerable in a more conventional style, blending jazz with modern dissonant elements and techniques; symphonies and movie scores comprise most of this category. Harry Partch (1901-) worked in the atmosphere of microtones, creating a forty-three tone octave and inventing instruments (guitars, marimbas and organs) capable of producing these tones. He focuses on highly refined tonal gradations to fuse and integrate music with speech. Inflections of speech (slight glidings up and down of the voice) and in general the build-up of tensions in dialogue are meticulously imitated or rather enhanced on the microtonal instruments. The score for a version of Sophicles' *Oedipus Rex* entitled *King Oedipus* (1952) exemplifies the treatment just discussed.

John Cage (1912-   ) has exploited overtone combinations obtained from a prepared piano as well as new sound possibilities of various percussion instruments. The strings of an ordinary piano are muted with various special objects so that when struck, they produce a curious variety of "pings" and "thuds". Curiously, the new, strange, often subtle, percussive sounds are generally contained within a strict formal framework. A set of sixteen sonatas and four interludes (1946-1948) impressively illustrate this method. There is no melodic line as such; the concept admits only successive clusters of different sounds. However, a basic principle of the composer is to use rhythm instead of harmony to organize the material; the end of each phrase is indicated by a rhythmic cadence (a retardation or cessation of movement) rather than by a harmonic cadence. Furthermore, each piece is controlled by a preconceived plan in which all the phrases of that piece are kept the same length. Although the rhythmic patterns are free and often rhapsodic, the organizational aspects of this technique give sufficient logic and formal containment to the most free and indeterminate sounds. Any plan such as this one that gives the average listener some recognizable structural elements with which to assemble the moving musical material is commendable and should be considered by many contemporary experimenters.

Lukas Foss, discussed earlier as a Neo-romanticist, has in recent years assumed the role of music experimenter. His latest works, usually for a small mixed instrumental group, show extremely free contrapuntal improvisation, with each part indulging in rhapsodic, cadenza-like melodies having wide range and many large interval skips. Like the melodies, the rhythms are the freest possible; the harmonies range from consonance to extreme dissonance and much of the time are unpredictable because any given vertical simultaneity of tones will usually vary with each performance because of the very nature of the style. Formally, the cadenzas are loosely held together by "motivic (figural) suggestion" which each performer, according to the inspiration of the moment, imparts to another performer in the ensemble. Hence, these "suggestions" also vary in each performance. In a most recent composition, Foss has combined the improvisational aspect with a horizontal-vertical ordered sequence plan: A fixed number of pseudo-improvisatory motivic groupings, unusual sound combinations and *sprechstimme* effects are precomposed but their order of linear succession and contrapuntal combination are arbitrarily set by the conductor at each performance. It can be seen that the same group of musical units can be combined in a great many ways to produce a similar but different composition each time. The extreme difficulty of achieving and maintaining the mathematically complicated dispersement of musical units affords a challenge and stimulation to the individual performers which, according to Foss, is an important goal of this style. After hearing several performances, one wonders to what extent the listening audience is meant to participate in this "checkerboard-contrived" music.

FOOTNOTES

[1]SesR, p. 148.
[2]BelI, p. 58.
[3]SeeR, p. 589.
[4]CowV, p. 47.
[5]BrunS, p. 185.

twelve-tone techniques

Atonality. In the early decades of the twentieth century, new systems of tonal organization evolved to take the place of the outworn, traditional major-minor tonal system. The term *atonal* has been applied to most of these new systems to indicate the absence of any relationships or implications of tonality. As tonality or key consciousness results from the interrelation and contrast of a selected group of triads, the less triadic contrast there is, the more indeterminate the key becomes, until, as in several of the new systems, the complete breakdown of triadic formation as a tonal-harmonic constructive principle results in no tonal, but atonal relationships of successive groups of tones. According to the eminent historian, Roger Sessions, atonality may be defined as a principle of construction "in which the composer deliberately avoids all procedures capable of evoking 'tonal' associations."[1]

Dominance of Harmonic Tonality. To attain a consciousness of complete atonality, however, is a most difficult goal. Again, Sessions reasons that the feeling of harmonic sense is an important dimension of music and once the listener has acquired an awareness of it, he cannot disregard its protrusion in the music he hears.[2] Furthermore, because all tones are heard in a horizontal or vertical relationship to one another, the ear cannot help but perceive them in patterns; inevitably, the one or more tones that are favored (from previous harmonic conditioning) establish a tonal grouping — a tone or tonal area of reference. This concept is corroborated by the astute contemporary music theorist, Edward T. Cone: "Where the cadence exists, it is impossible to hear music as completely atonal, even though one may be unable to define the key in conventional terms."[3] Hence, because many contemporary composers have forsaken harmonic tonality, including all of its ramifications of interrelationships of tones, cadences and so forth, they have of necessity been forced to fall back on sixteenth- and seventeenth-century polyphonic devices and to devise new ways to organize, articulate and unify their music material as substitutes for tonality.

Serial Twelve-tone Technique. One of the new organizing systems that at first was considered most radical but has since gradually achieved widespread use and acceptance was devised by the Austrian, Arnold Schoenberg (1874-1951). This system is based on arbitrary arrangements of the twelve equal chromatic tones in the octave; a selected row for a given piece has almost unlimited structural possibilities since the original order may be inverted, used in retrograde and retrograde inversion. Also, any of the orders may be transposed to any level of the half-step chromatic scale, and, finally, the rows may be used to form vertical chord combinations as well as horizontal melodic lines. The only basic rule is that, once a series is started, all of its twelve tones must be used before the series can be used again; in other words, any single tone of a series cannot be repeated until the other eleven tones of that series have been sounded. Careful analysis of Schoenberg's compositions, however, shows that occasionally a note is repeated, but most always in smaller subdivisions of the prevailing note values.

Although originating and developing the twelve-tone technique in Vienna, Schoenberg's residence of eighteen years in the United States and his eventual influence on native composers justify his inclusion in the American scene. Until 1925, he taught and composed in Vienna; in this year he was appointed Professor of Composition at the Prussian Academy of Fine Arts in Berlin; in 1933, anticipating trouble from Hitler, Schoenberg went to Paris and soon the United States, where he taught at the Malkin Conservatory in Boston, the University of Southern California and the University of California, Los Angeles. Schoenberg's music varies in style and form, including orchestral works, chamber music and choral and instrumental pieces.

Criticism of Serial Twelve-tone Technique. Some composers feel the serial twelve-tone technique is too mathematical, too intellectualized and antithetic to the emotional, personalized expression of music. Roger Sessions feels the value of music lies in its imaginative and emotive aspects rather than in the contrived technical system of its construction.[4] Paul Lang contends that the expressive aspects of moods and feelings cannot be serialized.[5] Other critics express the view that the unfolding mechanics of the technique cannot be heard by the listener as part of the expected intellectual enjoyment of music common to traditional techniques.

Advocates of Serial Twelve-tone Technique. The technique has become increasingly popular among composers who feel the structural possibilities of traditional tonal techniques, even in their most altered far out extenuations, have been exhaustively explored to their practical limits. The disciples argue that the recognition of the structural devices by the listener is not important or necessary to the understanding and enjoyment of this kind of music; the fact that the structural devices serve the composer in the technical manipulation and organization of the material is sufficient justification for their use.[6] Ernst Křenek (1900-   ) puts forth an esoteric justification of the system in which inspiration is likened to the factor of chance. He builds his premise as follows: It is the job of the composer to set up an "impersonal mechanism" of "premeditated patterns" which in the process of their unfoldment produce "unpredictable situations." The "creative act" is the organization of the premeditated structure; the "inspiration" is the chance element — the unpredictable tonal and rhythmic combinations that result.[7]

Modifications of Schoenberg's System. Many modern composers are liberalizing and broadening the use of Schoenberg's rules. One offshoot technique uses the twelve chromatic tones with complete equality and freedom of succession and position (atonality); each composer organizes and integrates the material into musical forms according to his individual taste and requirements. The application of one or more tonal centers to this technique has become a most prevalent and productive trend; Paul Hindemith and Ernst Toch, to name just two outstanding composers, have realized most fruitful results with such a blend. Also, since Schoenberg's tone-row rules apply only to successions of tones and their combinations, recent developments show the application of serial techniques to tonal durations and even to dynamics; basically, a rhythmic or dynamic unit cannot recur until all of a selected, ordered group of such units have been used.

Stefan Wolpe (1902-   ), a European by birth, settled in the United States to contribute toward the expansion of our musical horizons. He experimented with the addition of a harmonic element to Schoenberg's system: Each line of a twelve-tone composition is organized into its own harmonic zone; the different horizontal harmonic zones have a vertical relationship with a spatial organization between them. Milton Babbitt (1916-   ) has, in a sense, carried the development of the tone-row to extremes in exhausting the structural possibilities of each idea used; he has also experimented with structuralizing rhythms and dynamics according to serialized arrangements. Wallingford Riegger (1885-1961) combined a free use of the twelve-tone technique with traditional procedures to enlarge his technical possibilities without abandoning tonality. Ben Weber (1916-   ) combines a free use of the twelve-tone technique with the traditional devices of thematic recurrence and recapitulation. Harrison Kerr (1897-   ), Lou Harrison (1917-   ), Ross Lee Finney (1906-   ) and Leon Kirchner (1919-   ) are typical of a growing group of American composers striving to integrate a more or less free use of the twelve-tone technique with some feeling of tonal center. Even such tonal composers as Copland and Piston have, at times, used the technique of twelve equal tones to expand their tonal gamut with effective, expressive results. As is typical of the history of many innovations, the strict use of the twelve-tone technique may eventually be relaxed to blend with and include the more effective structural attributes of the traditional techniques.

FOOTNOTES

[1]SesP, p. 26.
[2]*Ibid.*, pp. 26-27.
[3]ConA, p. 45.
[4]SesP, p. 30.
[5]LanI, p. 13.
[6]ThoR, p. 182.
[7]KreE, pp. 90-91.

electronic music

MUSIQUE CONCRÈTE — ELEKTRONISCHE MUSIK

Initial Experimentation. In recent years the most *avant-garde* composers in their insatiable search for new sounds and techniques have become electronic engineers in both the production of sound and in its formal organization. About 1948 Pierre Schaeffer (1910-), working for Radio-diffusion Française in Paris, initiated a movement called *Musique Concrète* which involves the recording on magnetic tape of a variety of natural sounds. About the same time a similar group in Cologne began working with *elektronische musik* and expanded the tonal possibilities in the tape recording of synthetic sounds produced mostly by electronic frequency generators. A group in Italy under the direction of Luciano Berio (1925-) and Bruno Maderna (1920-) have been experimenting with both natural and synthetic sound composition.

Basic Techniques. But these pure, raw sounds are seldom used as originally recorded; rather, they are refined by several processes before becoming acceptable tonal material. In transmutation, an original pure sound is electronically manipulated through various speeds, durations and reverberations (successive, rapid duplications of a sound, resulting in recurring vibration beat effects); in transformation, the original sound is changed by cutting off the attack or ending, or by reversing the production of the sound; in modulation, new extraneous elements are added to the original sound. Each of a great variety of such sounds is recorded separately on an individual tape in building up a backlog of tonal possibilities.[1]

Preliminary Steps to Composing. The act of creative composition varies somewhat with individual composers, but generally follows a set sequence necessitated by the very nature of the materials and equipment. When a varied collection of taped sounds has been catalogued, it is usual for a composer to become familiar with his material through countless trial runs. This enables him to imagine in varying degrees not only the pure or raw sounds but the synthesized new material of pitch changes through variation of tape speed, prolongation of sound with the initial attack or ending cut-off, variation of tone quality through the filtering of harmonics and even to a degree, the playing backward of a taped sound. Next, the experimental blending of taped sound tracks in a kind of chance improvisation may reveal a wide range of creative possibilities.

Sequential Steps in Composing. The electronic composer then must make some detailed schema which includes the specific sounds, textures, order of sounds and rhythmic patterns to be used in a projected piece. The schema is carried out through two basic processes: One involves the organizational factors of rhythm and form; the other, the texture and harmonic (vertical) elements. The process of montage would seem to be the most crucial and difficult process in electronic composing since each sound to be used is cut or spliced so that the length of each, when played back, will fill the prescribed time indicated in the schema; in essence, the tape lengths determine the meters, rhythmic patterns, phrase lengths and overall form of a piece.[2]

In the second process, the tapes are set up in multiple machines so the composer can mix the sounds by superposition of the tapes; hence, the textures are assembled polyphonically although the characteristic lack of any recognizable melodic line results in the aesthetic focus on varying, vertical tonal densities. The mixing process, no doubt, after much trial and error experimentation, is recorded on a single tape which becomes the finished composition. Usually, the schema of a piece is notated on a four-line chart which shows the approximation of the main pitches used, the durations in terms of seconds (the characteristic rhythmic flexibility and independence of each line or texture requires precise timing) and dynamic indications on a decibel scale.

American Composers. In the United States, Vladimir Ussachevsky (1913-) and Otto Luening (1900-) are probably the first composers to experiment with tape-recorder music. They expanded the tonal gamut by combining electronically produced sounds with taped voice and instrumental parts; also, material on electronic tape is combined with live instrumental performance. The collaboration of Luening with Ussachevsky has resulted in a number of compositions which include *Rhapsodic Variations* (1954), *A Poem in Cycles and Bells* (1954), both for tape recorder and orchestra. Luening's *Theater Piece No. 2* (1956) is for tape recorder, voice and chamber orchestra. While Ussachevsky is interested in extending the range of sound and creating new tonal possibilities, he retains some traditional concepts of formal organization. Specifically, he seeks unification in a piece (1) through the use of pure (without overtones) electronic tones for tonal stabilization amid composite, mixed sonorities; in other words, the contrast of simple clarity versus noiselike, often complex indefiniteness; (2) by figural affinity and gradual change of material in a premediated overall shape; (3) in the use of an overall dynamic scheme. A *Piece for Tape Recorder* (1955) develops the above structural characteristics. Other Americans who have experimented with this medium are Edgar Varèse, Ernest Křenek and John Cage; Varèse has contrasted sounds in nature with orchestra sonorities in his *Deserts* (1954) for tape-recorded sound and orchestra.

Advantages of Electronic Music. In light of the ever-increasing interest aroused by the advent of electronic, tape-recorder music, it does not seem amiss to reflectively appraise the benefits and shortcomings of this creative process. One of its assets is the elimination of the middle-man performer — the composer can shape and hear his material as he proceeds. In other words, he can communicate directly with his audience. Of equal importance, the traditional tonal and rhythmic material as well as refinement of techniques can be extended to almost unheard-of limits; synthetic composite sounds, rhythmic complexities and control of all manner of juxtaposition which are impossible to produce by conventional musical means can now be realized.

Disadvantages of Electronic Music. On the other hand, critics contend that the electronic process of musical composing is unnatural — even antagonistic to the function of artistic creativity — when a plan for a complete piece, including all the minute structural intricacies, is conceived beforehand (premeditated) with the composer never knowing exactly how the eventually realized composition will sound; in effect, chance seems too strong a factor for any controlled, artistic creativity. As Křenek says, the audible results must always be at least partly incidental as the realization of the premeditated procedures can never be completely visualized ahead of time — mixtures of complex rhythmic patterns at various speeds make any specific aural forecast impossible.[3] Another common objection is that mechanized music lacks the spontaneity of individual, human performance in which each performance illuminates a work from a slightly different angle. Of more subtle effect is the unvarying regularity of mechanical rhythm, which tends to destroy the elements of anticipation and surprise that human performance instills in each successive phrase of a piece;[4] in short, we are in danger of dehumanization. Paul Lang has written that electronic composers "create a false relationship between acoustics and music, between objective nature and subjective art."[5] Continuing, he writes: "For the core of the musical process, of the creative process in music, is subject neither to physics, physiology, nor mathematics, but is an artistic thought process, a musical logic, virtually independent of the natural sciences. We are not dealing with physics but with music, not with science but with art; it is the human element that is decisive."[6]

RCA ELECTRONIC MUSIC SYNTHESIZER

Description. A more highly developed instrument that brings music reproduction (although original composition is possible) nearer complete automation is the Electronic Music Synthesizer developed by H. Olson and H. Belar at the RCA Acoustical Laboratory in Princeton, New Jersey. The elaborate device can, through electronic oscillators, reproduce almost every conceivable pitch, duration and intensity; this is accomplished by the build-up or superposition of oscillatory waves and the control of the wave forms. Any sounds or music may be reduced to a code of holes punched on an input tape; as the tape is fed into the machine, the coded holes are translated electronically into the desired sounds or music and recorded on disks.[7]

Pros and Cons in its Use. Although Ussachevsky and Babbit have conducted experiments with the machine, it seems unlikely that it will offer practical benefits to the composer since he still must conceive his music by some traditional (or electronic) method and then acquire the highly technical, acoustical knowledge to code the music on the input tape. But considered solely from the reproduction standpoint, the machine could serve the composer well as a quick and accurate means of performing works especially for large groups which might not otherwise, because of the costs of live performance, be heard. Of course, there is always the possibility that the electronic-acoustical technique of producing tones and the corresponding code of punched holes will be perfected to the point where a composer might work directly with the coded holes on the input tape. It would seem, however, that the use of nonmusical symbols far removed from the tones they represent could easily discourage all but the most enthusiastic objective and intellectually inclined composers.

PROGRAMMED DIGITAL COMPUTER MUSIC

A Tonal Organization Process. The newest concept of music creativity affects the total organization of a piece through the storage and programming of music material in an electronic, high-speed digital computer. The highly technical Information Theory and Monte Carlo Theory are involved. Unlike the techniques used in tape-recorder music and in the RCA Music Synthesizer, the newest technique is not concerned with new methods of creating sounds, but with the logic of musical organization and composition. Experiments began in 1955 with the digital computer at the University of Illinois by Lejaren A. Hiller, Jr. and Leonard M. Isaacson. The composition, *Illiac Suite for String Quartet* (1957), is the result of this experimentation.

Musical Justification in Use of Machine. The reasoning behind the experiments is as follows: A high-speed, electronic digital computer can efficiently select ordered sets of information from a "random universe" of information previously stored in the machine; similarly, a music composition is the imposition of order and form on selected material from a wide variety of musical possibilities, depending on a composer's total musical background. Hence, if ample musical material is stored in the computer and proper instructions are programmed or fed into the machine, ordered formulations of selected musical units should emerge to create a musical composition.

Structure Sequence: Information and Monte Carlo Theories. The simplified sequence plan of structuring a music composition is as follows: (1) Tones and rhythmic units including rests and dynamics are transferred to integers (numbers). (2) The Information Theory is now applied; according to the theory, the larger the number of units of information in a particular category of facts, the less organized are those facts. Hence, when innumerable random arrangements of the integers are fed to the machine to be multiplied greatly into millions of units and stored electronically in the machine, the large body of material approaches the neutral state of complete nonorganization (comparable to a composer's more or less subconscious background of material possibilities). (3) The sorting of these patterns (the raw material) into a finished piece depends on the interoperation of the coded rules of sequential selection fed the machine by the operator and the function of the Monte Carlo Theory. This theory is based on chance (probability); in essence, it functions on the premise that each item of a group of similar items has an equal chance of selection if the selective process is repeated often enough. Therefore, each stored integer pattern of a particular homogeneous group theoretically has an equal chance of being selected by the machine (as by a composer). The limitations of the coded rules, however, considerably limit the possibilities in each sequential selection by the machine. (4) Finally, the succession of machine-created and machine-selected integer patterns is transcribed into notes, rhythm and dynamics on a music staff to realize the completed composition.[8]

Freedom of Choice. One of the most fascinating aspects of digital computer composing is that the step-by-step sequential process allows the machine some freedom of choice. In order to create a confining tonality, rhythmic order and logic in a prospective composition, the choice of tones, intervals and rhythms are necessarily limited by a particular coded program fed the machine. But the machine is allowed by trial and error to select the interval or pattern that meets the coded instructions; interestingly, there usually are several possible choices in each successive sequential step. For example, if one choice resolves the leading tone downward instead of upward as required in the instructions, the machine will discard this choice and try another one until a correct resolution is obtained.

Future Musical Uses of Digital Computer. Looking ahead, the machine might prove an ideal instrument for the objective testing of new organizational techniques and hypotheses as it provides a practical experimental means for the application of the scientific method to music composition. Also, the machine could be used most advantageously for the analysis, screening and cataloguing (ordering) of specific characteristics of a large body or category of music.

Objections to Use of Total Organization. On the other hand, the traditionally minded composers have strong objections to the total organization method of music composition. The most obvious criticism is the nonmusical approach of working with mathematical substitutes for musical material. Also, because all the detailed intricacies of form must be preset by the composer, a spontaneous choice or change at any point, once the computer is activated, is eliminated. Furthermore, only the basic course of a composition can be foreseen by planned calculation because the machine has the liberty to make many of the possible choices; as a result, the specific outcome may vary considerably from the composer's original concept and may or may not produce an artistic expression.

A Compromise. Speaking of the RCA Electronic Synthesizer, the noted conductor, Alfred Wallenstein, has stated: "Depending on the perfection of the process, an entirely new concept of what is musically useful can be evolved. And the entire world of sound can be tapped for the creation of yet unheard of musical forms."[9] It may well be that because both traditional music and electronic music have their own acoustical and organizational strengths and weaknesses, each can exist side by side and develop its individual strengths. Possibly in the future the two now radically opposed methods will move toward some effective practical synthesis or amalgamation which will retain the favorable aspects of each.

FOOTNOTES

[1]MarM, p. 40.
[2]*Ibid.*, pp. 40-41.
[3]KreE, p. 83.
[4]SesP, p. 32.
[5]LanI, p. 15.
[6]*Ibid.*, p. 16.
[7]Ol-BelE, p. 595.
[8]Hil-IsaE p.p. 73-78.
[9]As quoted in MarE, p. 42.

discography

Symbols	Recording Company
AAFS	Archive of American Folksong (Lib. of Congress)
All.	Allegro
Ang.	Angel
Argo	Argo
ARS	American Recording Society
Art.	
ASC	American Stereophonic Corp.
Buena	Buena Vista
Cap.	Capitol
Col.	Columbia
CHS	Concert Hall Society
Con.	Concord
Contem.	Contemporary
CRI	Composers Recordings, Inc.
Dec.	Decca
Desto	Desto
Dorian	Dorian
Elek.	Elektra
EMS	
Epic	Epic (Columbia)
Ev.	Everest
Fam.	Family
Folk.	Folkways
Folk-Lyric	

GNP	GNP Crescendo
Greg.	Gregorian Institute
Har.	Harmony
Her.	Heritage
Imper.	Imperial
Lon.	London
	Louisianne
Lou.	Louisville
Lyr.	Lyric
Main.	Mainstream
Mer.	Mercury
Metro	
MGM	Metro-Goldwyn-Mayer
Mon.	Monitor
Mus.-Lib.	Music Library
NR	New Records
Over.	Overtone
Pick.	Pickwick
Riv.	Riverside
Seeco	
Son-Nova	
SPA	Society of Participating Artists
SPAMH	Society for the Preservation of the American Musical Heritage
Sti.	Stinson
Time	Time
Trad.	Tradition
Turn.	Turnabout
	Urania
Van.	Vanguard
Vic.	RCA Victor
Vox	
WCFM	
West.	Westminster
WFB	
WR	Washington Records

CHAPTER I   First Arrivals

| CATHOLIC MISSION MUSIC IN CALIFORNIA | NR 2001; SPAMH MIA 96 |
| BALLADS IN COLONIAL AMERICA | NR 2005; SPAMH MIA 97 |

CHAPTER II   The Psalters

BAY PSALM BOOK	SPAMH MIA 102
EARLY AMERICAN PSALMODY	Over. LP-2

CHAPTER III   The Rise of American Music

THE AMERICAN HARMONY	WR 418
BILLINGS, WILLIAM	
Chester	Col. ML-5496
(The Organ in America)	
Four Anthems	SPAMH MIA 114
American Psalms and Fuguing Tunes	Col. M-434
Lamentation Over Boston	SPAMH MIA 114;
	CHS 52
David's Lamentation	CHS 52
The Bird	Vic LM-57
I am the Rose of Sharon	Vic LM-57
Morpheus	WR 418
Hymns and Anthems	Folk. 2377
HOPKINSON, FRANCIS	
A Toast	All. 3148
(A Panorama of American	
Orchestral Music)	
HYMNS AND CAROLS	Folk. Fa 2361
(Early American Religious Songs)	
THE NEW ENGLAND HARMONY	Folk. FA 2377
READ, DANIEL	
Five Anthems	SPAMH MIA 114
SHAW, OLIVER	
Trip to Pawtucket	Col. ML-5496
(The Organ in America)	

CHAPTER IV   The Influx of Professional Musicians

BROWN, WILLIAM	
Rondo in G	Col. ML-5496
(The Organ in America)	
FRANCESCHINI, GAETANO	
Trio Sonata in B flat	NR 2006; SPAMH MIA 113
For Violins, Cello and	
Continuo	
GEHOT, JEAN	
Quartette in D	NR 2002; SPAMH MIA 101
Op. 7, No. 6	
GRAM, HANS	
Death Song of an Indian Chief	All. 3148
GUALDO, GIOVANNI	
Six Sonatas for Two	SPAMH MIA 112
Flutes and Continuo	

HAGEN, PETER ALBRECHT VAN
   All the World Shall Sing   COL. ML-5688 Vol. 2
HEWITT, JAMES
   Battle of Trenton   COL. ML-5496
   (The Organ in America)
JACKSON, GEORGE
   Dirge for General Washington   VIC. LM-57
LEAUMONT, MARIE ROBERT DE
   Duo Concertant   SPAMH MIA 113
   for Cello and Piano
MOLLER, JOHN
   Six Quartets   NR 2002; SPAMH MIA
                                    101, 107
   Sonata in D   COL. ML-5496
PACHELBEL, CHARLES
   Magnificat in C   SPAMH MIA 111
   Double Chorus and Continuo
PHILE, PHILLIP
   President's March   COL. ML-5496
   (The Organ in America)
REINAGLE, ALEXANDER
   Sonata for Piano   NR 2006; SPAMH MIA 101
SELBY, WILLIAM
   Fugue or Voluntary in D   COL. ML-5496
   (The Organ in America)
TAYLOR, RAYNOR
   Six Sonatas for Cello and Continuo   SPAMH MIA 108
   Sonata No. 4 and 6 for   NR 2004
   Cello and Continuo
YARNOLD, BENJAMIN
   March in D   COL. ML-5496
   (The Organ in America)

CHAPTER V The Minority Sects and Their Music

ANTES, JOHN
   Three Trios for Two Violins   NR 2016; COL. ML-6141
   and Cello, Op. 3
   Anthems   COL. ML-5688 Vol. 1, 2
DENCKE, JEREMIAH
   Anthems   SPAMH MIA 98, COL.
                                    ML-5688, vol. 2.
HERBST, JOHANNES
   I Will Go in the Strength   SPAMH MIA 98; COL.
   of the Lord   ML-5688
KELLNER, J. P.
   O Sacred Head Now Wounded   COL. ML-5688
LEINBACH, EDWARD W.
   Hosanna   COL. ML-5688

MICHAEL, DAVID
  I Love to Dwell in Spirit   SPAMH MIA 98
  Parthia (The Organ in America)   COL. ML-5496
  Hearken, Stay Close to Christ   COL. ML-5688
MORMON FOLK SONGS   FOLK. FA 2036 (36)
MÜLLER, GEORG
  My Savior Lies in Anguish   SPAMH MIA 98
OLD AMERICAN SONGS   COL. ML-2206
PETER, JOHANN
  Sinfonia in G (Arr. from   MER. 50163
    Quintet No. 3)
  Six Quintets   NR 2013
  Choral Music   SPAMH MIA 98
SONGS OF THE MORMONS AND   AAFS L 30
    THE WEST
WOLLE, PETER
  For Me, O Lord My God   COL. ML 5688

CHAPTER VI   Fasola, Doremi and Revivalism

GOSPEL SONGS   FOLK. FA 2357
  (White spirituals sung by
    Harry and Jeanie West)
INTRODUCTION TO GOSPEL SONG   FOLK. RF-S
OLD HARP SINGERS   FOLK. FA 2356 (56)
  (Hymns, anthems, fuging
    from Tennessee)
SACRED HARP SINGING   AAFS 51-55 (L 11)
  (ed. by G. P. Jackson)

CHAPTER VII   Patriotic and National Songs and Our Lighter Side

BALES, RICHARD
  The Confederacy   COL. SL-220
BALLADS OF THE CIVIL WAR   FOLK. FH 5004; 2187-8
BALLADS OF THE REVOLUTION
             Vol. 1 FOLK. FA 2151 (48/1)
             Vol. 2 FOLK. FA 2152 (48/2)
BALLADS OF THE REVOLUTION   FOLK. FH 5001; 2151-2
  (1767-81)
BALLADS OF THE WAR OF 1812
             Vol. 1 FOLK. FA 2163 (48/3)
             Vol. 2 FOLK. FA 2164 (48/4)
BALLADS OF THE WAR OF 1812   FOLK. FH 5002; 2163-4
CIVIL WAR SONGS   2-MER. 2-501; 2-901
  (Eastman Wind Ens.)   2-MER. 2-502; 2-902
DAYS OF THE '49. SONGS OF   FOLK. FH 5255
  THE GOLD RUSH

MUSIC OF THE AMERICAN REVOLUTION	WCFM Lp-1
MUSIC OF THE CIVIL WAR	FAM. 129; S-129
SONGS AND BALLADS OF AMERICAN HISTORY	AAFS L 29
SONGS OF THE CIVIL WAR	FOLK. FH 5717
SOLDIER SONGS, U.S.A.	FOLK. FH 5249
(From the Revolution to Korea)	

CHAPTER VIII   Nineteenth-Century Musical
Sophistication

BRISTOW, FREDERICK G.
Sixth Symphony   SPAMH MIA 132
BUCK, D.
Festival te Deum in E flat   VIC. 31781; 35674
Rock of Ages   VIC. 16269
FRY, WILLIAM HENRY
Santa Claus Symphony   SPAMH MIA 131
Childe Harolde Symphony
Overture to Macbeth   ALL. 3148
    (A Panorama of American
        Orchestral Music)
HOFFMAN, RICHARD
La Gazelle   SPAMH MIA 109
Caprice de Concert   SPAMH MIA 109
Polka de Concert   SPAMH MIA 109
LANIER, SYDNEY
Wind Song   SPAMH MIA 117
Blackbirds
Danse des Moucherons
MASON, WILLIAM
Monody, Op. 13   SPAMH MIA 109
Silver Springs, Op. 6   SPAMH MIA 109
Toujours, Op. 7, No. 2   SPAMH MIA 109
Lullaby, Op. 10   SPAMH MIA 109
PAINE, JOHN KNOWLES   VIC. M-608; VIC. 15658
Prelude to Oedipus Tyrannus, Op. 35
WOLLENHAUPT, HERMAN
Le Dernier Sourire   SPAMH MIA 110
Morceau en Forme d'Etude   SPAMH MIA 110

CHAPTER IX   New England Academicians

BEACH, MRS. H. H. A.
Five Improvisations for Piano   DORIAN 1006
Trio for Violin, Cello, Piano, Op. 150   DORIAN 1007
CHADWICK, GEORGE W.
Tam O'Shanter   ARS-29; DESTO 421; 6421

FOOTE, ARTHUR
  Night Piece for Flute and Strings — Epic LC-3754; BC-1116
  Suite for Strings in E, Op. 63 — Vic. DM-962; Mer. 40001 ARS-22

HILL, EDWARD BURLINGAME
  Sextet for Piano and Winds — Col. ML-4846

LOEFFLER, CHARLES M.
  A Pagan Poem, Op. 14 — Vic. M-876; Cap. P-8188
  Memories of My Childhood — Mer. 50085
  La Bonne Chanson — Mer. 50085
  Music for String Instruments — Vic. M-543

MACDOWELL, EDWARD
  Suite No. 2, Op. 48 (Indian Suite) — Desto 408; 6408; Mer. 50422; 90422
  ARS-3; Col. M-373; ML-54372
  Woodland Sketches, Op. 51 — Van. 1011; West. 9310
  Concerto No. 1 in A Minor for Piano, Op. 15 — West. 19012; 17012; 18367
  Concerto No. 2 in D Minor for Piano, Op. 23 — Vic. LM-2507; LSC-2507; Van. 1011; West. 19012; 17012; 18367

MASON, DANIEL G.
  Chanticleer (A Festival Overture) — ARS-20; Desto 409; 6409
  Quartet in G Minor on Negro Themes, Op. 19 — Vic. M-891

NEVIN, ETHELBERT
  Mighty Lak' a Rose — Vic. 89108; Vic. 64308; Col. 30486
  Narcissus — Vic. 16029
  The Rosary — Vic. 88108; Vic. 64502

PARKER, HORATIO W.
  Hora Novissima — 2-Desto 413/4; 6413/4; ARS-335

CHAPTER X   Music Education

WEBB, GEORGE
  Song Over a Child — Vic. LM-57

CHAPTER XI   Native Musical Activity

GOLDEN MARCH FAVORITES — Dec. 4453; 74453
  (Goldman Band)
PHONO-CYLINDERS — Folk. FS 3886; 3887
  (Reissues of early recordings)
SEMPER FIDELIS — SOUSA MARCHES — Har. 7001
  (Goldman Band)

SOUSA, JOHN P.
   Marches   MER. MG-40007

CHAPTER XII   Nationalistic Elements I

INDIAN MUSIC OF AMERICAN
   SOUTHWEST   FOLK. FW 8850
   Libr. of Congress   AAFS L 34-43
                                  AAFS 26-30 (L 6)
                                  AAFS 81-85 (L 17)
                                  AAFS 106-10 (L 22)
                                  AAFS L 23-25
                                  AAFS L 31, L 33, L 35
                                  AAFS L 35-43

MUSIC OF THE AMERICAN
   INDIANS   FOLK. FE 4420 (420)

SPANISH-MEXICAN AMERICAN SONGS

SPANISH AND MEXICAN MUSIC-   FOLK. FE 4426 (426)
   FOLK MUSIC OF NEW MEXICO
SPANISH AND MEXICAN SONGS   2 ELEK. 218
SPANISH SONGS OF NEW MEXICO   FOLK. FA 2204 (604)

CREOLE SONGS

BAHAMAN SONGS, FRENCH BALLADS   AAFS 21-25 (L 5)
   AND DANCE TUNES, SPANISH RE-
   LIGIOUS SONGS AND GAME SONGS
CAJUN MUSIC OF LOUISIANA   FOLK. FE 4438 (438)
CREOLE SONGS AND STREET CRIES   FOLK. FA 2202 (602)
FRENCH MUSIC OF SO. LOUISIANA   LOUISIANNE 107
LOUISIANA ACADIANS—FOLKSONGS   FOLK-LYRIC 4
LOUISIANA FOLKSONG JAMBALAYA   FOLK-LYRIC 2
NEW ORLEANS CREOLE SONGS AND   10" FOLK. 2202
   CRIES

NEGRO SONGS

AFRO-AMERICAN-NEGRO SONGS   AAFS 11-15 (L 3)
                                    AAFS 16-20 (L 4)
                                  AAFS 46-50 (L 10)
                                  AAFS L 59
FISK JUBILEE SINGERS   FOLK. FE 2372 (72)
   (Negro Spirituals)
NEGRO FOLK MUSIC OF AFRICA   2-FOLK. 4500
   AND AMERICA
NEGRO FOLK MUSIC OF ALABAMA
   (Secular)   FOLK. FE 4417 (417)
   (Religious)   FOLK. FE 4418 (418)
                                    FOLK. FE 4472 (472)
                                    FOLK. FE 4473 (473)
                                    FOLK. FE 4474 (474)

NEGRO PRISON SONGS	TRAD. 1020
(compiled by Lomax)	
NEGRO RHYTHMS	FOLK. 7654
NEGRO WORK SONGS	STINSON 87
SPIRITUALS AND BLUES	ELEK. 193; 7193
SHOUTS, SPIRITUALS	MON. 335; S335

FOLK MUSIC – ANGLO-AMERICAN BALLADS

AMERICAN FOLK BLUES FESTIVAL		DEC. 4392; 74392
AMERICAN SEA SONGS–SHANTIES		AAFS L 26; L 27
ANGLO-AMERICAN BALLADS		AAFS 1-5 (L 1)
(ed. by Lomax)		AAFS 6-10 (L 2)
(shanties, spirituals)		AAFS 31-35 (L 7)
		AAFS 36-40 (L 8)
		AAFS 56-60 (L 12)
		AAFS 66-70 (L 14)
		AAFS 96-100 (L 20)
		AAFS 101-105 (L 21)
		AAFS L 57, L 58
ANTHOLOGY OF AMERICAN FOLK MUSIC		
	Vol. 1	FOLK. FA 2951 (251)
	Vol. 2	FOLK. FA 2952 (252)
	Vol. 3	FOLK. FA 2953
BRITISH BROADSIDE BALLADS		FOLK. FW 8708
BROADSIDE BALLADS –		
LONDON	Vol. 1	FOLK. FW 3043
(1600-1700 Ewan MacColl)	Vol. 2	FOLK. FW 3044
CHILD BALLADS IN AMERICA		2-FOLK. 2301/2
EARLY AMERICAN BALLADS		VIC. M-604
FOLK MUSIC IN U.S.A.		FOLK. FE 4530
400 YEARS OF FOLK MUSIC		FOLK. FA 2404
TRADITIONAL BALLADS	Vol. 1	FOLK. FA 2301
(F. J. Child Collection)	Vol. 2	FOLK. FA 2302
TWO CENTURIES OF AMERICAN FOLK SONGS		VIC. P-41

COWBOY SONGS

COWBOY SONGS	AAFS L 28
COWBOY SONGS	DEC. 9105
(Carl Sandburg)	
COWBOY SONGS	FOLK. FA 2022 (22)

CHAPTER XIII Nationalistic Elements II

RAGTIME

ESSAY IN RAGTIME	FOLK. FG 3563
FATS WALLER (Valentine Stomp)	VIC. LPV-525
JELLY ROLL MORTON	VIC. LPM-1649

JOSEPH LAMB PLAYS RAGTIME   Folk. FG 3562
  (Study in classic ragtime)
ROGER SPRUNG   Folk. FA 2371
  (Ragtime Banjo)

BLUES-BOOGIE WOOGIE

BEST OF THE BLUES	Vol. 1	Imper. 9257
BLUES	Vol. 1	Argo 4026
	Vol. 2	Argo 4027
	Vol. 4	Argo 4042
RARE BLUES OF THE 20s		Hist. ASC-1
	Vol. 2	Hist. ASC-2
	Vol. 4	Hist. ASC-4
	Vol. 5	Hist. ASC-5
THE RURAL BLUES		Folk. RF-202

  (Extensive survey of traditional
    blues singers)

TRADITIONAL BLUES	Vol. 1	Folk. FA 2421
	Vol. 2	Folk. FA 2422
W. C. HANDY BLUES		Folk. FG 3540

  (Sung by his daughter)

JAZZ (General collect.)

ENCYCLOPEDIA OF JAZZ   4 Dec. DX-140 (8398/8401)
  (20s, 30s, 40s, 50s)
HISTORY OF JAZZ—NEW YORK SCENE   Folk. RF-1 (2823)
INTRODUCTION TO JAZZ   Dec. 8244
JAZZ Vol. 1 THE SOUTH WORK   Folk. FJ 2801 (53)
          SONGS, HOLLERS, ETC.
    Vol. 2 THE BLUES EARLY   Folk. FJ 2802 (55)
          SINGERS AND OR-
          CHESTRAS
    Vol. 3 DIXIELAND (NEW   Folk, FJ 2803 (57)
          ORLEANS EARLY RE-
          CORDINGS)
    Vol. 4 JAZZ SINGERS (MANY   Folk. FJ 2804 (59)
          SINGERS AND STYLES)
    Vol. 5 CHICAGO NO. 1 (EXAM-   Folk. FJ 2805 (63)
          PLES OF JAZZ ERA)
    Vol. 6 CHICAGO NO. 2 (MORE   Folk. FJ 2806 (65)
          EXAMPLES OF JAZZ
          ERA)
    Vol. 7 NEW YORK 1922-34   Folk. FJ 2807 (67)
          (Combos of the big city era)
    Vol. 8 BIG BANDS (From pre-   Folk. FJ 2808 (69)
          1935 period)
    Vol. 9 PIANO (Classics of the   Folk. FJ 2809 (71)
          jazz keyboard)

Vol. 10 BOOGIE WOOGIE (Jump and Kansas City styles)	FOLK. FJ 2810 (73)
Vol. 11 ADDENDA (A mixture of great jazz momentos)	FOLK, FJ 2811 (75)
THE STORY OF JAZZ	FOLK. FC 7312 (712)
WHAT IS JAZZ?	COL. CL-919

JAZZ (Classic — Dixieland)

BEST OF DIXIELAND	VIC. LPM-2982; LSP-2982
HOT JAZZ (Jelly Roll Morton)	VIC. LPV-524
MUSIC OF NEW ORLEANS	
Vol. 2 EUREKA BRASS BAND ORIGINALS	FOLK. FA 2462
Vol. 3 MUSIC OF THE DANCE HALLS	FOLK. FA 2463
Vol. 4 THE BIRTH OF JAZZ	FOLK. FA 2464
Vol. 5 NEW ORLEANS JAZZ FLOWERING	FOLK. FA 2465
TREASURES OF CLASSIC JAZZ	4-COL. C4L-18 (CL-1521/4)

JAZZ (Sweet and Swing)

BIG BAND, VERY BEST	MGM 4219; S4219
DUKE ELLINGTON ERA, Vol. 2, 1927-40	3-Col. C3L-39
ERA OF THE SWING TRUMPET	MAIN. 56017; 6017
JAZZ AT TOWN HALL (Live performance of one of the 40s great concerts)	FOLK. FJ 2841

JAZZ (Modern)

AFRO-COOL	GNP 48
BEBOP ERA	VIC. LPV-519
COOL JAZZ	SEECO 465
MILES DAVIS COMPOSITIONS	RIV. 3504; 93504
ROCK AND ROLL SOUND	FOLK. 2865

CHAPTER XIV   Nationalistic Composers I

BLOCH, ERNEST	
America, An Epic Rhapsody	VAN. 1056; 2065
Schelomo, Rhapsody for Cello and Orchestra	
CADMAN, C. W.	
At Dawning	VIC. 45170
From the Land of the Sky-Blue Water	VIC. 64190; VIC. 1115
FARWELL, A.	
Navajo War Dance, Op. 20, No. 1	VIC. M-764
Sourwood Mountain, Op. 78, No. 3	VIC. M-764

GILBERT, H. F.
  Dance in the Place Congo   Art   100-A
                                     Ev. 6118; 3118
  Pirate Song   Col. A-5778
GOTTSCHALK, L. M.
  Latin-American Sym.   Van. 1103; 2141
  Piano Music   Con.-Disc 1217; 217
  Cakewalk (Ballet Suite)   Col. ML-4616
  A Night in the Tropics   Van. VRS 1103
JACOBI, FREDERICK
  Hagiographia — Three Biblical   CRI-174
    Narratives for String Quartet
    and Piano
  Quartet No. 3   CRI-174
MUSIC OF STEPHEN FOSTER   Dec. 8923; 78923
                                     Cap. P-8501; SP-8501
SONGS OF STEPHEN FOSTER   Vic. LM-2295; LSC-2295
                                     Cap. P-8267; DP-8267
                                     Ars-15
POWELL, JOHN
  Negro Rhapsody for Piano and Orch.   Desto 409; 6409
                                     ARS-20

CHAPTER XV Nationalistic Composers II

CARPENTER, JOHN ALDEN
  Skyscrapers   Desto 407; 6407
                                     ARS-37
  Concertino for Piano and Orchestra   CRI-180
COPLAND, AARON
  Concerto for Piano and Orchestra   Col. ML-6098; MS-6698
    Music for the Theatre
  Piano Variations   Lyr. 104
  El Salon Mexico   Col. ML-5755; MS-6355
  Appalachian Spring Ballet   ARS-26
  Symphony No. 3   Ev. 6018; 3018
FINNEY, ROSS LEE
  Symphony No. 1   Lou. 652
  Symphony No. 2   Lou. 625
GERSHWIN, GEORGE
  Rhapsody in Blue   Col. CL-1495; CS-8286
  An American in Paris   Col. ML-5413; MS-6091
  Porgy and Bess   Dec. 9024; 79024
                                     Col. OL-5410; OS-2016
GOULD, MORTON
  Come Where My Love Lies Dreaming   All. 3148
GRUENBERG, LOUIS
  Concerto for Violin and Orchestra   Vic. LVT-1017

HARRIS, ROY
 Symphony No. 4 (Folk Song)   VAN. 1064; 2082
 Symphony No. 3   COL. ML-5703; MS-6303
  (Bernstein, N. Y. Phil.)   ARS-28
MOORE, DOUGLAS
 The Ballad of Baby Doe   3-MGM 3GC-1; 53-GC-1
 The Devil and Daniel Webster   DESTO 450; 6450
 Symphony in A Major   ARS-5
THOMSON, VIRGIL
 Four Saints in Three Acts   VIC. LM-2756
 Louisiana Story; Acadian Songs   EPIC LC-3809; BC-1147
  and Dances
VINCENT, JOHN
 Symphony in D   LOU. 57-2
 Consort for Piano and Strings   CONTEM. 6009

CHAPTER XVI   Contemporary Development of Traditional Styles

BARBER, SAMUEL
 Second Essay for Orchestra   ALL. 3148
 Adagio for Strings   MER. 50148; ARS-26
  Essay No. 1 for Orchestra
  Overture, School for Scandal
 Medea, Op. 23 (Ballet Suite)   MER. 50224; 90224
 Toccata Festiva, Op. 36 (1961)   COL. ML-5798; MS-6398
BERNSTEIN, LEONARD
 "Jeremiah" Symphony   COL. ML-5703; MS-6303
 Symphony No. 3—Kaddish   COL. KL-6005; KS-6605
 Candide Overture   COL. ML-6077; MS-6677
  On the Town (Ballet Music)
CRESTON, PAUL
 A Rumor   ALL. 3148
DELLO JOIO, NORMAN
 Epigraph   DESTO 416; 6416
    ARS-31
 Meditation on Ecclesiastes   CRI-110
DIAMOND, DAVID
 Rounds for String Orchestra   CAP. P-8245
    ARS-7

FOSS, LUKAS
 Parable of Death   COL. ML-4859
 Time Cycle   COL. ML-5680; MS-6280
GRIFFES, CHARLES T.
 Pleasure Dome of Kubla Khan   MER. 50085
    MER. 50422; 90422
 Roman Sketches   LYR. 105

Poem for Flute and Orchestra	MER. 50422; 90422
	COL. ML-4629
	EPIC LC-3754; BC-1116
	ARS-22
HANSON, HOWARD	
Merry Mount Suite	MER. 50423; 90423
Symphony No. 2 (Romantic)	MER. 50192; 90192
Symphony No. 4	MER. 50077
	ARS-6
MENNIN, PETER	
Symphony No. 5	MER. 50379; 90379
MENOTTI, GIAN CARLO	
Amahl and the Night Visitors	VIC. LM-2762; LSC-2762
The Consul	2-DEC. DX-101
The Medium	2-COL. OSL-154
PISTON, WALTER	
The Incredible Flutist	MER. 50423; 90423
Symphony No. 2	DESTO 410; 6410
	ARS-1
TAYLOR, DEEMS	
Through the Looking-Glass	VIC. LM-2807; LSC-2807
THOMPSON, RANDALL	
Alleluia	GREG. EL-19
	MUS.-LIB.-7085
The Peaceable Kingdom	MUS.-LIB.-7065
	LYR. 124; 7124
Symphony No. 2	ARS-4
YOUMANS, VINCENT	
Hit the Deck	MGM 3163

CHAPTER XVII   On New Paths

ANTHEIL, GEORGE	
Ballet Mechanique	URANIA 134; 5134
Symphony No. 5	SPA 16
CAGE, JOHN	
Sonatas and Interludes for	CRI-199
Prepared Piano	EV.-6132; 3132
Indeterminacy	2-FOLK. 3704
COWELL, HENRY D.	
Ongaku for Orchestra	LOU.-595
Persian Set	CRI-114
Quartets, No. 2, 3, 4	CRI-173
Symphony No. 15	LOU.-622
Symphony No. 16	CRI-179
FOSS, LUKAS	
Echoi	
Time Cycle	EPIC LC-3886; BC-1286

IVES, CHARLES
    Variations on America   Col. ML-5496
      (The Organ in America)
    Concord Sonata (No. 2)   CRI-150
    Symphony No. 4   Col. ML-6175; MS-6775
    Three Places in New England   Mer. 50149; 90149
                                    Ev. 6118; 3118
                                    ARS-27

PARTCH, HARRY
    Castor and Pollux, Cloud Chamber   CRI-193
      Music (and other select.)
RUGGLES, CARL
    Evocations; Lilacs; Portals   Col. ML-4986
    Sun-Treader   Col. ML-6201; MS-6801
SCHUMAN, WILLIAM
    American Festival Overture   Desto-404; 6404
                                    ARS-28
    Chester (Overture for Band)   Mer.-Dec. 8633; 78633
    Symphony No. 8   Col. ML-5912; MS-6512
SESSIONS, ROGER
    The Black Maskers Suite   Mer. 50423; 90423
                                    Desto-404; 6404
                                    ARS-11
    Sonata for Violin Solo   Folk. 3355
VARESE, EDGAR
    Deserts, Arcana, Offrandes   Col. ML-5762; MS-6362
    Ionisation   Col. ML-5478; MS-6146
    Octandre, Intégrales, Density   EMS-401

CHAPTER XVIII   Twelve-Tone Techniques

BABBITT, MILTON
    Composition for Four Instruments   CRI-138
HARRISON, LOU
    Canticle No. 3 for Percussion   Urania 106; 5106
      (1941)
    Suite for Symphonic Strings   Lou. 621
KERR, HARRISON
    Concerto for Violin and Orchestra   CRI-142
KIRCHNER, LEON
    Quartet No. 1 (1949)   Col. ML-4843
RIEGGER, WALLINGFORD
    Romanza, Dance Rhythms   CRI-117
    Symphony No. 4   Lou. 646; S-646

CHAPTER XIX   Electronic Music

BABBITT, MILTON
Composition for Synthesizer (1964)   Col. ML-5966; MS-6566
EIGHT ELECTRONIC PIECES   Folk. FM 3434
T. Dockstader
INDETERMINACY   Folk. FT 3704
(John Cage reads 90 stories to
electronic music)
USSACHEVSKY, VLADIMIR
Composition; Sonic Contours   Folk. 6160
Creation-Prologue   Col. ML-5966; MS-6566
Metamorphosis; Improvisation   Son-Nova-3; S-3
No. 4711
Piece for Tape Recorder   CRI-112

bibliography

Aiken, Jesse B., *The Christian Minstrel*, Philadelphia, 1850.

Ainsworth, Henry, *The Book of Psalmes*, Amsterdam, 1612.

Alter, Martha, "Howard Hanson," *Modern Music*, January/February, 1941, pp. 84-89.

AndG   Andrews, Edward D., *The Gift to be Simple*, Locust Valley, N.Y.: J. J. Augustin, Inc. — Publisher, 1940.

Armitage, Merle (ed.), *George Gershwin*, New York: Longmans, Green & Co., Inc., 1938.

Baker, Theodore, *Über die Musik der Nordamerikanischen Wilden*, Leipzig: Breitkopf & Härtel, 1882.

BarP   Barry, Philip, "The Part of the Folk Singer in the Making of Folk Balladry," in MacEdwards Leach and Tristram P. Coffin, *The Critics and the Ballad*, Carbondale: Southern Illinois University Press, 1961, pp. 59-76.

Bauer, Marion, *Twentieth Century Music*, New York: G. P. Putnam's Sons, 1933.

BayP   Bayard, Samuel P., "Prolegomena to a Study of the Principal Melodic Families of Folk Song," in MacEdwards Leach and Tristram P. Coffin, *The Critics and the Ballad*, Carbondale: Southern Illinois University Press, 1961, pp. 103-150.

Bayley, Daniel, *The American Harmony*, Newbury-Port, 1767.

Bay Psalm Booke (The Whole Booke of Psalmes Faithfully Translated into English Metre), Cambridge, 1640 and 1698 editions.

BeaR   Beard, Charles and Mary, *The Rise of American Civilization*, New York: The Macmillan Company, 1927.

BehP   Behrend, Jeanne (ed.), *Music of Louis Moreau Gottschalk*, Bryn Mawr, Pa.: Theodore Presser Company, 1956.

Behrend, Jeanne, *Notes of a Pianist,* New York: Alfred A. Knopf, Inc., 1964.

BelH   Belcher, Supply, *The Harmony of Maine,* Boston: Thomas and Andrews, 1794.

BelI   Bellamann, Henry, "Charles Ives: The Man and His Music," *Musical Quarterly* 19:45-58, January, 1933.

Berger, Arthur V., *Aaron Copland,* New York: Oxford University Press, Inc., 1953.

BilN   Billings, William, *The New-England Psalm-Singer: or American Chorister,* Boston: Edes and Gill, n.d. [1770].

BilS   —————, *The Singing Master's Assistant, or Key to Practical Music,* Boston: Draper and Folsom, 1778.

BirPS   Birge, Edward B., *History of Public School Music in the United States,* Boston: Oliver Ditson Company, 1928.

Blesh, Rudi and Janis, Harriet, *They All Played Ragtime: The True Story of an American Music,* New York: Alfred A. Knopf, Inc., 1950.

BorR   Bornemen, Ernest, *The Roots of Jazz,* New York: Holt, Rinehart and Winston, Inc., 1950.

BorC   Borowski, Felix, "John Alden Carpenter," *Musical Quarterly* 16:449-468, October, 1930.

Boyd, James M., *The Virginia Sacred Musical Repository,* Winchester, Va., 1818.

BrenM   Brennecke, E., *John Milton Elder and His Music,* New York: Columbia University Press, 1938.

Broder, Nathan, "The Music of Samuel Barber," *Musical Quarterly* 34:325-335, July, 1948.

—————, "The Music of William Schuman," *Musical Quarterly* 31:17-28, January, 1945.

BroI   Bronson, Bertrand H., "The Interdependence of Ballad Tunes and Texts," in MacEdwards Leach and Tristram P. Coffin, *The Critics and the Ballad,* Carbondale: Southern University Press, 1961, pp. 77-102.

Bruno, Anthony, "Two American Twelve-tone Composers," *Musical America* 22:170, February, 1951. [About Milton Babbitt and Ben Weber.]

BrunS   Brunswick, Mark, "Roger Huntington Sessions," *Modern Music* 10:182-187, May/June, 1933.

BucA   Buchanan, Annabel Morris, "Anglo-American Folk Music," *International Cyclopedia of Music and Musicians,* 9th ed., 1964, pp. 700-710.

BucH   —————, "American Folk Hymnody," *International Cyclopedia of Music and Musicians,* 9th ed., 1964, pp. 596-601.

BurA   Burton, Frederick R., *American Primitive Music,* New York: Moffat, Yard & Company, 1909.

Burton, Jack, *The Blue Book of Broadway Musicals,* Watkins Glen, N.Y.: Century House, Inc., 1952.

Calvin, John, *Aulcuns pseaulmes et cantiques,* Strasbourg, 1539.

—————, *Institutes of the Christian Religion,* translated by Thomas Norton, London, 1634.

Carden, Allen D., *The Missouri Harmony*, St. Louis, 1820.

Carter, Elliott, "American Figure, with Landscape," *Modern Music* May/June, 1943, pp. 219-225. [About Henry F. Gilbert.]

—————, "Ives Today: His Vision and Challenge," *Modern Music* May/June, 1944, pp. 199-202.

CarP   —————, "Walter Piston," *Musical Quarterly* 32:354-375, July, 1946.

Chadwick, George W., *Commemorative Tribute to Horatio Parker*, New Haven, Conn.: Yale University Press, 1921.

ChaC   Chandler, Theodore, "Aaron Copland," in Henry Cowell (ed.), *American Composers on American Music*, Stanford: Stanford University Press, 1933, pp. 49-56.

Chapin, N. and J. Dickerson, *The Musical Instructor*, Philadelphia, 1810.

ChaA   Chase, Gilbert, *America's Music*, New York: McGraw-Hill, Inc., 1955.

ChauR   Chauncey, Nathaniel, *Regular Singing Defended, and Proved to be the only true way of singing the songs of the Lord*, New London, Conn.: T. Green, 1728.

Citkowitz, Israel, "Walter Piston, Classicist," *Modern Music*, January/February, 1936, pp. 3-11.

ChrisS   Christy, Byron, *New Songster and Black Joker*, New York, 1863.

ColF   Coleman, R. V., *The First Frontier*, New York: Charles Scribner's Sons, 1948.

ConA   Cone, Edward T., "Analysis Today," in Paul Henry Lang (ed.), *Problems in Modern Music*, New York: W. W. Norton & Company, Inc., 1962, pp. 34-50.

Copland, Aaron, "Jazz Structure and Influence," *Modern Music* 4:9-14, January/February, 1927.

CopO   —————, *Our New Music; Leading Composers in Europe and America*, New York: McGraw-Hill, Inc., 1941.

CotS   Cotton, John, *Singing of Psalms a Gospel Ordinance. Or a Treatise wherein are handled these four particulars. I. touching the duty itself. II. Touching the matter to be sung. III. Touching the singers. IV. Touching the manner of singing*, Boston, 1647.

CovP   Covey, Cyclone, "Puritanism and Music in Colonial America," *William and Mary Quarterly* 8:378-388, 1951.

CowH   Cowell, Henry, "Roy Harris," *American Composers on American Music*, Stanford: Stanford University Press, 1933, pp. 64-69.

————— and Cowell, S., *Charles Ives and His Music*, New York: Oxford University Press, 1955.

—————, "Wallingford Riegger," *Musical America* 9:29, December 1, 1948.

CowV   —————, "Edgar Varèse," *American Composers on American Music*, Stanford: Stanford University Press, 1933, pp. 43-48.

Currier, T. P., "MacDowell as I Knew Him," *Musical Quarterly* 1:17-51, January, 1915.

Curtis, Natalie, *The Indians' Book*, New York: Harper & Brothers, [1907].

DaSM   Da Silva, Owen, *Mission Music of California*, Los Angeles: the Franciscan Fathers of California, W. L. Lewis, 1941.

DavE   David, Hans T., "Ephrata and Bethlehem in Pennsylvania: A Comparison," *Papers of the American Musicological Society*, 1941, printed by the Society, 1946, pp. 97-104.

Davis, A. J., *Music to Hymns and Anthems for Jewish Worship*, New York, 1887.

DavO   Davis, Ronald L., *A History of Opera in the American West*, New York: Prentice-Hall, Inc., 1965.

DavsK   Davisson, Ananias, *Kentucky Harmony*, (4th ed.). Harrisonburg, Va., 1821.

DayF   Day, Charles, *Fun in Black*, or *Sketches of Minstrel Life*, New York: R. M. De Witt, 1874.

Day, H. W. and Beale, F. F., *Boston Numeral Harmony*, Boston, 1845.

DenA   Densmore, Frances, *The American Indians and Their Music*, New York: The Women's Press, 1926.

—————, Bulletins on music of various American Indian Tribes issued by Bureau of American Ethnology, Washington, D.C.: Government Printing Office, 1910-1942.

Dexter, Dave, Jr., *Jazz Cavalcade: The Inside Story of Jazz*, New York: Criterion Music Corp., 1946.

Dictionary of American Biography, Articles on Bristow, Buck, Fry, Gilchrist, Gleason, Paine, Pratt.

DowR   Downey, James C., "Revivalism, The Gospel Songs and Social Reforms," *Journal of the Society of Ethnomusicology* 9:115-125, 1965.

Downes, Olin, "An American Composer," *Musical Quarterly* January, 1918, pp. 23-36. [About Henry F. Gilbert.]

DruA   Drummond, Robert R., "Alexander Reinagle and His Connection with the Musical Life of Philadelphia," *German-American Annals* 5:294-306, 1907.

DwiJ   Dwight, John Sullivan, (ed), *Dwight's Journal of Music*, February, 1853.

Edwards, Arthur C., *The Art of Melody*, New York: Philosophical Library, 1956.

—————, *Practical Lessons in Melody-Writing*, Dubuque, Iowa: Wm. C. Brown Company Publishers, 1963.

EllinR   Ellinwood, Leonard, *Religious Perspectives in American Culture*, Princeton: *Princeton University Press*, 1961, pp. 289-359.

ElsH   Elson, Louis C., *The History of American Music*, New York: The Macmillan Company, 1904, rev. ed., 1915 (New ed. revised by Arthur Elson, 1925.)

EngC Engel, Carl, "George W. Chadwick," *Musical Quarterly* 10:438-457, July, 1924.

————, "Charles Martin Loeffler," *International Cyclopedia of Music and Musicians*, 9th ed., 1964, p. 1226.

Erskine, John, "Edward MacDowell," *Dictionary of American Biography*, 12:24-27, 1928.

Est, Thomas, *The Whole Booke of Psalmes*, London, 1592.

Ewen, David, *American Composers Today*, New York: The H. W. Wilson Co., 1949.

EweM ————, *Music Comes to America*, New York: Allen, Towne & Heath, Inc., 1947.

EweP ————, *History of Popular Music*, New York: Barnes & Noble, Inc., 1961.

Farwell, Arthur, "Roy Harris," *Musical Quarterly* 18:18-32, January, 1932.

FauA Faulkner, H. U., *American Political and Social History*, New York: F. S. Crofts & Co., Inc., 1941.

FayG Fay, Amy, *Music Study in Germany*, Chicago, 1881.

FinH Finkelstein, Sidney, *How Music Expresses Ideas*, New York: International Publishers Co., Inc., 1952.

FisN Fisher, Miles M., *Negro Slave Songs in the United States*, Ithaca, N.Y.: Cornell University Press, 1953.

FisY Fisher, William Arms, *Ye Olde New England Psalm Tunes (1620-1820), with Historical Sketch.* Boston: Oliver Ditson Company, 1930.

Flagg, Josiah, *A Collection of the Best Psalm Tunes*, Boston, 1764.

Fletcher, Alice C., *Indian Story and Song from North America*, Boston: Small, Maynard & Co., 1900.

FleO ————, "A Study of Omaha Indian Music, with a Report on the Structural Peculiarities of the Music by John Comfort Fillmore," *Archaeological and Ethnological Papers of the Peabody Museum* 1:5, 1893.

FooT Foote, Henry W., *Three Centuries of American Hymnody*, Cambridge, Mass.: Harvard University Press, 1940.

ForJ Ford, Paul L., *The Writings of Thomas Jefferson*, ed. Paul L. Ford, New York: G. P. Putnam's Sons, 1892.

FosS Foster, Morrison, *Songs and Musical Compositions of Stephen Collins Foster*, Pittsburgh, 1896.

Frankenstein, Alfred, "William Schuman," *Modern Music* November/December, 1944, pp. 23-29.

FraQ Franklin, Benjamin, *Quatour pour 3 violons et violoncelle, transcription de Guillaume de Van*, Paris: Odette Lieutier, 1946.

French-Genevan Psalter, *Trente quatre pseaumes*, Geneva, 1551.

Funk, Joseph, *Genuine Church Music*, Mountain Valley, Va., 1832.

FurP   Furnivall, F. J., *Phillip Stubbe's Anatomy of the Abuses in Eng-
            land in Shakespeare's Youth*, London: N. Trubner & Co.,
            1877.

GerJ   Gershwin, George, "The Relation of Jazz to American Music"
            in Henry Cowell (ed.), *American Composers on Ameri-
            can Music*, Stanford: Stanford University Press, 1933,
            pp. 186-187.
            Glenn, R. A., *The Pleasant Hour, Philadelphia*, 1883.

GolL   Goldman, Richard Franko, *Landmarks of Early American
            Music, 1760-1800*, New York: G. Schirmer, Inc., 1943.
            Goss, Madeleine, *Modern Music-makers: Contemporary Ameri-
            can Composers*, New York: E. P. Dutton & Co., Inc.,
            1952.

GottN   Gottschalk, Louis M., *Notes of a Pianist* ed. Clara Gottschalk,
            Philadelphia: J. B. Lippincott Co., 1881.

GoulH   Gould, Nathaniel D., *History of Church Music in America*,
            Boston: A. N. Johnson, 1853.
            Grof, Herbert, *Opera and Its Future in America*, New York:
            W. W. Norton & Company, Inc., 1941.
            Handy, W. C. (ed.), *A Treasury of the Blues*, with an historical
            and critical text by Abbe Niles, New York: Charles
            Boni; distributed by Simon & Schuster, 1949.
            Harrison, Thomas, *The Sacred Harmonicon*, Cincinnati, 1845.
            Hearn, Lafcadio, *American Miscellany*, articles collected by Al-
            bert Mordell, 2 vols. New York: Dodd, Mead & Co.,
            1924.
            Hecht, Simon, *Jewish Hymns for Sabbath Schools and Families*,
            New York: Bloch Printing Co., 1896.

HiggH   Higginson, J. Vincent, "Hymnody in the American Indian Mis-
            sions," *Papers of the Hymn Society* 18:3-39, 1954.
            Hill, Richard S., "Schoenberg's Tone-Rows and the Music of
            the Future," *Musical Quarterly* 22:14-37, January, 1936.

Hil-IsaE   Hiller, Lejaren A. Jr., and Isaacson, Leonard M., *Experimental
            Music: Composition with an Electronic Computer*, New
            York: McGraw-Hill Book Company, Inc., 1959.

HodJ   Hodeir, André, *Jazz: Its Evolution and Essence*, translated by
            David Noakes, New York: Grove Press, Inc., 1956.
            Hood, George, *History of Music in New England*, Boston: Wil-
            kins, Carter, and Co., 1846.
            Hopkinson, Francis, *A Collection of Psalm Tunes*, Philadelphia,
            1753.
            ————, *Seven Songs for the Harpsichord or Forte Piano*,
            Philadelphia, 1788; modern facsimile edition by Harry
            Dichter, Philadelphia: Musical Americana, 1954.

HorB   Horan, Robert, "Samuel Barber," *Modern Music*, November/
            June, 1942-1943, pp. 161-169.

HowA   Howard, John Tasker, *Our American Music: Three Hundred
            Years of It*, 3rd ed., rev., New York: Thomas Y. Crowell
            Company, 1941.

————, *Our Contemporary Composers: American Music in the Twentieth Century,* New York: Thomas Y. Crowell Company, 1941.

HowP ————, *A Program of Early American Piano Pieces,* New York: J. Fisher and Brother, 1931.

————, *Charles Sanford Skilton,* New York: Carl Fischer, Inc., 1929.

How-BelM ———— and Bellows, George Kent, *Music in America,* New York: Thomas Y. Crowell Company, 1957.

Howe, M. A. De Wolfe, "John Knowles Paine," *Musical Quarterly* 25:257-267, July, 1939.

Hymns of Jesus Christ of Latter-day Saints, Kirtland, Ohio, 1835.

JacSF Jackson, George P., *Spiritual Folk-Songs of Early America,* Locust Valley, N.Y.: J. J. Augustin, Inc. — Publisher, 1937.

JacSW ————, *Another Sheaf of White Spirituals,* Gainesville, Fla.: University of Florida Press, 1952.

JacWN ————, White and Negro Spirituals, Locust Valley, N.Y.: J. J. Augustin, Inc. — Publisher, 1943.

JacWS ————, *White Spirituals in Southern Uplands,* Chapel Hill: University of North Carolina Press, 1933.

JohM Johnson, H. Earle, *Musical Interludes in Boston, 1795-1830,* New York: Columbia University Press, 1943.

JohR ————, "The Need for Research in the History of American Music," *Journal of Research in Music Education* 6:43-61, 1958.

Johnston, Thomas, *A Supplement to the New Version,* Boston, 1755.

KalMC Kallmann, Helmut, *A History of Music in Canada,* Toronto: University of Toronto Press, 1960.

KemJ Kemble, Frances Anne, *Journal of a Residence on a Georgian Plantation, 1838-39.*

Kolodin, Irving, *The Story of the Metropolitan Opera, 1883-1950. A Candid History,* New York: Alfred A. Knopf, Inc., 1953.

KreE Křenek, Ernst, "Extents and Limits of Serial Techniques," *Problems of Modern Music,* ed., Paul Henry Lang, New York: W. W. Norton & Company, Inc., 1962, pp. 72-94.

————, "New Development in Electronic Music," *Musical America* 75:8, September, 1955.

LanI Lang, Paul Henry, ed., "Introduction," *Problems of Modern Music,* New York: W. W. Norton & Company, Inc., 1962, pp. 7-16.

Langley, Allen L., "George Chadwick and the New England Conservatory of Music," *Musical Quarterly* 21:39-52, January, 1935.

LawM   Law, Andrew, *The Musical Primer, or the First Part of the Art of Singing*, New Haven, Conn., 1780.

Fry, Gilchrist, Gleason, Paine, Pratt.

Leonard, Silas, *The Christian Psalmist*, Louisville, Ky., 1850.

LogW   Loggins, Vernon, *Where the Word Ends*, Baton Rouge, La.: Louisiana State University Press, 1958.

LowB   Lowens, Irving, "The Bay Psalm Book in 17th Century New England," *Journal of the American Musicological Society* 8:22-29, 1955.

LowJ   —————, "John Wyeth's Repository of Sacred Music, Part Second: A Northern Precursor of Southern Folk Hymnody," *Journal of the American Musicological Society* 5:114-131, Summer, 1952.

LowM   —————, *Music and Musicians in Early America*, New York: W. W. Norton & Company, Inc., 1964.

LowO   —————, "The Origins of the American Fuging Tune," *Journal of the American Musicological Society* 6:43-52, Spring, 1953.

LueM   Luening, Otto, "Douglas Moore," *Modern Music* May/June, 1943, pp. 248-253.

Lyon, James, *Urania*, Philadelphia, 1762.

MacE   MacDougall, Hamilton C., *Early New England Psalmody, 1620-1820*, Brattleboro, N. H.: Stephen Daye Press, 1940.

MacS   Macknerness, E. D., *A Social History of English Music*, London: Routledge and Kegan Paul, Ltd., 1964.

MarE   Maren, R., "Electronic Music: Untouched by Human Hands," *The Reporter*, April 18, 1957, pp. 40-42.

MarM   —————, "Music by Montage and Mixing," *The Reporter*, October 6, 1955, pp. 38-42.

Marr N   Marrocco, W. Thomas, "The Notation in American Sacred Music Collections," *Acta Musicologica* 36:136-142, 1964, facsimile 2 and 3.

MarrSP   —————, "The Set Piece," *Journal of the American Musicological Society* 15:348-352, 1962.

Ma-GlA   —————, and Gleason, H., *Music in America* — An Anthology, New York: W. W. Norton & Company, Inc., 1964.

Mason, Daniel G., "Arthur Whiting," *Musical Quarterly* 23:26-36, January, 1937.

—————, *Music in My Time, and Other Reminiscences*, New York: The Macmillan Company, 1938.

Mason, Lowell, *The Boston Handel and Haydn Collection of Church Music*, 10th ed., Boston: Richardson, Lord and Holbrook, 1831.

—————, *Lyra Sacra*, Boston, 1832.

—————, *Sacred Harp or Eclectic Harmony*, Cincinnati, 1835.

Mattfeld, Julius, *A Hundred Years of Grand Opera in New York (1825-1925)*, New York: The New York Public Library, 1927.

Matthews, J. Brauder, *Commemorative Tributes to Edward MacDowell*, New York: American Academy of Arts and Letters, 1922.

Maurer, Maurer, "The 'Professor of Musick' in Colonial America," *Musical Quarterly* 36:511-524, October, 1950.

McAll McAllester, David P., *Indian Music in the Southwest*, Colorado Springs: The Taylor Museum, Colorado Springs Fine Arts Center, 1961.

McCracken, D. D., "The Monte Carlo Method," *Scientific American* 192:90-96, May, 1955.

McMC McMaster, Ann H., "Creole Songs," *International Cyclopedia of Music and Musicians*, 9th ed., 1964, pp. 715-16.

Mennonite Hymnary, Newton, Kansas: Board of Publication of the General Conference of the Mennonite Church of North America, 1940.

Metcalf, Frank J., *American Psalmody (1721-1820)*, New York: C. F. Hartman, 1917.

MetA ————, *American Writers and Compilers of Sacred Music*, New York: Abingdon Press, 1925.

MeyM Meyer, Sheldon, "Modern Jazz," in Rex Harris, *The Story of Jazz*, New York: Grosset & Dunlap, Inc., Publishers, 1960, pp. 245-261.

Mezzrow, Milton and Wolfe, Bernard, *Really the Blues*, New York: Random House, Inc., 1946.

MilP Milligan, Harold V., *Pioneer American Composers. A Collection of Early American Songs*, 2 vols., Boston: Arthur P. Schmidt Company, 1921.

Montani, Nicola, *The St. Gregory Hymnal*, Philadelphia: St. Gregory Guild, 1920.

MulB Muller, Joseph, *Bibliography of Francis Scott Key's The Star Spangled Banner*, New York: G. A. Baker & Company, Inc., 1935.

NatD Nathan, Hans, "Dixie," *Musical Quarterly* 35:60-84, January, 1949.

NefO Nef, Karl, *Outline of the History of Music*, New York: Columbia University Press, 1939.

NetI Nettl, Bruno, *An Introduction to Folk Music in the United States*, Detroit: Wayne State University Press, 1962.

NYMC *New York Musical Courier*, May, 1899, pp. 10-17.

Ol-BelE Olson, H. F. and Belar, H., "Electronic Music Synthesizer," *Journal of American Acoustical Society* 27:595-612, May, 1955.

Original Sacred Harp, Denison rev., Haleyville, Ala.: Sacred Harp Publishing Co., Inc., 1936.

PMB *Parish Mass Book*, Cincinnati: World Library of Sacred Music, 1959.

Parsons, William, *The Whole Psalmes in Foure Partes*, London, 1563.

Partch, Harry, *Genesis of a Music*, Madison: The University of Wisconsin Press, 1949.

PicM   Picchieri, Louis, *Music in New Hampshire*, New York: Columbia University Press, 1960.

Pinkerton, R. C., "Information Theory and Melody," *Scientific American* 194:77-86, February, 1956.

Piston, Walter, "Roy Harris," *Modern Music*, January/February, 1934, pp. 71-83.

Pius X Hymnal, Boston: McLaughlin & Reilly Co., 1953.

PlaI   Playford, John, *An Introduction to the Skill of Musick*, 11th ed., London, 1687.

PraM   Pratt, Waldo Selden, *The Music of the French Psalter of 1562*, New York: Columbia University Press, 1939.

PraM   ————, *The Music of the Pilgrims*, Boston: Oliver Ditson Company, 1921.

Proceedings of the Musical Convention Assembled in Boston, August 16 1838. Boston: Kidder and Wright, 1838.

PutM   *Putnam's Monthly Magazine*, I (Feb., June, Oct., 1853).

RavW   Ravenscroft, Thomas, *The Whole Booke of Psalmes: With the Hymnes Evangellical and Songs Spirituall. Composed into four parts by Sundry Authors*, London, 1621.

Redway, Virginia Larkin, "The Carrs, American Music Publishers," *Musical Quarterly* 18:150-157, January, 1932.

ReeR   Reese, Gustave, *Music in the Renaissance*, New York: W. W. Norton & Company, Inc., 1954.

Reis, Claire, *Composers in America; Biographical Sketches of Contemporary Composers with a Record of Their Works*, rev. ed., New York: The Macmillan Company, 1947.

RicS   Rich, Allen, "Karlheinz Stockhausen," *Cyclopedia of Music and Musicians*, 9th ed., 1964, pp. 2113-2117.

RitM   Ritter, Frederick Louis, *Music in America*, New York: Charles Scribner's Sons, 1883.

Roberts, Helen H., *Form in Primitive Music*, New York: W.W. Norton & Company, Inc., 1933.

RosH   Rosenfeld, Paul, *An Hour with American Music*, Philadelphia: J. B. Lippincott Company, 1929.

RoyH   Royce, Edward, "Howard Hanson," *American Composers on American Music*, ed., Henry Cowell, Stanford: Stanford University Press, 1933, pp. 97-100.

SacM   Sachse, Julius F., *Music of the Ephrata Cloister*, Lancaster, Pa.: Published by the author, 1903.

SacJ   ————, *The Journal of Johannes Kelpius, Magister of the Hermits of the Ridge in Pennsylvania 1694-1708*, Philadelphia, 1893.

SarJ   Sargent, Winthrop, *Jazz: A History*, original title: *Jazz: Hot and Hybrid*, New York: McGraw-Hill Book Company, 1964.

SchoP   Scholes, Percy A., *The Puritans and Music in England and New England*, New York: Oxford University Press, 1934.

Schubart, Mark A., "Roger Sessions," *Musical Quarterly* 32:196-214, April, 1946.

Scottish Psalter, *The CL Psalmes of David,* Edinburgh, 1615.

SeeC   Seeger, Charles, "Contrapuntal Style in the Three-Voice Shape-Note Hymns," *Musical Quarterly* 26:483-493, October, 1940.

SeeR   —————, "Carl Ruggles," *Musical Quarterly* 18:578-592, October, 1932.

Sessions, Roger, *The Musical Experience of Composer, Performer, Listener,* Princeton, N. J.: Princeton University Press, 1950.

SesP   —————, "Problems and Issues Facing the Composer Today," Paul Henry Lang, ed., *Problems of Modern Music,* New York: W. W. Norton & Company, Inc., 1962, pp. 21-33.

SesR   —————, *Reflections on the Music Life in the United States,* New York: Merlin Press, 1956.

SewD   Sewall, Samuel, *Diary,* Boston: Massachusetts Historical Society, 1878-1882.

Seward, Theodore, *The Church Praise Book,* New York and Chicago, 1888.

Skilton, Charles S., "American Indian Music," *International Cyclopedia of Music and Musicians,* 9th ed., 1964, pp. 46-48.

Skulsky, Abraham, "Arnold Schoenberg," *Musical America,* 5:34, September, 1951.

Slonimsky, Nicolas, *Music Since 1900,* 3rd ed., revised, New York: Coleman-Ross Co., Inc., 1949.

—————. "Roy Harris," *Musical Quarterly* 33:17-37, January, 1947.

SmiE   Smith, Carleton Sprague, *Early Psalmody in America. Series I. The Ainsworth Psalter,* Psalm 65 settings by Claude Goudimel, New York: The New York Public Library, 1938.

Smith, Cecil, *Musical Comedy in America,* New York: Theatre Arts Books, 1950.

Smith, David Stanley, "A Study of Horatio Parker," *Musical Quarterly* 16:153-169, April, 1930.

Smith, W. and W. Little, *The Easy Instructor,* New York, 1802.

SonB   Sonneck, Oscar G., *Bibliography of Early American Secular Music,* Washington, D. C.: H. L. McQueen, 1905; revised and enlarged by William Treat Upton, Washington, D. C.: The Library of Congress, 1945.

SonE   —————, *Early Concert Life in America,* Leipzig: Breitkopf & Härtel, 1907.

SonO   —————, *Early Opera in America,* New York: G. Schirmer, Inc., 1915.

SonS   —————, *The Star-Spangled Banner,* revised and enlarged from the report of 1909, Washington, D. C.: Library of Congress, Government Printing Office, 1914.

SowM   Sower, David, *Musical Teacher*, Norristown, Pa., 1832.
             Spaeth, Sigmund, *A History of Popular Music in America*, New
                  York: Random House, Inc., 1948.
StarL   Starke, Aubrey H., *Sidney Lanier: A Biographical and Critical
                  Study*, Chapel Hill: The University of North Carolina
                  Press, 1933.
             —————, "Sidney Lanier as a Musician," *Musical Quarterly*
                  20:384-400, October, 1934.
             Sternhold and Hopkins, *The Whole Booke of Psalmes*, London,
                  1562.
SteP   Stevenson, Robert M., *Patterns of Protestant Church Music*,
                  Durham, N. C.: Duke University Press, 1953.
             Tans'ur, William, *The Royal Melody Compleat*, London, 1734.
             Tate and Brady, *A Supplement to the New Version of the
                  Psalms of David*, London, 1700.
             Thomson, Virgil, "George Gershwin," *Modern Music*, Novem-
                  ber/December, 1935, pp. 13-19.

ThoR   —————, *Music, Right and Left*, New York: Henry Holt and
                  Co., Inc., 1951.
             Thorpe, Harry C., "Sidney Lanier: A Poet for Musicians,"
                  Musical Quarterly 11:373-382, July, 1925.
             Tozer, J. Edmunds, *Catholic Church Hymnal*, New York: J.
                  Fischer & Bros., 1905.
TudN   Tudor, Henry, *Narrative of a Tour in North America*, London,
                  1834.
TufV   Tufts, John, *A Very Plain and Easy Introduction to the Singing
                  of Psalm Tunes*, 5th ed., Boston, 1726. Modern Facsimile
                  edition by Harry Dichter, Philadelphia: Musical Ameri-
                  cana, 1954.
             Tuthill, Burnet C., "Mrs. H. H. A. Beach," *Musical Quarterly*
                  26:297-310, July, 1940.
TutH   —————, "Howard Hanson," *Musical Quarterly* 22:140-153,
                  April, 1936.
             Ulanov, Barry, *A History of Jazz in America*, New York: The
                  Viking Press, Inc., 1952.

             Union Hymnal, New York, 1897.
             Upton, William Treat, *Anthony Philip Heinrich*, New York:
                  Columbia University Press, 1939.
             —————, *William Henry Fry, American Journalist and Com-
                  poser-Critic*, New York: Thomas Y. Crowell Company,
                  1954.

VanP   Van Tassel, T., *The Phonographic Harmonist*, Syracuse, 1846.

WalC   Walker, William, *The Christian Harmony*, Spartanburg, S. C.,
                  1866.
WalS   —————, *The Southern Harmony*, Philadephia: E. W. Miller,
                  1854.

WalG   Walter, Thomas, *The Grounds and Rules of Music Explained* or
            An Introduction to the Art of Singing by Note, Boston:
            Printed by J. Franklin for S. Gerrish, near the Brick
            Church in Cornhill, 1721.
WesC   Wesley, John, *A Collection of Psalms and Hymns,* Charlestown,
            S. C.: Printed by L. Timothy, 1737.
WKSH   White, B. F. and King, E. J., *The Sacred Harp,* 1844; repub-
            lished as *The Original Sacred Harp,* Atlanta: United
            Harp Musical Association, 1911.
            Wilgus, Donald K., *Anglo-American Folk Song Scholarship
            Since 1898,* New Brunswick, N. J.: Rutgers University
            Press, 1959.
WitT   Wittke, Carl, *Tambo and Bones, a History of the American
            Minstrel Stage,* Durham, N. C.: Duke University Press,
            1930.
            Wyeth, John, *Repository of Sacred Music Part Second,* Harris-
            burgh, Penn., 1820.

index

Academy of Music (New York), 62, 63
Ainsworth, Henry, 5
Ainsworth Psalter, 5, 6, 102
Alda, Frances, 63
American College of Musicians, 56
American Conservatory, 55
American History: Ballads, 148
American Recording Society, 64
Anglicans, 20
Antes, John, 20, 146
Antheil, George, 129, 156
Anthem, 13
"Archers, The" (Carr), 17
Armstrong, Louis, 89
Arne, Thomas, 14
Atonality, 132

Babbitt, Milton, 134, 135, 139, 157, 158
Bacon, Ernest, 107
Baker, Theodore, 66
Bales, Richard, 147
Baltimore Symphony, 60
Bands, 60
    Gilmore, 39, 58
    Goldman, 149
    Sousa, 149, 150
Barber, Samuel, 113, 155
Barbirolli, Sir John, 58
Barry, Philip, 70
Bartók, Béla, x, 111, 120
Basie, William "Count", 89
"Battle Hymn of the Republic, The," 39
Bay Psalm Book, 6, 8
Bayley, Daniel, 10
Beach, H. H. A., 51, 148
Becker, John J., 128
Beggar's Opera, 13

Beissel, Conrad, 21
Belcher, Supply, 12
Belknap, Daniel, 12
Bellamann, Henry, 124
Berger, Arthur, 121
Berlin, Irving, 79, 116
Berliner, Emile, 64
Bernstein, Leonard, 58, 114, 115, 117, 155
Billings, William, 12, 57, 145
Bing, Rudolph, 63
Blitzstein, Marc, 115
Bloch, Ernest, 27, 98, 118, 153
Blues, 79
    Afro-American Influence, 79, 80
    Boogie-Woogie, 82
    Musical Instruments, 82
    Organization, 80, 81
    Performers, 82
    Records, 152
    Rhythm, 80
    Tonal Elements, 80
Bolden, Charles "Buddy," 89
Boogie-Woogie, 82
Borowski, Felix, 104
Boston News Letter, 10
Boston Opera, 63
Boston Symphony, 58
Bowles, Paul, 121
Bradbury, William, 54
Brennecke, Ernest, 3
"Brief Introduction to the Skill of Music" (John Playford), 7
Bristow, George Frederick, 43, 148
Bronson, Bertrand Harris, 70, 72
Brown, William, 145
Browning, John, 64
Brunswick, Mark, 128

Buchanan, Annabel, 70
Buck, Dudley, 44, 148
Budapest String Quartet, 64
Bull, Ole, 41
"Bunker Hill," 13
Burke, Edmund, 14
Burleigh, Henry T., 97
Burton, Frederick, 66

Cadman, Charles Wakefield, 93, 153
Cage, John, 130, 138, 156, 158
Cakewalk, 73, 78
Calinda, 73
Calvé, Emma, 62
Calvin, John, 3
Calvinistic Puritans, 4
Carpenter, John Alden, 45, 104, 154
Carr, Benjamin, 17, 18
Carter, Elliott, 121
Cartier, Jacques, 2
Caruso, Enrico, 62
Casals, Pablo, 64
Catholics, 20
    Hymnals, 25, 26
Cennick, John, 12, 30
Chadwick, George W., 48, 148
Chaliapin, Feodor, 63
Charleston (S.C.), 14
Chauncey, Nathaniel, 8
"Chester," 13
Chicago Musical College, 55
Chicago Opera, 63
Chicago Symphony, 59
Childs, Francis James, 70, 72
Choral Societies, 57, 58
Christensen, Alex, 79
Christy, Byron, 94
Cincinnati Conservatory, 55
Cincinnati Opera, 63
Civil War Ballads, 147, 148
Cleveland Symphony, 60
Cliburn, Van, 64
Cohan, George M., 116
"Collection of Psalms and Hymns"
    (Wesley), 12
Columbia (Records), 64
Common Way, 7
Cone, Edward T., 132, 133
Conried, Heinrich, 62
Contredanse, 73
Converse, Charles C., 37, 45
Converse, Frederick Shepherd, 112
Copland, Aaron, 106, 107, 154
Cortot, Alfred, 64
Covey, Cyclone, 4
Cowell, Henry, 126, 128, 129, 156
Cowper, William, 12
Creston, Paul, 121, 155
Curtis Institute of Music, 55
Curtis, Natalie, 66

Dahl, Ingolf, 121
Damon's Psalter, 22
Damrosch, Frank, 55
Damrosch, Leopold, 62
Damrosch, Walter, 58, 105
Datheen, Peter, 2
Davis, Miles, 89
Davis, Ronald, 60, 61
Day, Charles, 94
Day, John, 26
"Death Song of an Indian Chief," 18
"Death Song of Cherokee Indian," 17
De Koven, Reginald, 116
Dello Joio, Norman, 120, 121, 155
De Luca, Giuseppe, 63
Dencke, Jeremiah, 146
Densmore, Frances, 66
Detroit Symphony, 60
Diamond, David, 120, 155
Dicho, 73
Digital Computer Music, 140
    Freedom of Choice, 141
    Future Musical Uses, 141
    Information Theory, 140
    Justification in use of, 140
    Monte Carlo Theory, 140, 141
    Objections to use of, 141
    Organization Process, 140
"Dixie's Land," 39
Dixon, Geo. Washington, 94
Doolittle, Eliakim, 12
Doremi Notation, 33
Dorsey, Tommy, 89
Dukelsky, Vladimir (Duke, Vernon),
    121
Dunster, Henry Rev., 7
Dutch (influence), 2
Dvorak's influence, 97
Dwight's Musical Journal, 96

Eastman Rochester Symphony, 64
Eastman School of Music, 55, 112, 120
Easton, Florence, 63
Eckhard, Jacob, 18
Edison (records), 64
Edson, Lewis, 12
Edwards, Jonathan, 11, 35
Elektronische Musik, (See Musique Con-
    crète)
Ellington, Edward "Duke," 89
Ellinwood, Leonard, 2
Elliott, John, 6
Elman, Mischa, 64
Elson, Louis C., 48
Emmett, Daniel Decatur, 39, 94
English (influence), 2
Est, Thomas, 2, 22
Euterpean Society (N.Y.C.), 57
Ewen, David, ix

Farrar, Geraldine, 62
Farwell, Arthur, 92, 153
Fasola, Notation, 30, 31, 32, 33
Father Cristobal de Quinones, 1
Father Duran, 2
Father Jean Enjalran, 2
Father Juniper Serra, 1
Fay, Amy, 96
Fine, Irving, 121
Finkelstein, Sidney, ix, 77
Finney, Ross Lee, 101, 102, 135, 154
Fisher, William Arms, 97
Flagstad, Kirsten, 63
Fletcher, Alice C., 44, 66
Folk Hymns, 30
Folk Music, 69
    Composite Category, 72, 73
    Creole Songs, 73, 150
    Definition, 69
    English-Scottish-Irish influences, 69
    Harmony, 71
    Instruments, 74, 75
    Investigations, 69
    Native Song, 72, 151
    Old World Ballads, 72, 151
    Organization, 74
    Other influences, 69
    Rhythm, 71
    Scales, 70
    Spanish-Mexican-American Songs, 73, 150
    Stages of Development, 71
    Transposition, 70
Folksy Religious Songs, 29
Folkways (records), 64
Foote, Arthur, 45, 47, 149
Foss, Lukas, 115, 130, 131, 155, 156
Foster, Stephen Collins, 95, 154
Four-Syllable Notation, 30
Franceschini, Gaetano, 145
Franklin, Benjamin, 14
Franklin, James, 9
French (influence), 2
French, Jacob, 12
Friml, Rudolph, 116
Fry, William Henry, 42, 148
Fuging Tune, 12

Gabrilowitsch, Ossip, 59, 60
Garden, Mary, 63
Gatti-Gasazza, Giulio, 62, 63
Gehot, Jean, 17, 145
Geneva Psalter, 6, 22
"Genuine Church Music" (Joseph Funk), 30
Gericke, Wilhelm, 59
Germania Musical Society, 41
Gershwin, George, 105, 106, 107, 117, 154
Getz, Stan, 89

Gilbert, Henry Franklin Belknap, 93, 97, 154
Gilchrist, William Wallace, 46, 59
Gillespie, "Dizzy," 89
Gillis, Don, 107
Gilman, Benjamin Ives, 66
Gilmore, Patrick (Louis Lambert), 39, 58, 60
Gleason, Frederick Grant, 45
Gloria Dei Church, 22
"Glory, Hallelujah," 39
Goeb, Roger, 115
Goetchius, Percy, 50
Gold Rush Songs, 149
Goodman, Benny, 89
Goosens, Eugene, 60
Gordon, R. W., 70
Gospel Songs, 147
Gottschalk, Louis Moreau, 96, 154
Gould, Morton, 154
Gram, Hans, 18, 145
Graupner, Gottlieb, 18
Griffes, Charles Tomlinson, 117, 118, 155
Grofé, Ferde, 105
Gruenberg, Louis, 105, 154
Gualdo, Giovanni, 16, 145
Guion, David, 107
Gummere, Francis B., 70

Habanera, 73
Hagen, van Peter A., 17, 146
Hail Columbia (Phile), 18, 39
Hammerstein, Oscar, 63, 117
Hampton, Lionel, 89
Handel and Haydn Choral Society, 18, 57, 58
Handy, William C., 82
Hanson, Howard, 64, 112, 113, 156
Harney, Ben R., 79
Harp Singers (Sacred, Old), 147
Harris, Roy, 77, 102, 103, 126, 155
Harrison, Lou, 135, 157
Harvard University, 55
Hastings, Thomas, 53
Hecht, Simon, 26
Heifetz, Jascha, 64
Heinrich, Anton Philip, 91, 92
Hempel, Frieda, 63
Henderson, Fletcher, 89
Henschel, George, 59
Herbert, Victor, 116
Herbst, Johannes, 146
Herman, Woody, 89
Hess, Myra, 64
Hewitt, James, 17, 18, 39, 57
Hewitt, John Hill, 40, 146
Higginson, Henry Lee, 58, 59
Hill, Bertha "Chippie," 82
Hill, Edward Burlingame, 50, 51, 149
Hill, Ureli Corelli, 58

Hiller, Lejaren A., Jr., 140
Hindemith, Paul, x, 111, 122, 134
Hodeir, André, 89, 90
Hoffman, Richard, 148
Hofmann, Josef, 64
Holden, Oliver, 12, 18
Holyoke, Samuel, 12, 18
Homer, Louise, 63
Hopkinson, Francis, 2, 14, 33, 145
Hopkinson, Joseph, 39
Horan, Robert, 114
Horn, Charles, 40
Horowitz, Vladimir, 64
Hovhannes, Alan, 121
Howard, John Tasker, 108
Howe, Julia Ward, 39
Hudson, Henry, 2
Huguenots, 2
Hymns and Psalms (Watts), 11, 12

Impressionism, 110
Indian Tribal Music, 66
    Conflicting Rhythms, 68
    General Characteristics, 66
    Instruments, 68
    Investigations, 66
    Organization, 68
    Records, 150
    Rhythm, 67
    Tonal Elements, 67
Indianapolis Symphony, 60
Ingalls, Jeremiah, 12
Institute of Musical Art (N.Y.C.), 55
Instrumental Virtuosi, 64
Isaacson, Leonard M., 140
Ives, Charles Edward, 123, 124, 157

Jackson, Anthony, 79
Jackson, George K., 18, 146
Jackson, Geo. Pullen, 30, 70
Jacobi, Frederick, 93, 154
James, Harry, 89
Jazz, 82
    Bebop, Cool, Progressive, 87, 153
    Classic Style, 86, 153
    Composite Improvisational Style, 82
    Influences, 89, 90
    Instruments, 88, 89
    Organization, 84, 85, 86
    Performers, 89
    Periods of Development, 83
    Records (General), 152
    Rhythm, 83, 84
    Sweet Style, 86, 87, 153
    Tonal Elements, 83
Jefferson, Thomas, 13
Jenks, Stephen, 12
Jeritza, Maria, 63
Jewish Hymnals, 26, 27
"Jim Crow," 94
Johnson, Edward, 63
Johnson, James P., 79

Johnston, Thomas, 10
Joplin, Scott, 79
Juilliard School of Music, 55, 126
Juilliard String Quartet, 64
Jullien, Louis Antoine, 42

Kellner, J. P., 146
Kelly, Edgar Stillman, 115
Kelpius, Johannes, 22
Ken, Bishop, 27
Kenton, Stan, 89
"Kentucky Harmony" (Ananias Davisson), 30
Keppard, Freddie, 89
Kern, Jerome, 116
Kerr, Harrison, 135, 157
Key, Francis Scott, 38
Kimball, Jacob, 12
King, James I., 1
Kirchner, Leon, 135, 157
Kittredge, Geo. L., 70
Kittredge, Walter, 39
Knight, Joseph, 40
Koussevitsky, Sergei, 59, 114
Kreisler, Fritz, 64
Kremenliev, Boris, 107
Křenek, Ernst, 134, 138
Krueger, Karl, 65
Krupa, Gene, 89

Laine, Jack "Papa," 89
Lang, Paul Henry, 133, 139
Lanier, Sidney, 44, 148
Law, Andrew, 12, 32
Leadbetter, Huddie, 82
Leaumont, Chev. Marie Robert de, 18, 146
Lee, Phillip L., 16
Lehmann, Lilli, 62
Leinbach, Edward W., 146
Leinsdorf, Erich, 59
Leland, John, 30
Lerner, Allen, 117
Lind, Jenny, 41, 61
Little, William, 32
Loeffler, Charles Martin, 49, 149
Loewe, Frederick, 117
Lomax, Allan, 76
Lomax, John A., 70
Loomis, Harvey W., 97
Los Angeles Philharmonic, 60
Los Pastores, 73
Lowens, Irving, 7, 29
Luening, Otto, 100, 101, 137, 138
Lutherans, 20
Lyon, James, 39
Lyon, Richard, 7

MacDowell, Edward, ix, 51, 52, 149
Mackerness, E. D., 3
Manhattan Opera House, 63
Mapleson, James Henry, 62

"Marching Through Georgia," 39
Martinelli, Giovanni, 63
Mason, Daniel Gregory, 45, 50, 149
Mason, Lowell, 33, 39, 53, 54, 55
Mason, William, 44, 148
"Massachusetts Compiler," 18
Mather, Cotton, 3, 8
Mather, Robert, 6
McDonald, Harl, 115
McKay, George, 107
Medley, Samuel, 27
Melba, Nellie, 62
Mengelberg, Willem, 58
Mennin, Peter, 115, 156
Mennonite Hymnary, 1940, 22
Mennonite, 20, 21
Menotti, Gian-Carlo, 113, 156
Menuhin, Yehudi, 64
Merulo, Gaetano, 63
"Messiah," 18
Metropolitan Opera House, 62, 63
Meyer, Sheldon, 87, 88
Michael, David Moritz, 21, 147
"Mighty Lak A Rose," 51
Milhaud, Darius, 27
Miller, Glen, 89
Milton, John, 3
Minneapolis Symphony, 60
Minstrel Show Music, 93
"Missouri Harmony" (Allen D. Carden),
    30
Moller, John, 17, 146
Montani, Nicola, 25
Monte Carlo Theory, 140, 141
Moody, Dwight L., 37
Moore, Douglas, 100, 155
Moravians, 20
Moravian Music Foundation, 20
Morgan, Justin, 12
Morgan, W. S., 16
Morley, Thomas, 3
Mormons, 27
    Folk Songs, 146
    Hymnal, 27
Morton, Ferdinand "Jelly Roll," 79, 89
Muck, Karl, 59
Müller, Georg, 147
Music Teachers National Association, 56
Musical Fund Society (Phila.), 57
Musique Concrète, 136
    Advantages of, 138
    Basic Techniques, 136
    Disadvantages of, 138, 139
    Experimentation, 136
    Preliminary Steps to Composing, 137
    Records, 158
    Sequential Steps to Composing, 137
"My Country 'Tis of Thee," 39

National Symphony, 60
"Nearer My God to Thee," 53
Neo-classicism, 110, 111

Neo-romanticism, 109, 110
Negro Music, 75
    Melodic Structure, 76
    Musical Heritage, 77
    Records, 150, 151
    Types of Songs, 76
Nevin, Arthur, 93
Nevin, Ethelbert, 51, 149
New England Conservatory, 55
New Orleans Opera, 60, 61
Newton, John, 12, 30
"New Version of the Psalms of David"
    (Tate and Brady), 9, 26
New York College of Music, 55
New York Opera, 61, 62, 63
New York Philharmonic, 58
Nichols, George, 94
Nikisch, Arthur, 59
Nilsson, Christine, 62
Nordica, Lillian, 62, 63
Numeral Notation, 33

Oberhoffer, Emil, 60
Oberlin Conservatory, 55
Oliver, Joseph "King," 89
Opera (New York), 61, 62, 63
Operetta: Musical Comedy, 115, 117
Ormandy, Eugene, 59

Pachelbel, Charles, 146
Pachelbel, Theodore, 16
Paderewski, Ignace, 64
Paine, John Knowles, 45, 148
Paine, Thomas Treat, 38
Palma, John, 15, 16
Parker, Charlie, 89
Parker, Horatio, 49, 123, 149
Partch, Harry, 129, 130, 157
Patriotic Tunes, 13
Patti, Adelina, 61, 62
Pauer, Emil, 58
Peabody Institute, 55
Peace Jubilees, 58
Pelham, Peter, 13
Pelissier, Victor, 18
Penn, John Gov., 14
Penn, William, 20, 21
Persichetti, Vincent, 115
Pestalozzi Method, 54
Peter, Johann Friedrich, 21, 147
Philadelphia, 14
Philadelphia Musical Academy, 55
Philadelphia Symphony, 59
Phile, Phillip, 18, 39, 146
Phillips, Burrill, 121
Phono-cylinders, 149
Phonograph records, 64
Piatigorsky, Gregor, 64
Picchieri, Louis, 18
Pietists, 20, 22

Pilgrims, 1, 5
Piston, Walter, 114, 119, 120, 156
Pons, Lily, 63
Porter, Cole, 116
Post-revolution, 16
Pound, Louise, 70
Powell, John, 70, 97, 154
Pratt, Silas Gamaliel, 46
Pre-revolution, 16

Quakers, 14, 20

Rachmaninoff, Sergei, 64
Ragtime, 78
    Instruments: Performers, 79
    Organization, 79
    Records, 151, 152
    Style, 78
Rainey, Gertrude "Ma," 82
Rathbun, Valentine, 24
Ravenscroft's Psalter, 6, 7, 22
RCA Music Synthesizer, 140
Read, Daniel, 12, 145
Read, Gardner, 121
Regular way, 8
Reinagle, Alexander, 16, 17, 146
Reiner, Fritz, 60
Religious Ballads, 30
Relly, James, 12
"Repository of Sacred Music, Part Sec-
    ond" (John Wyeth), 30
Revival Spiritual Songs, 30
Revolution Ballads, 147, 148
Ricci, Ruggiero, 64
Rice, Thomas Dartmouth, 94
Riegger, Wallingford, 135, 157
Ritter, Frederic Louis, 76
Robertson, Leroy J., 115
"Rocked in the Cradle of the Deep," 40
Rodgers, Richard, 117
Rogers, Bernard, 121
Romberg, Sigmund, 116
Root, George F., 37, 55
"Rosary, The," 51
Roth String Quartet, 64
Rothwell, Walter H., 60
Rubinstein, Arthur, 64
Ruggles, Carl, 124, 125, 157
Russell, Henry, 40

St. Augustine, Fla., 1
St. Cecilia Society (Charleston), 57
"Sacred Harp, The" (White and King),
    30
Sandburg, Carl, 70
San Felipe, N. M., 1
San Francisco Opera, 63
Sängerbund, 58
Sankey, Ira, 37
Sargeant, Winthrop, 84
Scheel, Fritz, 59

Schelling, Ernest, 112
Schnabel, Arthur, 64
Schoenberg, Arnold, x, 27, 124, 125, 133
Schumann-Heink, Ernestine, 62
Schuman, William, 126, 127, 128, 157
Scottish Psalter, 22
Scott, James S., 79
Seeger, Charles, 125
Seeger, Ruth Crawford, 129
Selby, William, 16, 146
Sembrich, Marcella, 62
Sentence, 12, 13
Sentimental Ballads, 40
Serial Twelve-tone Technique, 133
Serkin, Rudolf, 64
Sessions, Roger, 89, 108, 120, 123, 127,
    128, 133, 157
Set Piece, 12
Seven-Syllable Notation, 33
Seventh Day Baptists, 21
Sewall, Judge, 9
Shakers, 22, 24, 25
    "Millenial Praises"
    Shaker Hymnal, 25
Shapero, Harold, 115
Sharp, Cecil J., 70
Shaw, Artie, 89
Shaw, Oliver, 145
Shepherd, Arthur, 112
Siegmeister, Elie, 107
Sister Marie, 2
    de l'incarnation
Skilton, Charles Sanford, 92
Smith, Bessie, 82
Smith, C. Alphonso, 70
Smith, Clarence "Pinetop," 82
Smith, David Stanley, 112
Smith, Samuel Francis Rev., 39
Smith, Wm. and Little Wm., 32
Society for Preservation of the American
    Musical Heritage, 65
Sokoloff, Nikolai, 60
Soldier Songs, 148
Sousa, John Philip, 60
"Southern Harmony" (William Walker),
    30, 35
Sower, David Jr., 33
Sowerby, Leo, 115
Spalding, Walter Raymond, 118
Spaniards (influence), 1, 73
Speedwell, 1
"Star Spangled Banner," 38, 39
Steffe, William, 39
Stern, Isaac, 64
Sternhold and Hopkins Psalter, 5, 6, 7
Stevens, Halsey, 121
Still, William Grant, 98
Stock, Frederick, 59
Stokowski, Leopold, 59, 60
Stoughton Musical Society, 57
Stravinsky, Igor, x, 106, 111, 120, 127

Stringfield, Lamar, 107
Strube, Gustave, 60
Stubbes, Phillip, 2
Swan, Timothy, 12
Swanson, Howard, 115
Symmes, Thomas Rev., 8
Szigeti, Josef, 64

"Tammany" (Hewitt), 17
Tans'ur, William, 10
Taylor, Deems, 115, 156
Taylor, Raynor, 16, 17, 146
"Tenting on the Old Camp Ground," 39
Thalberg, Sigismund, 41
Thomas, Theodore, 58, 59
Thompson, Randall, 118, 119, 156
Thomson, Virgil, 101, 155
Thunder, Henry Gordon, 59
Toch, Ernst, 122, 134
Toscanini, Arturo, 58, 63
Tourjée, Eben, 55
Tozer, A. Edmonds, 25
"Tramp, Tramp, Tramp," 55
Tristano, Lennie, 89
"Triumphs of Oriana," 3
Tuckey, William, 18
Tufts, John, 8, 9, 32
Tune Books, 29
Turpin, Thomas M., 79
Tuthill, Burnet C., 112
Twain, Mark, 93

"Urania" (James Lyon), 39
Ussachevsky, Valdimir, 137, 138, 139, 158

Vardell, Charles, 107
Varèse, Edgar, 125, 126, 138, 157
Victor (records), 64
Vincent, John, 15n, 103, 104, 155

"Virginia Sacred Musical Repository" (James Boyd), 30

Wagenaar, Bernard, 120
Wallenstein, Alfred, 142
Waller, Thomas "Fats," 79
Walter, Bruno, 58
Walter, Thomas, 8, 9
War of 1812: Ballads, 147
Ward, Robert, 115
Washington, George, 14, 39
Watts, Isaac, 11, 27, 29, 30
Wa-Wan Press, 93
Webb, George, 53, 54, 149
Weber, Ben, 135
Weill, Kurt, 117
Weingartner, Felix, 59
Weld, Thomas, 6
Wesley, Charles, 12, 27
Wesley, John, 12, 27
"When Jesus Wept," 12
"When Johnny Comes Marching Home," 39
Whitefield, George, 11
Whiteman, Paul, 89, 105
Whiting, Arthur, 50, 51
Wilgus, D. K., 70
Williams, Aaron, 11
Williamsburg, 13
Wolle, Peter, 147
Wollenhaupt, Herman, 148
Wolpe, Stefan, 134
Wood, Abraham, 12
Woodbury, Isaac, 54, 55
"Woodman Spare That Tree," 40

Yancy, Jimmy, 82
"Yankee Doodle," 38
Yarnold, Benjamin, 146
Youmans, Vincent, 116, 156